2015 STATUTORY AND CASE SUPPLEMENT TO

COMPUTER CRIME LAW

Third Edition

■ ■ ■

by

Orin S. Kerr

Fred C. Stevenson Research Professor
George Washington University Law School

AMERICAN CASEBOOK SERIES®

Mat #41727917

American Casebook Series is a trademark registered in the U.S. Patent and Trademark Office.

© 2014 LEG, Inc. d/b/a West Academic
© 2015 LEG, Inc. d/b/a West Academic
      444 Cedar Street, Suite 700
      St. Paul, MN 55101
      1-877-888-1330

West, West Academic Publishing, and West Academic are trademarks of West Publishing Corporation, used under license.

Printed in the United States of America

ISBN: 978-1-63459-268-0

PREFACE

This supplement serves two purposes. First, it provides the current text of the federal computer crime statutes. Second, it provides supplemental materials consisting of recent case developments that have followed the publication of the Third Edition of *Computer Crime Law*.

ORIN S. KERR
WASHINGTON, D.C.

November 2014

TABLE OF CONTENTS

PART B. CASELAW SUPPLEMENT

2015 STATUTORY AND CASE SUPPLEMENT TO

COMPUTER CRIME LAW

Third Edition

PART A

STATUTORY SUPPLEMENT

■ ■ ■

18 U.S.C. § 641. PUBLIC MONEY, PROPERTY OR RECORDS

Whoever embezzles, steals, purloins, or knowingly converts to his use or the use of another, or without authority, sells, conveys or disposes of any record, voucher, money, or thing of value of the United States or of any department or agency thereof, or any property made or being made under contract for the United States or any department or agency thereof; or

Whoever receives, conceals, or retains the same with intent to convert it to his use or gain, knowing it to have been embezzled, stolen, purloined or converted—

Shall be fined under this title or imprisoned not more than ten years, or both; but if the value of such property in the aggregate, combining amounts from all the counts for which the defendant is convicted in a single case, does not exceed the sum of $1,000, he shall be fined under this title or imprisoned not more than one year, or both.

The word "value" means face, par, or market value, or cost price, either wholesale or retail, whichever is greater.

18 U.S.C. § 875. INTERSTATE COMMUNICATIONS

(a) Whoever transmits in interstate or foreign commerce any communication containing any demand or request for a ransom or reward for the release of any kidnapped person, shall be fined under this title or imprisoned not more than twenty years, or both.

(b) Whoever, with intent to extort from any person, firm, association, or corporation, any money or other thing of value, transmits in interstate or foreign commerce any communication containing any threat to kidnap any person or any threat to injure the person of another, shall be fined under this title or imprisoned not more than twenty years, or both.

(c) Whoever transmits in interstate or foreign commerce any communication containing any threat to kidnap any person or any threat to injure the person of another, shall be fined under this title or imprisoned not more than five years, or both.

(d) Whoever, with intent to extort from any person, firm, association, or corporation, any money or other thing of value, transmits in interstate or foreign commerce any communication containing any threat to injure the property or reputation of the addressee or of another or the reputation of a deceased person or any threat to accuse the addressee or any other person of a crime, shall be fined under this title or imprisoned not more than two years, or both.

18 U.S.C. § 1028. FRAUD AND RELATED ACTIVITY IN CONNECTION WITH IDENTIFICATION DOCUMENTS, AUTHENTICATION FEATURES, AND INFORMATION

(a) Whoever, in a circumstance described in subsection (c) of this section—

(1) knowingly and without lawful authority produces an identification document, authentication feature, or a false identification document;

(2) knowingly transfers an identification document, authentication feature, or a false identification document knowing that such document or feature was stolen or produced without lawful authority;

(3) knowingly possesses with intent to use unlawfully or transfer unlawfully five or more identification documents (other than those issued lawfully for the use of the possessor), authentication features, or false identification documents;

(4) knowingly possesses an identification document (other than one issued lawfully for the use of the possessor), authentication feature, or a false identification document, with the intent such document or feature be used to defraud the United States;

(5) knowingly produces, transfers, or possesses a document-making implement or authentication feature with the intent such document-making implement or authentication feature will be used in the production of a false identification document or another document-making implement or authentication feature which will be so used;

(6) knowingly possesses an identification document or authentication feature that is or appears to be an identification document or authentication feature of the United States or a sponsoring entity of an event designated as a special event of national significance which is stolen or produced without lawful authority knowing that such document or feature was stolen or produced without such authority;

(7) knowingly transfers, possesses, or uses, without lawful authority, a means of identification of another person with the intent to commit, or to aid or abet, or in connection with, any unlawful

activity that constitutes a violation of Federal law, or that constitutes a felony under any applicable State or local law; or

(8) knowingly traffics in false or actual authentication features for use in false identification documents, document-making implements, or means of identification; shall be punished * * *.

* * *

(c) The circumstance referred to in subsection (a) of this section is that—

(1) the identification document, authentication feature, or false identification document is or appears to be issued by or under the authority of the United States or a sponsoring entity of an event designated as a special event of national significance or the document-making implement is designed or suited for making such an identification document, authentication feature, or false identification document;

(2) the offense is an offense under subsection (a) (4) of this section; or

(3) either—

(A) the production, transfer, possession, or use prohibited by this section is in or affects interstate or foreign commerce, including the transfer of a document by electronic means; or

(B) the means of identification, identification document, false identification document, or document-making implement is transported in the mail in the course of the production, transfer, possession, or use prohibited by this section.

(d) In this section and section 1028A—

(1) the term "authentication feature" means any hologram, watermark, certification, symbol, code, image, sequence of numbers or letters, or other feature that either individually or in combination with another feature is used by the issuing authority on an identification document, document-making implement, or means of identification to determine if the document is counterfeit, altered, or otherwise falsified;

(2) the term "document-making implement" means any implement, impression, template, computer file, computer disc, electronic device, or computer hardware or software, that is specifically configured or primarily used for making an identification document, a false identification document, or another document-making implement;

(3) the term "identification document" means a document made or issued by or under the authority of the United States Government, a State, political subdivision of a State, a sponsoring entity of an event designated as a special event of national significance, a foreign government, political subdivision of a foreign government, an international governmental or an international quasi-governmental organization which, when completed with information concerning a particular individual, is of a type intended or commonly accepted for the purpose of identification of individuals;

(4) the term "false identification document" means a document of a type intended or commonly accepted for the purposes of identification of individuals that—

    (A) is not issued by or under the authority of a governmental entity or was issued under the authority of a governmental entity but was subsequently altered for purposes of deceit; and

    (B) appears to be issued by or under the authority of the United States Government, a State, a political subdivision of a State, a sponsoring entity of an event designated by the President as a special event of national significance, a foreign government, a political subdivision of a foreign government, or an international governmental or quasi-governmental organization;

(5) the term "false authentication feature" means an authentication feature that—

    (A) is genuine in origin, but, without the authorization of the issuing authority, has been tampered with or altered for purposes of deceit;

    (B) is genuine, but has been distributed, or is intended for distribution, without the authorization of the issuing authority and not in connection with a lawfully made identification document, document-making implement, or means of identification to which such authentication feature is intended to be affixed or embedded by the respective issuing authority; or

    (C) appears to be genuine, but is not;

(6) the term "issuing authority"—

    (A) means any governmental entity or agency that is authorized to issue identification documents, means of identification, or authentication features; and

    (B) includes the United States Government, a State, a political subdivision of a State, a sponsoring entity of an event designated by the President as a special event of national significance, a foreign government, a political subdivision of a foreign government, or an international government or quasi-governmental organization;

(7) the term "means of identification" means any name or number that may be used, alone or in conjunction with any other information, to identify a specific individual, including any—

(A) name, social security number, date of birth, official State or government issued driver's license or identification number, alien registration number, government passport number, employer or taxpayer identification number;

(B) unique biometric data, such as fingerprint, voice print, retina or iris image, or other unique physical representation;

(C) unique electronic identification number, address, or routing code; or

(D) telecommunication identifying information or access device (as defined in section 1029(e));

(8) the term "personal identification card" means an identification document issued by a State or local government solely for the purpose of identification;

(9) the term "produce" includes alter, authenticate, or assemble;

(10) the term "transfer" includes selecting an identification document, false identification document, or document-making implement and placing or directing the placement of such identification document, false identification document, or document-making implement on an online location where it is available to others;

(11) the term "State" includes any State of the United States, the District of Columbia, the Commonwealth of Puerto Rico, and any other commonwealth, possession, or territory of the United States; and

(12) the term "traffic" means—

(A) to transport, transfer, or otherwise dispose of, to another, as consideration for anything of value; or

(B) to make or obtain control of with intent to so transport, transfer, or otherwise dispose of.

(e) This section does not prohibit any lawfully authorized investigative, protective, or intelligence activity of a law enforcement agency of the United States, a State, or a political subdivision of a State, or of an intelligence agency of the United States, or any activity authorized under chapter 224 of this title.

(f) **Attempt and conspiracy.**—Any person who attempts or conspires to commit any offense under this section shall be subject to the same penalties as those prescribed for the offense, the commission of which was the object of the attempt or conspiracy.

18 U.S.C. § 1028A.   AGGRAVATED IDENTITY THEFT

(a) **Offenses.**

(1) **In general.** Whoever, during and in relation to any felony violation enumerated in subsection (c), knowingly transfers, possesses, or uses, without lawful authority, a means of identification of another person shall, in addition to the punishment provided for such felony, be sentenced to a term of imprisonment of 2 years.

(2) **Terrorism offense.** Whoever, during and in relation to any felony violation enumerated in section 2332b(g)(5)(B), knowingly transfers, possesses, or uses, without lawful authority, a means of identification of another person or a false identification document shall, in addition to the punishment provided for such felony, be sentenced to a term of imprisonment of 5 years.

* * *

(c) **Definition.** For purposes of this section, the term "felony violation enumerated in subsection (c)" means any offense that is a felony violation of—

(1) section 641 (relating to theft of public money, property, or records), section 656 (relating to theft, embezzlement, or misapplication by bank officer or employee), or section 664 (relating to theft from employee benefit plans);

(2) section 911 (relating to false personation of citizenship);

(3) section 922(a)(6) (relating to false statements in connection with the acquisition of a firearm);

(4) any provision contained in this chapter (relating to fraud and false statements), other than this section or section 1028(a)(7);

(5) any provision contained in chapter 63 (relating to mail, bank, and wire fraud);

(6) any provision contained in chapter 69 (relating to nationality and citizenship);

(7) any provision contained in chapter 75 (relating to passports and visas);

(8) section 523 of the Gramm-Leach-Bliley Act (15 U.S.C. 6823) (relating to obtaining customer information by false pretenses);

(9) section 243 or 266 of the Immigration and Nationality Act (8 U.S.C. 1253 and 1306) (relating to willfully failing to leave the United States after deportation and creating a counterfeit alien registration card);

(10) any provision contained in chapter 8 of title II of the Immigration and Nationality Act (8 U.S.C. 1321 et seq.) (relating to various immigration offenses); or

(11) section 208, 811, 1107(b), 1128B(a), or 1632 of the Social Security Act (42 U.S.C. 408, 1011, 1307(b), 1320a–7b(a), and 1383a) (relating to false statements relating to programs under the Act).

18 U.S.C. § 1029. FRAUD AND RELATED ACTIVITY IN CONNECTION WITH ACCESS DEVICES

(a) Whoever—

(1) knowingly and with intent to defraud produces, uses, or traffics in one or more counterfeit access devices;

(2) knowingly and with intent to defraud traffics in or uses one or more unauthorized access devices during any one-year period, and by such conduct obtains anything of value aggregating $1,000 or more during that period;

(3) knowingly and with intent to defraud possesses fifteen or more devices which are counterfeit or unauthorized access devices;

(4) knowingly, and with intent to defraud, produces, traffics in, has control or custody of, or possesses device-making equipment;

(5) knowingly and with intent to defraud effects transactions, with 1 or more access devices issued to another person or persons, to receive payment or any other thing of value during any 1-year period the aggregate value of which is equal to or greater than $1,000;

(6) without the authorization of the issuer of the access device, knowingly and with intent to defraud solicits a person for the purpose of—

(A) offering an access device; or

(B) selling information regarding or an application to obtain an access device;

(7) knowingly and with intent to defraud uses, produces, traffics in, has control or custody of, or possesses a telecommunications instrument that has been modified or altered to obtain unauthorized use of telecommunications services;

(8) knowingly and with intent to defraud uses, produces, traffics in, has control or custody of, or possesses a scanning receiver;

(9) knowingly uses, produces, traffics in, has control or custody of, or possesses hardware or software, knowing it has been configured to insert or modify telecommunication identifying information associated with or contained in a telecommunications instrument so that such instrument may be used to obtain telecommunications service without authorization; or

(10) without the authorization of the credit card system member or its agent, knowingly and with intent to defraud causes or arranges for another person to present to the member or its agent, for payment, 1 or more evidences or records of transactions made by an access device;

shall, if the offense affects interstate or foreign commerce, be punished as provided in subsection (c) of this section.

(b)(1) Whoever attempts to commit an offense under subsection (a) of this section shall be subject to the same penalties as those prescribed for the offense attempted.

(2) Whoever is a party to a conspiracy of two or more persons to commit an offense under subsection (a) of this section, if any of the parties engages in any conduct in furtherance of such offense, shall be fined an amount not greater than the amount provided as the maximum fine for such offense under subsection (c) of this section or imprisoned not longer than one-half the period provided as the maximum imprisonment for such offense under subsection (c) of this section, or both.

* * *

(e) As used in this section—

(1) the term "access device" means any card, plate, code, account number, electronic serial number, mobile identification number, personal identification number, or other telecommunications service, equipment, or instrument identifier, or other means of account access that can be used, alone or in conjunction with another access device, to obtain money, goods, services, or any other thing of value, or that can be used to initiate a transfer of funds (other than a transfer originated solely by paper instrument);

(2) the term "counterfeit access device" means any access device that is counterfeit, fictitious, altered, or forged, or an identifiable component of an access device or a counterfeit access device;

(3) the term "unauthorized access device" means any access device that is lost, stolen, expired, revoked, canceled, or obtained with intent to defraud;

(4) the term "produce" includes design, alter, authenticate, duplicate, or assemble;

(5) the term "traffic" means transfer, or otherwise dispose of, to another, or obtain control of with intent to transfer or dispose of;

(6) the term "device-making equipment" means any equipment, mechanism, or impression designed or primarily used for making an access device or a counterfeit access device;

(7) The term "credit card system member" means a financial institution or other entity that is a member of a credit card system, including an entity, whether affiliated with or identical to the credit card issuer, that is the sole member of a credit card system;

(8) the term "scanning receiver" means a device or apparatus that can be used to intercept a wire or electronic communication in violation of chapter 119 or to intercept an electronic serial number, mobile identification number, or other identifier of any telecommunications service, equipment, or instrument;

(9) the term "telecommunications service" has the meaning given such term in section 3 of title I of the Communications Act of 1934 (47 U.S.C. § 153);

(10) the term "facilities-based carrier" means an entity that owns communications transmission facilities, is responsible for the operation and maintenance of those facilities, and holds an operating license issued by the Federal Communications Commission under the authority of title III of the Communications Act of 1934; and

(11) the term "telecommunication identifying information" means electronic serial number or any other number or signal that identifies a specific telecommunications instrument or account, or a specific communication transmitted from a telecommunications instrument.

(f) This section does not prohibit any lawfully authorized investigative, protective, or intelligence activity of a law enforcement agency of the United States, a State, or a political subdivision of a State, or of an intelligence agency of the United States, or any activity authorized under chapter 224 of this title. For purposes of this subsection, the term "State" includes a State of the United States, the District of Columbia, and any commonwealth, territory, or possession of the United States.

(g)(1) It is not a violation of subsection (a)(9) for an officer, employee, or agent of, or a person engaged in business with, a facilities-based carrier, to engage in conduct (other than trafficking) otherwise prohibited by that subsection for the purpose of protecting the property or legal rights of that carrier, unless such conduct is for the purpose of obtaining telecommunications service provided by another facilities-based carrier without the authorization of such carrier.

(2) In a prosecution for a violation of subsection (a)(9), (other than a violation consisting of producing or trafficking) it is an affirmative defense (which the defendant must establish by a preponderance of the evidence) that the conduct charged was engaged in for research or development in connection with a lawful purpose.

(h) Any person who, outside the jurisdiction of the United States, engages in any act that, if committed within the jurisdiction of the United States, would constitute an offense under subsection (a) or (b) of this section, shall be subject to the fines, penalties, imprisonment, and forfeiture provided in this title if—

(1) the offense involves an access device issued, owned, managed, or controlled by a financial institution, account issuer, credit card system member, or other entity within the jurisdiction of the United States; and

(2) the person transports, delivers, conveys, transfers to or through, or otherwise stores, secrets, or holds within the jurisdiction of the United States, any article used to assist in the commission of the offense or the proceeds of such offense or property derived therefrom.

18 U.S.C. § 1030. F<small>RAUD AND</small> R<small>ELATED</small> A<small>CTIVITY IN</small> C<small>ONNECTION WITH</small> C<small>OMPUTERS</small>

(a) Whoever—

(1) having knowingly accessed a computer without authorization or exceeding authorized access, and by means of such conduct having obtained information that has been determined by the United States Government pursuant to an Executive order or statute to require protection against unauthorized disclosure for reasons of national defense or foreign relations, or any restricted data, as defined in paragraph y. of section 11 of the Atomic Energy Act of 1954, with reason to believe that such information so obtained could be used to the injury of the United States, or to the advantage of any foreign nation willfully communicates, delivers, transmits, or causes to be communicated, delivered, or transmitted, or attempts to communicate, deliver, transmit or cause to be communicated, delivered, or transmitted the same to any person not entitled to receive it, or willfully retains the same and fails to deliver it to the officer or employee of the United States entitled to receive it;

(2) intentionally accesses a computer without authorization or exceeds authorized access, and thereby obtains—

(A) information contained in a financial record of a financial institution, or of a card issuer as defined in section 1602(n) of title 15, or contained in a file of a consumer reporting agency on a consumer, as such terms are defined in the Fair Credit Reporting Act (15 U.S.C. 1681 et seq.);

(B) information from any department or agency of the United States; or

(C) information from any protected computer;

(3) intentionally, without authorization to access any nonpublic computer of a department or agency of the United States, accesses such a computer of that department or agency that is exclusively for the use of the Government of the United States or, in the case of a computer not exclusively for such use, is used by or for the Government of the United States and such conduct affects that use by or for the Government of the United States;

(4) knowingly and with intent to defraud, accesses a protected computer without authorization, or exceeds authorized access, and by means of such conduct furthers the intended fraud and obtains anything of value, unless the object of the fraud and the thing obtained consists only of the use of the computer and the value of such use is not more than $5,000 in any 1-year period;

(5)(A) knowingly causes the transmission of a program, information, code, or command, and as a result of such conduct, intentionally causes damage without authorization, to a protected computer;

(B) intentionally accesses a protected computer without authorization, and as a result of such conduct, recklessly causes damage; or

(C) intentionally accesses a protected computer without authorization, and as a result of such conduct, causes damage and loss.

(6) knowingly and with intent to defraud traffics (as defined in section 1029) in any password or similar information through which a computer may be accessed without authorization, if—

(A) such trafficking affects interstate or foreign commerce; or

(B) such computer is used by or for the Government of the United States;

(7) with intent to extort from any person any money or other thing of value, transmits in interstate or foreign commerce any communication containing any—

(A) threat to cause damage to a protected computer;

(B) threat to obtain information from a protected computer without authorization or in excess of authorization or to impair the confidentiality of information obtained from a protected computer without authorization or by exceeding authorized access; or

(C) demand or request for money or other thing of value in relation to damage to a protected computer, where such damage was caused to facilitate the extortion;

shall be punished as provided in subsection (c) of this section.

(b) Whoever conspires to commit or attempts to commit an offense under subsection (a) of this section shall be punished as provided in subsection (c) of this section.

(c) The punishment for an offense under subsection (a) or (b) of this section is—

(1)(A) a fine under this title or imprisonment for not more than ten years, or both, in the case of an offense under subsection (a)(1) of this section which does not occur after a conviction for another offense under this section, or an attempt to commit an offense punishable under this subparagraph; and

(B) a fine under this title or imprisonment for not more than twenty years, or both, in the case of an offense under subsection (a)(1) of this section which occurs after a conviction for another offense under this section, or an attempt to commit an offense punishable under this subparagraph;

(2)(A) except as provided in subparagraph (B), a fine under this title or imprisonment for not more than one year, or both, in the case of an offense under subsection (a)(2), (a)(3), or (a)(6) of this section which does not occur after a conviction for another offense under this section, or an attempt to commit an offense punishable under this subparagraph;

(B) a fine under this title or imprisonment for not more than 5 years, or both, in the case of an offense under subsection (a)(2), or an attempt to commit an offense punishable under this subparagraph, if—

(i) the offense was committed for purposes of commercial advantage or private financial gain;

(ii) the offense was committed in furtherance of any criminal or tortious act in violation of the Constitution or laws of the United States or of any State; or

(iii) the value of the information obtained exceeds $5,000; and

(C) a fine under this title or imprisonment for not more than ten years, or both, in the case of an offense under subsection (a)(2), (a)(3) or (a)(6) of this section which occurs after a conviction for another offense under this section, or an attempt to commit an offense punishable under this subparagraph;

(3)(A) a fine under this title or imprisonment for not more than five years, or both, in the case of an offense under subsection (a)(4) or (a)(7) of this section which does not occur after a conviction for another offense under this section, or an attempt to commit an offense punishable under this subparagraph; and

(B) a fine under this title or imprisonment for not more than ten years, or both, in the case of an offense under subsection (a)(4) or (a)(7) of this section which occurs after a conviction for another offense under this section, or an attempt to commit an offense punishable under this subparagraph;

(4)(A) except as provided in subparagraphs (E) and (F), a fine under this title, imprisonment for not more than 5 years, or both, in the case of—

(i) an offense under subsection (a)(5)(B), which does not occur after a conviction for another offense under this section, if the offense caused (or, in the case of an attempted offense, would, if completed, have caused)—

(I) loss to 1 or more persons during any 1-year period (and, for purposes of an investigation, prosecution, or other proceeding brought by the United States only, loss resulting from a related course of conduct affecting 1 or more other protected computers) aggregating at least $5,000 in value;

(II) the modification or impairment, or potential modification or impairment, of the medical examination, diagnosis, treatment, or care of 1 or more individuals;

(III) physical injury to any person;

(IV) a threat to public health or safety;

(V) damage affecting a computer used by or for an entity of the United States Government in furtherance of the administration of justice, national defense, or national security; or

(VI) damage affecting 10 or more protected computers during any 1-year period; or

(ii) an attempt to commit an offense punishable under this subparagraph;

(B) except as provided in subparagraphs (E) and (F), a fine under this title, imprisonment for not more than 10 years, or both, in the case of—

(i) an offense under subsection (a)(5)(A), which does not occur after a conviction for another offense under this section, if the offense caused (or, in the case of an attempted offense, would, if completed, have caused) a harm provided in subclauses (I) through (VI) of subparagraph (A)(i); or

(ii) an attempt to commit an offense punishable under this subparagraph;

(C) except as provided in subparagraphs (E) and (F), a fine under this title, imprisonment for not more than 20 years, or both, in the case of—

(i) an offense or an attempt to commit an offense under subparagraphs (A) or (B) of subsection (a)(5) that occurs after a conviction for another offense under this section; or

(ii) an attempt to commit an offense punishable under this subparagraph;

(D) a fine under this title, imprisonment for not more than 10 years, or both, in the case of—

(i) an offense or an attempt to commit an offense under subsection (a)(5)(C) that occurs after a conviction for another offense under this section; or

(ii) an attempt to commit an offense punishable under this subparagraph;

(E) if the offender attempts to cause or knowingly or recklessly causes serious bodily injury from conduct in violation of subsection (a)(5)(A), a fine under this title, imprisonment for not more than 20 years, or both;

(F) if the offender attempts to cause or knowingly or recklessly causes death from conduct in violation of subsection (a)(5)(A), a fine under this title, imprisonment for any term of years or for life, or both; or

(G) a fine under this title, imprisonment for not more than 1 year, or both, for—

(i) any other offense under subsection (a)(5); or

(ii) an attempt to commit an offense punishable under this subparagraph.

(d)(1) The United States Secret Service shall, in addition to any other agency having such authority, have the authority to investigate offenses under this section.

(2) The Federal Bureau of Investigation shall have primary authority to investigate offenses under subsection (a)(1) for any cases involving espionage, foreign counterintelligence, information protected against unauthorized disclosure for reasons of national defense or foreign relations, or Restricted Data (as that term is defined in section 11y of the Atomic Energy Act of 1954 (42 U.S.C. 2014(y)), except for offenses affecting the duties of the United States Secret Service pursuant to section 3056(a) of this title.

(3) Such authority shall be exercised in accordance with an agreement which shall be entered into by the Secretary of the Treasury and the Attorney General.

(e) As used in this section—

(1) the term "computer" means an electronic, magnetic, optical, electrochemical, or other high speed data processing device performing logical, arithmetic, or storage functions, and includes any data storage facility or communications facility directly related to or operating in conjunction with such device, but such term does not include an automated typewriter or typesetter, a portable hand held calculator, or other similar device;

(2) the term "protected computer" means a computer—

(A) exclusively for the use of a financial institution or the United States Government, or, in the case of a computer not exclusively for such use, used by or for a financial institution or the United States Government and the conduct constituting the offense affects that use by or for the financial institution or the Government; or

(B) which is used in or affecting interstate or foreign commerce or communication, including a computer located outside the United States that is used in a manner that affects interstate or foreign commerce or communication of the United States;

(3) the term "State" includes the District of Columbia, the Commonwealth of Puerto Rico, and any other commonwealth, possession or territory of the United States;

(4) the term "financial institution" means—

(A) an institution, with deposits insured by the Federal Deposit Insurance Corporation;

(B) the Federal Reserve or a member of the Federal Reserve including any Federal Reserve Bank;

(C) a credit union with accounts insured by the National Credit Union Administration;

(D) a member of the Federal home loan bank system and any home loan bank;

(E) any institution of the Farm Credit System under the Farm Credit Act of 1971;

(F) a broker-dealer registered with the Securities and Exchange Commission pursuant to section 15 of the Securities Exchange Act of 1934;

(G) the Securities Investor Protection Corporation;

(H) a branch or agency of a foreign bank (as such terms are defined in paragraphs (1) and (3) of section 1(b) of the International Banking Act of 1978); and

(I) an organization operating under section 25 or section 25(a) of the Federal Reserve Act;

(5) the term "financial record" means information derived from any record held by a financial institution pertaining to a customer's relationship with the financial institution;

(6) the term "exceeds authorized access" means to access a computer with authorization and to use such access to obtain or alter information in the computer that the accesser is not entitled so to obtain or alter;

(7) the term "department of the United States" means the legislative or judicial branch of the Government or one of the executive departments enumerated in section 101 of title 5;

(8) the term "damage" means any impairment to the integrity or availability of data, a program, a system, or information;

(9) the term "government entity" includes the Government of the United States, any State or political subdivision of the United States, any foreign country, and any state, province, municipality, or other political subdivision of a foreign country;

(10) the term "conviction" shall include a conviction under the law of any State for a crime punishable by imprisonment for more than 1 year, an element of which is unauthorized access, or exceeding authorized access, to a computer;

(11) the term "loss" means any reasonable cost to any victim, including the cost of responding to an offense, conducting a damage assessment, and restoring the data, program, system, or information to its condition prior to the offense, and any revenue lost, cost incurred, or other consequential damages incurred because of interruption of service; and

(12) the term "person" means any individual, firm, corporation, educational institution, financial institution, governmental entity, or legal or other entity.

(f) This section does not prohibit any lawfully authorized investigative, protective, or intelligence activity of a law enforcement agency of the United States, a State, or a political subdivision of a State, or of an intelligence agency of the United States.

(g) Any person who suffers damage or loss by reason of a violation of this section may maintain a civil action against the violator to obtain compensatory damages and injunctive relief or other equitable relief. A civil action for a violation of this section may be brought only if the conduct involves 1 of the factors set forth in subclauses (I), (II), (III), (IV), or (V) of subsection (c)(4)(A)(i). Damages for a violation involving only conduct described in subsection (c)(4)(A)(i)(I) are limited to economic damages. No action may be brought under this subsection unless such action is begun within 2 years of the date of the act complained of or the date of the discovery of the damage. No action may be brought under this subsection for the negligent design or manufacture of computer hardware, computer software, or firmware.

(h) The Attorney General and the Secretary of the Treasury shall report to the Congress annually, during the first 3 years following the date of the enactment of this subsection, concerning investigations and prosecutions under subsection (a)(5).

(i)(1) The court, in imposing sentence on any person convicted of a violation of this section, or convicted of conspiracy to violate this section, shall order, in addition to any other sentence imposed and irrespective of any provision of State law, that such person forfeit to the United States—

(A) such person's interest in any personal property that was used or intended to be used to commit or to facilitate the commission of such violation; and

(B) any property, real or personal, constituting or derived from, any proceeds that such person obtained, directly or indirectly, as a result of such violation.

(2) The criminal forfeiture of property under this subsection, any seizure and disposition thereof, and any judicial proceeding in relation thereto, shall be governed by the provisions of section 413 of the Comprehensive Drug Abuse Prevention and Control Act of 1970 (21 U.S.C. 853), except subsection (d) of that section.

(j) For purposes of subsection (i), the following shall be subject to forfeiture to the United States and no property right shall exist in them:

(1) Any personal property used or intended to be used to commit or to facilitate the commission of any violation of this section, or a conspiracy to violate this section.

(2) Any property, real or personal, which constitutes or is derived from proceeds traceable to any violation of this section, or a conspiracy to violate this section.

18 U.S.C. § 1084. TRANSMISSION OF WAGERING INFORMATION; PENALTIES

(a) Whoever being engaged in the business of betting or wagering knowingly uses a wire communication facility for the transmission in interstate or foreign commerce of bets or wagers or information assisting in the placing of bets or wagers on any sporting event or contest, or for the transmission of a wire communication which entitles the recipient to receive money or credit as a result of bets or wagers, or for information assisting in the placing of bets or wagers, shall be fined under this title or imprisoned not more than two years, or both.

(b) Nothing in this section shall be construed to prevent the transmission in interstate or foreign commerce of information for use in news reporting of sporting events or contests, or for the transmission of information assisting in the placing of bets or wagers on a sporting event or contest from a State or foreign country where betting on that sporting event or contest is legal into a State or foreign country in which such betting is legal.

(c) Nothing contained in this section shall create immunity from criminal prosecution under any laws of any State.

(d) When any common carrier, subject to the jurisdiction of the Federal Communications Commission, is notified in writing by a Federal, State, or local law enforcement agency, acting within its jurisdiction, that any facility furnished by it is being used or will be used for the purpose of transmitting or receiving gambling information in interstate or foreign commerce in violation of Federal, State or local law, it shall discontinue or refuse, the leasing, furnishing, or maintaining of such facility, after reasonable notice to the subscriber, but no damages, penalty or forfeiture, civil or criminal, shall be found against any common carrier for any act done in compliance with any notice received from a law enforcement agency. Nothing in this section shall be deemed to prejudice the right of any person affected thereby to secure an appropriate determination, as otherwise provided by law, in a Federal court or in a State or local tribunal or agency, that such facility should not be discontinued or removed, or should be restored.

(e) As used in this section, the term "State" means a State of the United States, the District of Columbia, the Commonwealth of Puerto Rico, or a commonwealth, territory or possession of the United States.

18 U.S.C. § 1343. FRAUD BY WIRE, RADIO, OR TELEVISION

Whoever, having devised or intending to devise any scheme or artifice to defraud, or for obtaining money or property by means of false or fraudulent pretenses, representations, or promises, transmits or causes to be transmitted by means of wire, radio, or television communication in interstate or foreign commerce, any writings, signs, signals, pictures, or sounds for the purpose of executing such scheme or artifice, shall be fined under this title or imprisoned not more than 20 years, or both. If the violation occurs in relation to, or involving any benefit authorized, transported, transmitted, transferred, disbursed, or paid in connection with, a presidentially declared major disaster or emergency (as those terms are defined in section 102 of the Robert T. Stafford Disaster Relief and Emergency Assistance Act (42 U.S.C. 5122)), or affects a financial institution, such person shall be fined not more than $1,000,000 or imprisoned not more than 30 years, or both.

18 U.S.C. § 1462. IMPORTATION OR TRANSPORTATION OF OBSCENE MATTERS

Whoever brings into the United States, or any place subject to the jurisdiction thereof, or knowingly uses any express company or other common carrier or interactive computer service (as defined in section 230(e)(2) of the Communications Act of 1934), for carriage in interstate or foreign commerce—

(a) any obscene, lewd, lascivious, or filthy book, pamphlet, picture, motion-picture film, paper, letter, writing, print, or other matter of indecent character; or

(b) any obscene, lewd, lascivious, or filthy phonograph recording, electrical transcription, or other article or thing capable of producing sound; or

(c) any drug, medicine, article, or thing designed, adapted, or intended for producing abortion, or for any indecent or immoral use;

or any written or printed card, letter, circular, book, pamphlet, advertisement, or notice of any kind giving information, directly or indirectly, where, how, or of whom, or by what means any of such mentioned articles, matters, or things may be obtained or made; or

Whoever knowingly takes or receives, from such express company or other common carrier or interactive computer service (as defined in section 230(e)(2) of the Communications Act of 1934) any matter or thing the carriage or importation of which is herein made unlawful—

Shall be fined under this title or imprisoned not more than five years, or both, for the first such offense and shall be fined under this title or imprisoned not more than ten years, or both, for each such offense thereafter.

18 U.S.C. § 1465. PRODUCTION AND TRANSPORTATION OF OBSCENE MATTERS FOR SALE OR DISTRIBUTION

Whoever knowingly produces with the intent to transport, distribute, or transmit in interstate or foreign commerce, or whoever knowingly transports or travels in, or uses a facility or means of, interstate or foreign commerce or an interactive computer service (as defined in section 230(e)(2) of the Communications Act of 1934) in or affecting such commerce, for the purpose of sale or distribution of any obscene, lewd, lascivious, or filthy book, pamphlet, picture, film, paper, letter, writing, print, silhouette, drawing, figure, image, cast, phonograph recording, electrical transcription or other article capable of producing sound or any other matter of indecent or immoral character, shall be fined under this title or imprisoned not more than five years, or both.

The transportation as aforesaid of two or more copies of any publication or two or more of any article of the character described above, or a combined total of five such publications and articles, shall create a presumption that such publications or articles are intended for sale or distribution, but such presumption shall be rebuttable.

18 U.S.C. § 1831. ECONOMIC ESPIONAGE

(a) **In general.**—Whoever, intending or knowing that the offense will benefit any foreign government, foreign instrumentality, or foreign agent, knowingly—

(1) steals, or without authorization appropriates, takes, carries away, or conceals, or by fraud, artifice, or deception obtains a trade secret;

(2) without authorization copies, duplicates, sketches, draws, photographs, downloads, uploads, alters, destroys, photocopies, replicates, transmits, delivers, sends, mails, communicates, or conveys a trade secret;

(3) receives, buys, or possesses a trade secret, knowing the same to have been stolen or appropriated, obtained, or converted without authorization;

(4) attempts to commit any offense described in any of paragraphs (1) through (3); or

(5) conspires with one or more other persons to commit any offense described in any of paragraphs (1) through (3), and one or more of such persons do any act to effect the object of the conspiracy,

shall, except as provided in subsection (b), be fined not more than $500,000 or imprisoned not more than 15 years, or both.

(b) **Organizations.**—Any organization that commits any offense described in subsection (a) shall be fined not more than $10,000,000.

18 U.S.C. § 1832. THEFT OF TRADE SECRETS

(a) Whoever, with intent to convert a trade secret, that is related to a product or service used in or intended for use in interstate or foreign commerce, to the economic benefit of anyone other than the owner thereof, and intending or knowing that the offense will, injure any owner of that trade secret, knowingly—

(1) steals, or without authorization appropriates, takes, carries away, or conceals, or by fraud, artifice, or deception obtains such information;

(2) without authorization copies, duplicates, sketches, draws, photographs, downloads, uploads, alters, destroys, photocopies, replicates, transmits, delivers, sends, mails, communicates, or conveys such information;

(3) receives, buys, or possesses such information, knowing the same to have been stolen or appropriated, obtained, or converted without authorization;

(4) attempts to commit any offense described in paragraphs (1) through (3); or

(5) conspires with one or more other persons to commit any offense described in paragraphs (1) through (3), and one or more of such persons do any act to effect the object of the conspiracy,

shall, except as provided in subsection (b), be fined under this title or imprisoned not more than 10 years, or both.

(b) Any organization that commits any offense described in subsection (a) shall be fined not more than $5,000,000.

18 U.S.C. § 1839. DEFINITIONS

As used in this chapter—

(1) the term "foreign instrumentality" means any agency, bureau, ministry, component, institution, association, or any legal, commercial, or business organization, corporation, firm, or entity that is substantially owned, controlled, sponsored, commanded, managed, or dominated by a foreign government;

(2) the term "foreign agent" means any officer, employee, proxy, servant, delegate, or representative of a foreign government;

(3) the term "trade secret" means all forms and types of financial, business, scientific, technical, economic, or engineering information, including patterns, plans, compilations, program devices, formulas, designs, prototypes, methods, techniques, processes, procedures, programs, or codes, whether tangible or intangible, and whether or how stored, compiled, or memorialized physically, electronically, graphically, photographically, or in writing if—

(A) the owner thereof has taken reasonable measures to keep such information secret; and

(B) the information derives independent economic value, actual or potential, from not being generally known to, and not being readily ascertainable through proper means by, the public; and

(4) the term "owner", with respect to a trade secret, means the person or entity in whom or in which rightful legal or equitable title to, or license in, the trade secret is reposed.

18 U.S.C. § 2251. SEXUAL EXPLOITATION OF CHILDREN

(a) Any person who employs, uses, persuades, induces, entices, or coerces any minor to engage in, or who has a minor assist any other person to engage in, or who transports any minor in or affecting interstate or foreign commerce, or in any Territory or Possession of the United States, with the intent that such minor engage in, any sexually explicit conduct for the purpose of producing any visual depiction of such conduct or for the purpose of transmitting a live visual depiction of such conduct, shall be punished as provided under subsection (e), if such person knows or has reason to know that such visual depiction will be transported or transmitted using any means or facility of interstate or foreign commerce or in or affecting interstate or foreign commerce or mailed, if that visual depiction was produced or transmitted using materials that have been mailed, shipped, or transported in or affecting interstate or foreign commerce by any means, including by computer, or if such visual depiction has actually been transported or transmitted using any means or facility of interstate or foreign commerce or in or affecting interstate or foreign commerce or mailed.

(b) Any parent, legal guardian, or person having custody or control of a minor who knowingly permits such minor to engage in, or to assist any other person to engage in, sexually explicit conduct for the purpose of producing any visual depiction of such conduct or for the purpose of transmitting a live visual depiction of such conduct shall be punished as provided under subsection (e) of this section, if such parent, legal guardian, or person knows or has reason to know that such visual depiction will be transported or transmitted using any means or facility of interstate or foreign commerce or in or affecting interstate or foreign commerce or mailed, if that visual depiction was produced or transmitted using materials that have been mailed, shipped, or transported in or affecting interstate or foreign commerce by any means, including by computer, or if such visual depiction has actually been transported or transmitted using any means or facility of interstate or foreign commerce or in or affecting interstate or foreign commerce or mailed.

(c)(1) Any person who, in a circumstance described in paragraph (2), employs, uses, persuades, induces, entices, or coerces any minor to engage in, or who has a minor assist any other person to engage in, any sexually explicit conduct outside of the United States, its territories or possessions, for the purpose of producing any visual depiction of such conduct, shall be punished as provided under subsection (e).

(2) The circumstance referred to in paragraph (1) is that—

(A) the person intends such visual depiction to be transported to the United States, its territories or possessions, by any means, including by using any means or facility of interstate or foreign commerce or mail; or

(B) the person transports such visual depiction to the United States, its territories or possessions, by any means, including by using any means or facility of interstate or foreign commerce or mail.

(d)(1) Any person who, in a circumstance described in paragraph (2), knowingly makes, prints, or publishes, or causes to be made, printed, or published, any notice or advertisement seeking or offering—

(A) to receive, exchange, buy, produce, display, distribute, or reproduce, any visual depiction, if the production of such visual depiction involves the use of a minor engaging in sexually explicit conduct and such visual depiction is of such conduct; or

(B) participation in any act of sexually explicit conduct by or with any minor for the purpose of producing a visual depiction of such conduct:

shall be punished as provided under subsection (e).

(2) The circumstance referred to in paragraph (1) is that—

(A) such person knows or has reason to know that such notice or advertisement will be transported using any means or facility of interstate or foreign commerce or in or affecting interstate or foreign commerce by any means including by computer or mailed; or

(B) such notice or advertisement is transported using any means or facility of interstate or foreign commerce or in or affecting interstate or foreign commerce by any means including by computer or mailed.

(e) Any individual who violates, or attempts or conspires to violate, this section shall be fined under this title and imprisoned not less than 15 years nor more than 30 years, but if such person has one prior conviction under this chapter, section 1591, chapter 71, chapter 109A, or chapter 117, or under section 920 of title 10 (article 120 of the Uniform Code of Military Justice), or under the laws of any State relating to aggravated sexual abuse, sexual abuse, abusive sexual contact involving a minor or ward, or sex trafficking of children, or the production, possession, receipt, mailing, sale, distribution, shipment, or transportation of child pornography, such person shall be fined under this title and imprisoned for not less than 25 years nor more than 50 years, but if such person has 2 or more prior convictions under this chapter, chapter 71, chapter 109A, or chapter 117, or under section 920 of title 10 (article 120 of the Uniform Code of Military Justice), or under the laws of any State relating to the sexual exploitation of children, such person shall be fined under this title and imprisoned not less than 35 years nor more than life. Any organization that violates, or attempts or conspires to violate, this section shall be fined under this title. Whoever, in the course of an offense under this section, engages in conduct that results in the death of a person, shall be punished by death or imprisoned for not less than 30 years or for life.

18 U.S.C. § 2252. CERTAIN ACTIVITIES RELATING TO MATERIAL INVOLVING THE SEXUAL EXPLOITATION OF MINORS

(a) Any person who—

(1) knowingly transports or ships using any means or facility of interstate or foreign commerce or in or affecting interstate or foreign commerce by any means including by computer or mails, any visual depiction, if—

(A) the producing of such visual depiction involves the use of a minor engaging in sexually explicit conduct; and

(B) such visual depiction is of such conduct;

(2) knowingly receives, or distributes, any visual depiction using any means or facility of interstate or foreign commerce or that has been mailed, or has been shipped or transported in or affecting interstate or foreign commerce, or which contains materials which have been mailed or so shipped or transported, by any means including by computer, or knowingly reproduces any visual depiction for distribution using any means or facility of interstate or foreign commerce or in or affecting interstate or foreign commerce or through the mails, if—

(A) the producing of such visual depiction involves the use of a minor engaging in sexually explicit conduct; and

(B) such visual depiction is of such conduct;

(3) either—

(A) in the special maritime and territorial jurisdiction of the United States, or on any land or building owned by, leased to, or otherwise used by or under the control of the Government of the United States, or in the Indian country as defined in section 1151 of this title, knowingly sells or possesses with intent to sell any visual depiction; or

(B) knowingly sells or possesses with intent to sell any visual depiction that has been mailed, shipped, or transported using any means or facility of interstate or foreign commerce, or has been shipped or transported in or affecting interstate or foreign commerce, or which was produced using materials which have been mailed or so shipped or transported using any means or facility of interstate or foreign commerce, including by computer, if—

(i) the producing of such visual depiction involves the use of a minor engaging in sexually explicit conduct; and

(ii) such visual depiction is of such conduct; or

(4) either—

(A) in the special maritime and territorial jurisdiction of the United States, or on any land or building owned by, leased to, or otherwise used by or under the control of the Government of the United States, or in the Indian country as defined in section 1151 of this title, knowingly possesses, or knowingly accesses with intent to view, 1 or more books, magazines, periodicals, films, video tapes, or other matter which contain any visual depiction; or

(B) knowingly possesses, or knowingly accesses with intent to view, 1 or more books, magazines, periodicals, films, video tapes, or other matter which contain any visual depiction that has been mailed, or has been shipped or transported using any means or facility of interstate or foreign commerce or in or affecting interstate or foreign commerce, or which was produced using materials which have been mailed or so shipped or transported, by any means including by computer, if—

(i) the producing of such visual depiction involves the use of a minor engaging in sexually explicit conduct; and

(ii) such visual depiction is of such conduct;

shall be punished as provided in subsection (b) of this section.

(b)(1) Whoever violates, or attempts or conspires to violate, paragraph (1), (2), or (3) of subsection (a) shall be fined under this title and imprisoned not less than 5 years and not more than 20 years, but if such person has a prior conviction under this chapter, section 1591, chapter 71, chapter 109A, chapter 117, or under section 920 of title 10 (article 120 of the Uniform Code of Military Justice), or under the laws of any State relating to aggravated sexual abuse, sexual abuse, or abusive sexual conduct involving a minor or ward, or the production, possession, receipt, mailing, sale, distribution, shipment, or transportation of child pornography, or sex trafficking of children, such person shall be fined under this title and imprisoned for not less than 15 years nor more than 40 years.

(2) Whoever violates, or attempts or conspires to violate, paragraph (4) of subsection (a) shall be fined under this title or imprisoned not more than 10 years, or both, but if such person has a prior conviction under this chapter, chapter 71, chapter 109A, or chapter 117, or under section 920 of Title 10 (article 120 of the Uniform Code of Military Justice), or under the laws of any State relating to aggravated sexual abuse, sexual abuse, or abusive sexual conduct involving a minor or ward, or the production, possession, receipt, mailing, sale, distribution, shipment, or transportation of child pornography, such person shall be fined under this title and imprisoned for not less than 10 years nor more than 20 years.

(c) Affirmative defense.—It shall be an affirmative defense to a charge of violating paragraph (4) of subsection (a) that the defendant—

(1) possessed less than three matters containing any visual depiction proscribed by that paragraph; and

(2) promptly and in good faith, and without retaining or allowing any person, other than a law enforcement agency, to access any visual depiction or copy thereof—

(A) took reasonable steps to destroy each such visual depiction; or

(B) reported the matter to a law enforcement agency and afforded that agency access to each such visual depiction.

18 U.S.C. § 2252A. CERTAIN ACTIVITIES RELATING TO MATERIAL CONSTITUTING OR CONTAINING CHILD PORNOGRAPHY

(a) Any person who—

(1) knowingly mails, or transports or ships using any means or facility of interstate or foreign commerce or in or affecting interstate or foreign commerce by any means, including by computer, any child pornography;

(2) knowingly receives or distributes—

(A) any child pornography that has been mailed, or using any means or facility of interstate or foreign commerce shipped or transported in or affecting interstate or foreign commerce by any means, including by computer; or

(B) any material that contains child pornography that has been mailed, or using any means or facility of interstate or foreign commerce shipped or transported in or affecting interstate or foreign commerce by any means, including by computer;

(3) knowingly—

(A) reproduces any child pornography for distribution through the mails, or using any means or facility of interstate or foreign commerce or in or affecting interstate or foreign commerce by any means, including by computer; or

(B) advertises, promotes, presents, distributes, or solicits through the mails, or using any means or facility of interstate or foreign commerce or in or affecting interstate or foreign commerce by any means, including by computer, any material or purported material in a manner that reflects the belief, or that is intended to cause another to believe, that the material or purported material is, or contains—

(i) an obscene visual depiction of a minor engaging in sexually explicit conduct; or

(ii) a visual depiction of an actual minor engaging in sexually explicit conduct;

(4) either—

(A) in the special maritime and territorial jurisdiction of the United States, or on any land or building owned by, leased to, or otherwise used by or under the control of the United States Government, or in the Indian country (as defined in section 1151), knowingly sells or possesses with the intent to sell any child pornography; or

(B) knowingly sells or possesses with the intent to sell any child pornography that has been mailed, or shipped or transported using any means or facility of interstate or foreign commerce or in or affecting interstate or foreign commerce by any means, including by computer, or that was produced using materials that have been mailed, or shipped or transported in or affecting interstate or foreign commerce by any means, including by computer;

(5) either—

(A) in the special maritime and territorial jurisdiction of the United States, or on any land or building owned by, leased to, or otherwise used by or under the control of the United States Government, or in the Indian country (as defined in section 1151), knowingly possesses, or knowingly accesses with intent to view, any book, magazine, periodical, film, videotape, computer disk, or any other material that contains an image of child pornography; or

(B) knowingly possesses, or knowingly accesses with intent to view, any book, magazine, periodical, film, videotape, computer disk, or any other material that contains an image of child pornography that has been mailed, or shipped or transported using any means or facility of interstate or foreign commerce or in or affecting interstate or foreign commerce by any means, including by computer, or that was produced using materials that have been mailed, or shipped or transported in or affecting interstate or foreign commerce by any means, including by computer;

(6) knowingly distributes, offers, sends, or provides to a minor any visual depiction, including any photograph, film, video, picture, or computer generated image or picture, whether made or produced by electronic, mechanical, or other means, where such visual depiction is, or appears to be, of a minor engaging in sexually explicit conduct—

(A) that has been mailed, shipped, or transported using any means or facility of interstate or foreign commerce or in or affecting interstate or foreign commerce by any means, including by computer;

(B) that was produced using materials that have been mailed, shipped, or transported in or affecting interstate or foreign commerce by any means, including by computer; or

(C) which distribution, offer, sending, or provision is accomplished using the mails or any means or facility of interstate or foreign commerce,

for purposes of inducing or persuading a minor to participate in any activity that is illegal; or

(7) knowingly produces with intent to distribute, or distributes, by any means, including a computer, in or affecting interstate or foreign commerce, child pornography that is an adapted or modified depiction of an identifiable minor.

shall be punished as provided in subsection (b).

(b)(1) Whoever violates, or attempts or conspires to violate, paragraph (1), (2), (3), (4), or (6) of subsection (a) shall be fined under this title and imprisoned not less than 5 years and not more than 20 years, but, if such person has a prior conviction under this chapter, section 1591, chapter 71, chapter 109A, chapter 117, or under section 920 of title 10 (article 120 of the Uniform Code of Military Justice), or under the laws of any State relating to aggravated sexual abuse, sexual abuse, or abusive sexual conduct involving a minor or ward, or the production, possession, receipt, mailing, sale, distribution, shipment, or transportation of child pornography, or sex trafficking of children, such person shall be fined under this title and imprisoned for not less than 15 years nor more than 40 years.

(2) Whoever violates, or attempts or conspires to violate, subsection (a)(5) shall be fined under this title or imprisoned not more than 10 years, or both, but, if such person has a prior conviction under this chapter, chapter 71, chapter 109A, or chapter 117, or under section 920 of title 10 (article 120 of the Uniform Code of Military Justice), or under the laws of any State relating to aggravated sexual abuse, sexual abuse, or abusive sexual conduct involving a minor or ward, or the production, possession, receipt, mailing, sale, distribution, shipment, or transportation of child pornography, such person shall be fined under this title and imprisoned for not less than 10 years nor more than 20 years.

(3) Whoever violates, or attempts or conspires to violate, subsection (a)(7) shall be fined under this title or imprisoned not more than 15 years, or both.

(c) It shall be an affirmative defense to a charge of violating paragraph (1), (2), (3)(A), (4), or (5) of subsection (a) that—

    (1)(A) the alleged child pornography was produced using an actual person or persons engaging in sexually explicit conduct; and

      (B) each such person was an adult at the time the material was produced; or

      (2) the alleged child pornography was not produced using any actual minor or minors.

No affirmative defense under subsection (c)(2) shall be available in any prosecution that involves child pornography as described in section 2256(8)(C). A defendant may not assert an affirmative defense to a charge of violating paragraph (1), (2), (3)(A), (4), or (5) of subsection (a) unless, within the time provided for filing pretrial motions or at such time prior to trial as the judge may direct, but in no event later than 10 days before the commencement of the trial, the defendant provides the court and the United States with notice of the intent to assert such defense and the substance of any expert or other specialized testimony or evidence upon which the defendant intends to rely. If the defendant fails to comply with this subsection, the court shall, absent a finding of extraordinary circumstances that prevented timely compliance, prohibit the defendant from asserting such defense to a charge of violating paragraph (1), (2), (3)(A), (4), or (5) of subsection (a) or presenting any evidence for which the defendant has failed to provide proper and timely notice.

(d) **Affirmative defense.** It shall be an affirmative defense to a charge of violating subsection (a)(5) that the defendant—

    (1) possessed less than three images of child pornography; and

    (2) promptly and in good faith, and without retaining or allowing any person, other than a law enforcement agency, to access any image or copy thereof—

      (A) took reasonable steps to destroy each such image; or

      (B) reported the matter to a law enforcement agency and afforded that agency access to each such image.

(e) **Admissibility of evidence.** On motion of the government, in any prosecution under this chapter or section 1466A, except for good cause shown, the name, address, social security number, or other nonphysical identifying information, other than the age or approximate age, of any minor who is depicted in any child pornography shall not be admissible and may be redacted from any otherwise admissible evidence, and the jury shall be instructed, upon request of the United States, that it can draw no inference from the absence of such evidence in deciding whether the child pornography depicts an actual minor.

(f) **Civil remedies.—**

(1) *In general.* Any person aggrieved by reason of the conduct prohibited under subsection (a) or (b) or section 1466A may commence a civil action for the relief set forth in paragraph (2).

(2) *Relief.* In any action commenced in accordance with paragraph (1), the court may award appropriate relief, including—

> (A) temporary, preliminary, or permanent injunctive relief;

> (B) compensatory and punitive damages; and

> (C) the costs of the civil action and reasonable fees for attorneys and expert witnesses.

(g) **Child exploitation enterprises.**

(1) Whoever engages in a child exploitation enterprise shall be fined under this title and imprisoned for any term of years not less than 20 or for life.

(2) A person engages in a child exploitation enterprise for the purposes of this section if the person violates section 1591, section 1201 if the victim is a minor, or chapter 109A (involving a minor victim), 110 (except for sections 2257 and 2257A), or 117 (involving a minor victim), as a part of a series of felony violations constituting three or more separate incidents and involving more than one victim, and commits those offenses in concert with three or more other persons.

18 U.S.C. § 2256. DEFINITIONS FOR CHAPTER

For the purposes of this chapter, the term—

(1) "minor" means any person under the age of eighteen years;

(2)(A) Except as provided in subparagraph (B), "sexually explicit conduct" means actual or simulated—

> (i) sexual intercourse, including genital-genital, oral-genital, anal-genital, or oral-anal, whether between persons of the same or opposite sex;

> (ii) bestiality;

> (iii) masturbation;

> (iv) sadistic or masochistic abuse; or

> (v) lascivious exhibition of the genitals or pubic area of any person;

(B) For purposes of subsection 8(B) of this section, "sexually explicit conduct" means—

(i) graphic sexual intercourse, including genital-genital, oral-genital, anal-genital, or oral-anal, whether between persons of the same or opposite sex, or lascivious simulated sexual intercourse where the genitals, breast, or pubic area of any person is exhibited;

(ii) graphic or lascivious simulated;

(I) bestiality;

(II) masturbation; or

(III) sadistic or masochistic abuse; or

(iii) graphic or simulated lascivious exhibition of the genitals or pubic area of any person;

(3) "producing" means producing, directing, manufacturing, issuing, publishing, or advertising;

(4) "organization" means a person other than an individual;

(5) "visual depiction" includes undeveloped film and videotape, data stored on computer disk or by electronic means which is capable of conversion into a visual image, and data which is capable of conversion into a visual image that has been transmitted by any means, whether or not stored in a permanent format;

(6) "computer" has the meaning given that term in section 1030 of this title;

(7) "custody or control" includes temporary supervision over or responsibility for a minor whether legally or illegally obtained;

(8) "child pornography" means any visual depiction, including any photograph, film, video, picture, or computer or computer-generated image or picture, whether made or produced by electronic, mechanical, or other means, of sexually explicit conduct, where—

(A) the production of such visual depiction involves the use of a minor engaging in sexually explicit conduct;

(B) such visual depiction is a digital image, computer image, or computer-generated image that is, or is indistinguishable from, that of a minor engaging in sexually explicit conduct; or

(C) such visual depiction has been created, adapted, or modified to appear that an identifiable minor is engaging in sexually explicit conduct.

(9) "identifiable minor"—

(A) means a person—

(i)(I) who was a minor at the time the visual depiction was created, adapted, or modified; or

(II) whose image as a minor was used in creating, adapting, or modifying the visual depiction; and

(ii) who is recognizable as an actual person by the person's face, likeness, or other distinguishing characteristic, such as a unique birthmark or other recognizable feature; and

(B) shall not be construed to require proof of the actual identity of the identifiable minor.

(10) "graphic", when used with respect to a depiction of sexually explicit conduct, means that a viewer can observe any part of the genitals or pubic area of any depicted person or animal during any part of the time that the sexually explicit conduct is being depicted; and

(11) the term "indistinguishable" used with respect to a depiction, means virtually indistinguishable, in that the depiction is such that an ordinary person viewing the depiction would conclude that the depiction is of an actual minor engaged in sexually explicit conduct. This definition does not apply to depictions that are drawings, cartoons, sculptures, or paintings depicting minors or adults.

18 U.S.C. § 2258A. REPORTING REQUIREMENTS OF ELECTRONIC COMMUNICATION SERVICE PROVIDERS AND REMOTE COMPUTING SERVICE PROVIDERS

(a) **Duty to report.**

(1) **In general.** Whoever, while engaged in providing an electronic communication service or a remote computing service to the public through a facility or means of interstate or foreign commerce, obtains actual knowledge of any facts or circumstances described in paragraph (2) shall, as soon as reasonably possible—

(A) provide to the CyberTipline of the National Center for Missing and Exploited Children, or any successor to the CyberTipline operated by such center, the mailing address, telephone number, facsimile number, electronic mail address of, and individual point of contact for, such electronic communication service provider or remote computing service provider; and

(B) make a report of such facts or circumstances to the CyberTipline, or any successor to the CyberTipline operated by such center.

(2) **Facts or circumstances.** The facts or circumstances described in this paragraph are any facts or circumstances from which there is an apparent violation of—

(A) section 2251, 2251A, 2252, 2252A, 2252B, or 2260 that involves child pornography; or

(B) section 1466A.

(b) **Contents of report.** To the extent the information is within the custody or control of an electronic communication service provider or a remote computing service provider, the facts and circumstances included in each report under subsection (a)(1) may include the following information:

(1) **Information about the involved individual.** Information relating to the identity of any individual who appears to have violated a Federal law described in subsection (a)(2), which may, to the extent reasonably practicable, include the electronic mail address, Internet Protocol address, uniform resource locator, or any other identifying information, including self-reported identifying information.

(2) **Historical reference.** Information relating to when and how a customer or subscriber of an electronic communication service or a remote computing service uploaded, transmitted, or received apparent child pornography or when and how apparent child pornography was reported to, or discovered by the electronic communication service provider or remote computing service provider, including a date and time stamp and time zone.

(3) **Geographic location information.**

(A) *In general.* Information relating to the geographic location of the involved individual or website, which may include the Internet Protocol address or verified billing address, or, if not reasonably available, at least 1 form of geographic identifying information, including area code or zip code.

(B) *Inclusion.* The information described in subparagraph (A) may also include any geographic information provided to the electronic communication service or remote computing service by the customer or subscriber.

(4) **Images of apparent child pornography.** Any image of apparent child pornography relating to the incident such report is regarding.

(5) **Complete communication.** The complete communication containing any image of apparent child pornography, including—

(A) any data or information regarding the transmission of the communication; and

(B) any images, data, or other digital files contained in, or attached to, the communication.

(c) **Forwarding of report to law enforcement.**

(1) **In general.** The National Center for Missing and Exploited Children shall forward each report made under subsection (a)(1) to any appropriate law enforcement agency designated by the Attorney General under subsection (d)(2).

(2) **State and local law enforcement.** The National Center for Missing and Exploited Children may forward any report made under subsection (a)(1) to an appropriate law enforcement official of a State or political subdivision of a State for the purpose of enforcing State criminal law.

(3) **Foreign law enforcement.**

(A) *In general.* The National Center for Missing and Exploited Children may forward any report made under subsection (a)(1) to any appropriate foreign law enforcement agency designated by the Attorney General under subsection (d)(3), subject to the conditions established by the Attorney General under subsection (d)(3).

(B) *Transmittal to designated Federal agencies.* If the National Center for Missing and Exploited Children forwards a report to a foreign law enforcement agency under subparagraph (A), the National Center for Missing and Exploited Children shall concurrently provide a copy of the report and the identity of the foreign law enforcement agency to—

(i) the Attorney General; or

(ii) the Federal law enforcement agency or agencies designated by the Attorney General under subsection (d)(2).

(d) **Attorney general responsibilities.**

(1) **In general.** The Attorney General shall enforce this section.

(2) **Designation of Federal agencies.** The Attorney General shall designate promptly the Federal law enforcement agency or agencies to which a report shall be forwarded under subsection (c)(1).

(3) **Designation of foreign agencies.** The Attorney General shall promptly—

(A) in consultation with the Secretary of State, designate the foreign law enforcement agencies to which a report may be forwarded under subsection (c)(3);

(B) establish the conditions under which such a report may be forwarded to such agencies; and

(C) develop a process for foreign law enforcement agencies to request assistance from Federal law enforcement agencies in obtaining evidence related to a report referred under subsection (c)(3).

(4) **Reporting designated foreign agencies.** The Attorney General shall maintain and make available to the Department of State, the National Center for Missing and Exploited Children, electronic communication service providers, remote computing service providers, the Committee on the Judiciary of the Senate, and the Committee on the Judiciary of the House of Representatives a list of the foreign law enforcement agencies designated under paragraph (3).

(5) **Sense of Congress regarding designation of foreign agencies.** It is the sense of Congress that—

(A) combating the international manufacturing, possession, and trade in online child pornography requires cooperation with competent, qualified, and appropriately trained foreign law enforcement agencies; and

(B) the Attorney General, in cooperation with the Secretary of State, should make a substantial effort to expand the list of foreign agencies designated under paragraph (3).

(6) **Notification to providers.** If an electronic communication service provider or remote computing service provider notifies the National Center for Missing and Exploited Children that the electronic communication service provider or remote computing service provider is making a report under this section as the result of a request by a foreign law enforcement agency, the National Center for Missing and Exploited Children shall—

(A) if the Center forwards the report to the requesting foreign law enforcement agency or another agency in the same country designated by the Attorney General under paragraph (3), notify the electronic communication service provider or remote computing service provider of—

(i) the identity of the foreign law enforcement agency to which the report was forwarded; and

(ii) the date on which the report was forwarded; or

(B) notify the electronic communication service provider or remote computing service provider if the Center declines to forward the report because the Center, in consultation with the Attorney General, determines that no law enforcement agency in the foreign country has been designated by the Attorney General under paragraph (3).

(e) **Failure to report.** An electronic communication service provider or remote computing service provider that knowingly and willfully fails to make a report required under subsection (a)(1) shall be fined—

(1) in the case of an initial knowing and willful failure to make a report, not more than $150,000; and

(2) in the case of any second or subsequent knowing and willful failure to make a report, not more than $300,000.

(f) **Protection of privacy.** Nothing in this section shall be construed to require an electronic communication service provider or a remote computing service provider to—

(1) monitor any user, subscriber, or customer of that provider;

(2) monitor the content of any communication of any person described in paragraph (1); or

(3) affirmatively seek facts or circumstances described in sections (a) and (b).

(g) **Conditions of disclosure information contained within report.**

(1) **In general.** Except as provided in paragraph (2), a law enforcement agency that receives a report under subsection (c) shall not disclose any information contained in that report.

(2) **Permitted disclosures by law enforcement.**

(A) *In general.* A law enforcement agency may disclose information in a report received under subsection (c)—

(i) to an attorney for the government for use in the performance of the official duties of that attorney;

(ii) to such officers and employees of that law enforcement agency, as may be necessary in the performance of their investigative and recordkeeping functions;

(iii) to such other government personnel (including personnel of a State or subdivision of a State) as are determined to be necessary by an attorney for the government to assist the attorney in the performance of the official duties of the attorney in enforcing Federal criminal law;

(iv) if the report discloses a violation of State criminal law, to an appropriate official of a State or subdivision of a State for the purpose of enforcing such State law;

(v) to a defendant in a criminal case or the attorney for that defendant, subject to the terms and limitations under section 3509(m) or a similar State law, to the extent the information relates to a criminal charge pending against that defendant;

(vi) subject to subparagraph (B), to an electronic communication service provider or remote computing provider if necessary to facilitate response to legal process issued in connection to a criminal investigation, prosecution, or post-conviction remedy relating to that report; and

(vii) as ordered by a court upon a showing of good cause and pursuant to any protective orders or other conditions that the court may impose.

(B) *Limitations.*

(i) *Limitations on further disclosure.* The electronic communication service provider or remote computing service provider shall be prohibited from disclosing the contents of a report provided under subparagraph (A)(vi) to any person, except as necessary to respond to the legal process.

(ii) *Effect.* Nothing in subparagraph (A)(vi) authorizes a law enforcement agency to provide child pornography images to an electronic communications service provider or a remote computing service.

(3) Permitted disclosures by the National Center for Missing and Exploited Children.—The National Center for Missing and Exploited Children may disclose information received in a report under subsection (a) only—

(A) to any Federal law enforcement agency designated by the Attorney General under subsection (d)(2);

(B) to any State, local, or tribal law enforcement agency involved in the investigation of child pornography, child exploitation, kidnapping, or enticement crimes;

(C) to any foreign law enforcement agency designated by the Attorney General under subsection (d)(3); and

(D) to an electronic communication service provider or remote computing service provider as described in section 2258C.

(h) Preservation.

(1) **In general.** For the purposes of this section, the notification to an electronic communication service provider or a remote computing service provider by the CyberTipline of receipt of a report under subsection (a)(1) shall be treated as a request to preserve, as if such request was made pursuant to section 2703(f).

(2) **Preservation of report.** Pursuant to paragraph (1), an electronic communication service provider or a remote computing service shall preserve the contents of the report provided pursuant to subsection (b) for 90 days after such notification by the CyberTipline.

(3) **Preservation of commingled images.** Pursuant to paragraph (1), an electronic communication service provider or a remote computing service shall preserve any images, data, or other digital files that are commingled or interspersed among the images of apparent child pornography within a particular communication or user-created folder or directory.

(4) **Protection of preserved materials.** An electronic communications service or remote computing service preserving materials under this section shall maintain the materials in a secure location and take appropriate steps to limit access by agents or employees of the service to the materials to that access necessary to comply with the requirements of this subsection.

(5) **Authorities and duties not affected.** Nothing in this section shall be construed as replacing, amending, or otherwise interfering with the authorities and duties under section 2703.

18 U.S.C. § 2261A. STALKING

Whoever—

(1) travels in interstate or foreign commerce or within the special maritime and territorial jurisdiction of the United States, or enters or leaves Indian country, with the intent to kill, injure, harass, or place under surveillance with intent to kill, injure, harass, or intimidate another person, and in the course of, or as a result of, such travel places that person in reasonable fear of the death of, or serious bodily injury to, or causes substantial emotional distress to that person, a member of the immediate family (as defined in section 115) of that person, or the spouse or intimate partner of that person; or

(2) with the intent—

(A) to kill, injure, harass, or place under surveillance with intent to kill, injure, harass, or intimidate, or cause substantial emotional distress to a person in another State or tribal jurisdiction or within the special maritime and territorial jurisdiction of the United States; or

(B) to place a person in another State or tribal jurisdiction, or within the special maritime and territorial jurisdiction of the United States, in reasonable fear of the death of, or serious bodily injury to—

(i) that person;

(ii) a member of the immediate family (as defined in section 115) of that person; or

(iii) a spouse or intimate partner of that person;

uses the mail, any interactive computer service, or any facility of interstate or foreign commerce to engage in a course of conduct that causes substantial emotional distress to that person or places that person in reasonable fear of the death of, or serious bodily injury to, any of the persons described in clauses (i) through (iii) of subparagraph (B);

shall be punished as provided in section 2261(b) of this title.

18 U.S.C. § 2314. TRANSPORTATION OF STOLEN GOODS, SECURITIES, MONEYS, FRAUDULENT STATE TAX STAMPS, OR ARTICLES USED IN COUNTERFEITING

Whoever transports, transmits, or transfers in interstate or foreign commerce any goods, wares, merchandise, securities or money, of the value of $5,000 or more, knowing the same to have been stolen, converted or taken by fraud; or

Whoever, having devised or intending to devise any scheme or artifice to defraud, or for obtaining money or property by means of false or fraudulent pretenses, representations, or promises, transports or causes to be transported, or induces any person or persons to travel in, or to be transported in interstate or foreign commerce in the execution or concealment of a scheme or artifice to defraud that person or those persons of money or property having a value of $5,000 or more; or

Whoever, with unlawful or fraudulent intent, transports in interstate or foreign commerce any falsely made, forged, altered, or counterfeited securities or tax stamps, knowing the same to have been falsely made, forged, altered, or counterfeited; or

Whoever, with unlawful or fraudulent intent, transports in interstate or foreign commerce any traveler's check bearing a forged countersignature; or

Whoever, with unlawful or fraudulent intent, transports in interstate or foreign commerce, any tool, implement, or thing used or fitted to be used in falsely making, forging, altering, or counterfeiting any security or tax stamps, or any part thereof—

Shall be fined under this title or imprisoned not more than ten years, or both.

This section shall not apply to any falsely made, forged, altered, counterfeited or spurious representation of an obligation or other security of the United States, or of an obligation, bond, certificate, security, treasury note, bill, promise to pay or bank note issued by any foreign government. This section also shall not apply to any falsely made, forged, altered, counterfeited, or spurious representation of any bank note or bill issued by a bank or corporation of any foreign country which is intended by the laws or usage of such country to circulate as money.

18 U.S.C. § 2319. CRIMINAL INFRINGEMENT OF A COPYRIGHT

(a) Any person who violates section 506(a) (relating to criminal offenses) of title 17 shall be punished as provided in subsections (b), (c), and (d) and such penalties shall be in addition to any other provisions of title 17 or any other law.

(b) Any person who commits an offense under section 506(a)(1)(A) of title 17—

(1) shall be imprisoned not more than 5 years, or fined in the amount set forth in this title, or both, if the offense consists of the reproduction or distribution, including by electronic means, during any 180-day period, of at least 10 copies or phonorecords, of 1 or more copyrighted works, which have a total retail value of more than $2,500;

(2) shall be imprisoned not more than 10 years, or fined in the amount set forth in this title, or both, if the offense is a felony and is a second or subsequent offense under subsection (a); and

(3) shall be imprisoned not more than 1 year, or fined in the amount set forth in this title, or both, in any other case.

(c) Any person who commits an offense under section 506(a)(1)(B) of title 17—

(1) shall be imprisoned not more than 3 years, or fined in the amount set forth in this title, or both, if the offense consists of the reproduction or distribution of 10 or more copies or phonorecords of 1 or more copyrighted works, which have a total retail value of $2,500 or more;

(2) shall be imprisoned not more than 6 years, or fined in the amount set forth in this title, or both, if the offense is a felony and is a second or subsequent offense under subsection (a); and

(3) shall be imprisoned not more than 1 year, or fined in the amount set forth in this title, or both, if the offense consists of the reproduction or distribution of 1 or more copies or phonorecords of 1 or more copyrighted works, which have a total retail value of more than $1,000.

(d) Any person who commits an offense under section 506(a)(1)(C) of title 17—

(1) shall be imprisoned not more than 3 years, fined under this title, or both;

(2) shall be imprisoned not more than 5 years, fined under this title, or both, if the offense was committed for purposes of commercial advantage or private financial gain;

(3) shall be imprisoned not more than 6 years, fined under this title, or both, if the offense is a felony and is a second or subsequent offense under subsection (a); and

(4) shall be imprisoned not more than 10 years, fined under this title, or both, if the offense is a felony and is a second or subsequent offense under paragraph (2).

(e)(1) During preparation of the presentence report pursuant to Rule 32(c) of the Federal Rules of Criminal Procedure, victims of the offense shall be permitted to submit, and the probation officer shall receive, a victim impact statement that identifies the victim of the offense and the extent and scope of the injury and loss suffered by the victim, including the estimated economic impact of the offense on that victim.

(2) Persons permitted to submit victim impact statements shall include—

(A) producers and sellers of legitimate works affected by conduct involved in the offense;

(B) holders of intellectual property rights in such works; and

(C) the legal representatives of such producers, sellers, and holders.

(f) As used in this section—

(1) the terms "phonorecord" and "copies" have, respectively, the meanings set forth in section 101 (relating to definitions) of title 17;

(2) the terms "reproduction" and "distribution" refer to the exclusive rights of a copyright owner under clauses (1) and (3) respectively of section 106 (relating to exclusive rights in copyrighted works), as limited by sections 107 through 122, of title 17;

(3) the term "financial gain" has the meaning given the term in section 101 of title 17; and

(4) the term "work being prepared for commercial distribution" has the meaning given the term in section 506(a) of title 17.

17 U.S.C. § 506.   CRIMINAL OFFENSES

(a) Criminal infringement.

(1) *In general.* Any person who willfully infringes a copyright shall be punished as provided under section 2319 of title 18, if the infringement was committed—

(A) for purposes of commercial advantage or private financial gain;

(B) by the reproduction or distribution, including by electronic means, during any 180-day period, of 1 or more copies or phonorecords of 1 or more copyrighted works, which have a total retail value of more than $1,000; or

(C) by the distribution of a work being prepared for commercial distribution, by making it available on a computer network accessible to members of the public, if such person knew or should have known that the work was intended for commercial distribution.

(2) *Evidence.* For purposes of this subsection, evidence of reproduction or distribution of a copyrighted work, by itself, shall not be sufficient to establish willful infringement of a copyright.

(3) *Definition.* In this subsection, the term "work being prepared for commercial distribution" means—

(A) a computer program, a musical work, a motion picture or other audiovisual work, or a sound recording, if, at the time of unauthorized distribution—

(i) the copyright owner has a reasonable expectation of commercial distribution; and

(ii) the copies or phonorecords of the work have not been commercially distributed; or

(B) a motion picture, if, at the time of unauthorized distribution, the motion picture—

(i) has been made available for viewing in a motion picture exhibition facility; and

(ii) has not been made available in copies for sale to the general public in the United States in a format intended to permit viewing outside a motion picture exhibition facility.

(b) **Forfeiture, destruction, and restitution.** Forfeiture, destruction, and restitution relating to this section shall be subject to section 2323 of title 18, to the extent provided in that section, in addition to any other similar remedies provided by law.

(c) **Fraudulent Copyright Notice.** Any person who, with fraudulent intent, places on any article a notice of copyright or words of the same purport that such person knows to be false, or who, with fraudulent intent, publicly distributes or imports for public distribution any article bearing such notice or words that such person knows to be false, shall be fined not more than $2,500.

(d) **Fraudulent Removal of Copyright Notice.** Any person who, with fraudulent intent, removes or alters any notice of copyright appearing on a copy of a copyrighted work shall be fined not more than $2,500.

(e) **False Representation.** Any person who knowingly makes a false representation of a material fact in the application for copyright registration provided for by section 409, or in any written statement filed in connection with the application, shall be fined not more than $2,500.

(f) **Rights of Attribution and Integrity.** Nothing in this section applies to infringement of the rights conferred by section 106A(a).

18 U.S.C. § 2422. COERCION AND ENTICEMENT

(a) Whoever knowingly persuades, induces, entices, or coerces any individual to travel in interstate or foreign commerce, or in any Territory or Possession of the United States, to engage in prostitution, or in any sexual activity for which any person can be charged with a criminal offense, or attempts to do so, shall be fined under this title or imprisoned not more than 20 years, or both.

(b) Whoever, using the mail or any facility or means of interstate or foreign commerce, or within the special maritime and territorial jurisdiction of the United States knowingly persuades, induces, entices, or coerces any individual who has not attained the age of 18 years, to engage in prostitution or any sexual activity for which any person can be charged with a criminal offense, or attempts to do so, shall be fined under this title and imprisoned not less than 10 years or for life.

18 U.S.C. § 2423. TRANSPORTATION OF MINORS

(a) **Transportation with intent to engage in criminal sexual activity.** A person who knowingly transports an individual who has not attained the age of 18 years in interstate or foreign commerce, or in any commonwealth, territory or possession of the United States, with intent that the individual engage in prostitution, or in any sexual activity for which any person can be charged with a criminal offense, shall be fined under this title and imprisoned not less than 10 years or for life.

(b) **Travel with intent to engage in illicit sexual conduct.** A person who travels in interstate commerce or travels into the United States, or a United States citizen or an alien admitted for permanent residence in the United States who travels in foreign commerce, for the purpose of engaging in any illicit sexual conduct with another person shall be fined under this title or imprisoned not more than 30 years, or both.

(c) **Engaging in illicit sexual conduct in foreign places.** Any United States citizen or alien admitted for permanent residence who travels in foreign commerce, and engages in any illicit sexual conduct with another person shall be fined under this title or imprisoned not more than 30 years, or both.

(d) **Ancillary offenses.** Whoever, for the purpose of commercial advantage or private financial gain, arranges, induces, procures, or facilitates the travel of a person knowing that such a person is traveling in interstate commerce or foreign commerce for the purpose of engaging in illicit sexual conduct shall be fined under this title, imprisoned not more than 30 years, or both.

(e) **Attempt and conspiracy.** Whoever attempts or conspires to violate subsection (a), (b), (c), or (d) shall be punishable in the same manner as a completed violation of that subsection.

(f) **Definition.** As used in this section, the term "illicit sexual conduct" means (1) a sexual act (as defined in section 2246) with a person under 18 years of age that would be in violation of chapter 109A if the sexual act occurred in the special maritime and territorial jurisdiction of the United States; or (2) any commercial sex act (as defined in section 1591) with a person under 18 years of age.

(g) **Defense.** In a prosecution under this section based on illicit sexual conduct as defined in subsection (f)(2), it is a defense, which the defendant must establish by a preponderance of the evidence, that the defendant reasonably believed that the person with whom the defendant engaged in the commercial sex act had attained the age of 18 years.

18 U.S.C. § 2510. DEFINITIONS

As used in this chapter—

(1) "wire communication" means any aural transfer made in whole or in part through the use of facilities for the transmission of communications by the aid of wire, cable, or other like connection between the point of origin and the point of reception (including the use of such connection in a switching station) furnished or operated by any

person engaged in providing or operating such facilities for the transmission of interstate or foreign communications or communications affecting interstate or foreign commerce;

(2) "oral communication" means any oral communication uttered by a person exhibiting an expectation that such communication is not subject to interception under circumstances justifying such expectation, but such term does not include any electronic communication;

(3) "State" means any State of the United States, the District of Columbia, the Commonwealth of Puerto Rico, and any territory or possession of the United States;

(4) "intercept" means the aural or other acquisition of the contents of any wire, electronic, or oral communication through the use of any electronic, mechanical, or other device.

(5) "electronic, mechanical, or other device" means any device or apparatus which can be used to intercept a wire, oral, or electronic communication other than—

    (A) any telephone or telegraph instrument, equipment or facility, or any component thereof, (i) furnished to the subscriber or user by a provider of wire or electronic communication service in the ordinary course of its business and being used by the subscriber or user in the ordinary course of its business or furnished by such subscriber or user for connection to the facilities of such service and used in the ordinary course of its business; or (ii) being used by a provider of wire or electronic communication service in the ordinary course of its business, or by an investigative or law enforcement officer in the ordinary course of his duties;

    (B) a hearing aid or similar device being used to correct subnormal hearing to not better than normal;

(6) "person" means any employee, or agent of the United States or any State or political subdivision thereof, and any individual, partnership, association, joint stock company, trust, or corporation;

(7) "Investigative or law enforcement officer" means any officer of the United States or of a State or political subdivision thereof, who is empowered by law to conduct investigations of or to make arrests for offenses enumerated in this chapter, and any attorney authorized by law to prosecute or participate in the prosecution of such offenses;

(8) "contents", when used with respect to any wire, oral, or electronic communication, includes any information concerning the substance, purport, or meaning of that communication;

(9) "Judge of competent jurisdiction" means—

(A) a judge of a United States district court or a United States court of appeals; and

(B) a judge of any court of general criminal jurisdiction of a State who is authorized by a statute of that State to enter orders authorizing interceptions of wire, oral, or electronic communications;

(10) "communication common carrier" has the meaning given that term in section 3 of the Communications Act of 1934;

(11) "aggrieved person" means a person who was a party to any intercepted wire, oral, or electronic communication or a person against whom the interception was directed;

(12) "electronic communication" means any transfer of signs, signals, writing, images, sounds, data, or intelligence of any nature transmitted in whole or in part by a wire, radio, electromagnetic, photoelectronic or photooptical system that affects interstate or foreign commerce, but does not include—

(A) any wire or oral communication;

(B) any communication made through a tone-only paging device;

(C) any communication from a tracking device (as defined in section 3117 of this title); or

(D) electronic funds transfer information stored by a financial institution in a communications system used for the electronic storage and transfer of funds;

(13) "user" means any person or entity who—

(A) uses an electronic communication service; and

(B) is duly authorized by the provider of such service to engage in such use;

(14) "electronic communications system" means any wire, radio, electromagnetic, photooptical or photoelectronic facilities for the transmission of wire or electronic communications, and any computer facilities or related electronic equipment for the electronic storage of such communications;

(15) "electronic communication service" means any service which provides to users thereof the ability to send or receive wire or electronic communications;

(16) "readily accessible to the general public" means, with respect to a radio communication, that such communication is not—

(A) scrambled or encrypted;

(B) transmitted using modulation techniques whose essential parameters have been withheld from the public with the intention of preserving the privacy of such communication;

(C) carried on a subcarrier or other signal subsidiary to a radio transmission;

(D) transmitted over a communication system provided by a common carrier, unless the communication is a tone only paging system communication; or

(E) transmitted on frequencies allocated under part 25, subpart D, E, or F of part 74, or part 94 of the Rules of the Federal Communications Commission, unless, in the case of a communication transmitted on a frequency allocated under part 74 that is not exclusively allocated to broadcast auxiliary services, the communication is a two-way voice communication by radio;

(17) "electronic storage" means—

(A) any temporary, intermediate storage of a wire or electronic communication incidental to the electronic transmission thereof; and

(B) any storage of such communication by an electronic communication service for purposes of backup protection of such communication;

(18) "aural transfer" means a transfer containing the human voice at any point between and including the point of origin and the point of reception;

(19) "foreign intelligence information", for purposes of section 2517(6) of this title, means—

(A) information, whether or not concerning a United States person, that relates to the ability of the United States to protect against—

(i) actual or potential attack or other grave hostile acts of a foreign power or an agent of a foreign power;

(ii) sabotage or international terrorism by a foreign power or an agent of a foreign power; or

(iii) clandestine intelligence activities by an intelligence service or network of a foreign power or by an agent of a foreign power; or

(B) information, whether or not concerning a United States person, with respect to a foreign power or foreign territory that relates to—

(i) the national defense or the security of the United States; or

(ii) the conduct of the foreign affairs of the United States;

(20) "protected computer" has the meaning set forth in section 1030; and

(21) "computer trespasser"—

(A) means a person who accesses a protected computer without authorization and thus has no reasonable expectation of privacy in any communication transmitted to, through, or from the protected computer; and

(B) does not include a person known by the owner or operator of the protected computer to have an existing contractual relationship with the owner or operator of the protected computer for access to all or part of the protected computer.

18 U.S.C. § 2511. INTERCEPTION AND DISCLOSURE OF WIRE, ORAL, OR ELECTRONIC COMMUNICATIONS PROHIBITED

(1) Except as otherwise specifically provided in this chapter any person who—

(a) intentionally intercepts, endeavors to intercept, or procures any other person to intercept or endeavor to intercept, any wire, oral, or electronic communication;

(b) intentionally uses, endeavors to use, or procures any other person to use or endeavor to use any electronic, mechanical, or other device to intercept any oral communication when—

(i) such device is affixed to, or otherwise transmits a signal through, a wire, cable, or other like connection used in wire communication; or

(ii) such device transmits communications by radio, or interferes with the transmission of such communication; or

(iii) such person knows, or has reason to know, that such device or any component thereof has been sent through the mail or transported in interstate or foreign commerce; or

(iv) such use or endeavor to use (A) takes place on the premises of any business or other commercial establishment the operations of which affect interstate or foreign commerce; or (B) obtains or is for the purpose of obtaining information relating to the operations of any business or other commercial establishment the operations of which affect interstate or foreign commerce; or

(v) such person acts in the District of Columbia, the Commonwealth of Puerto Rico, or any territory or possession of the United States;

(c) intentionally discloses, or endeavors to disclose, to any other person the contents of any wire, oral, or electronic communication, knowing or having reason to know that the information was obtained through the interception of a wire, oral, or electronic communication in violation of this subsection;

(d) intentionally uses, or endeavors to use, the contents of any wire, oral, or electronic communication, knowing or having reason to know that the information was obtained through the interception of a wire, oral, or electronic communication in violation of this subsection; or

(e)(i) intentionally discloses, or endeavors to disclose, to any other person the contents of any wire, oral, or electronic communication, intercepted by means authorized by sections 2511(2)(a)(ii), 2511(2)(b)–(c), 2511(2)(e), 2516, and 2518 of this chapter, (ii) knowing or having reason to know that the information was obtained through the interception of such a communication in connection with a criminal investigation, (iii) having obtained or received the information in connection with a criminal investigation, and (iv) with intent to improperly obstruct, impede, or interfere with a duly authorized criminal investigation,

shall be punished as provided in subsection (4) or shall be subject to suit as provided in subsection (5).

(2)(a)(i) It shall not be unlawful under this chapter for an operator of a switchboard, or an officer, employee, or agent of a provider of wire or electronic communication service, whose facilities are used in the transmission of a wire or electronic communication, to intercept, disclose, or use that communication in the normal course of his employment while engaged in any activity which is a necessary incident to the rendition of his service or to the protection of the rights or property of the provider of that service, except that a provider of wire communication service to the public shall not utilize service observing or random monitoring except for mechanical or service quality control checks.

(ii) Notwithstanding any other law, providers of wire or electronic communication service, their officers, employees, and agents, landlords, custodians, or other persons, are authorized to provide information, facilities, or technical assistance to persons authorized by law to intercept wire, oral, or electronic communications or to conduct electronic surveillance, as defined in section 101 of the Foreign Intelligence Surveillance Act of 1978, if such provider, its officers, employees, or agents, landlord, custodian, or other specified person, has been provided with—

(A) a court order directing such assistance or a court order pursuant to section 704 of the Foreign Intelligence Surveillance Act of 1978 signed by the authorizing judge, or

(B) a certification in writing by a person specified in section 2518(7) of this title or the Attorney General of the United States that no warrant or court order is required by law, that all statutory requirements have been met, and that the specified assistance is required,

setting forth period of time during which the provision of the information, facilities, or technical assistance is authorized and specifying the information, facilities, or technical assistance required. No provider of wire or electronic communication service, officer, employee, or agent thereof, or landlord, custodian, or other specified person shall disclose the existence of any interception or surveillance or the device used to accomplish the interception or surveillance with respect to which the person has been furnished a court order or certification under this chapter, except as may otherwise be required by legal process and then only after prior notification to the Attorney General or to the principal prosecuting attorney of a State or any political subdivision of a State, as may be appropriate. Any such disclosure, shall render such person liable for the civil damages provided for in section 2520. No cause of action shall lie in any court against any provider of wire or electronic communication service, its officers, employees, or agents, landlord, custodian, or other specified person for providing information, facilities, or assistance in accordance with the terms of a court order, statutory authorization, or certification under this chapter.

(iii) If a certification under subparagraph (ii)(B) for assistance to obtain foreign intelligence information is based on statutory authority, the certification shall identify the specific statutory provision and shall certify that the statutory requirements have been met.

(b) It shall not be unlawful under this chapter for an officer, employee, or agent of the Federal Communications Commission, in the normal course of his employment and in discharge of the monitoring responsibilities exercised by the Commission in the enforcement of chapter 5 of title 47 of the United States Code, to intercept a wire or electronic communication, or oral communication transmitted by radio, or to disclose or use the information thereby obtained.

(c) It shall not be unlawful under this chapter for a person acting under color of law to intercept a wire, oral, or electronic communication, where such person is a party to the communication or one of the parties to the communication has given prior consent to such interception.

(d) It shall not be unlawful under this chapter for a person not acting under color of law to intercept a wire, oral, or electronic communication where such person is a party to the communication or where one of the parties to the communication has given prior consent to such interception unless such communication is intercepted for the purpose of committing any criminal or tortious act in violation of the Constitution or laws of the United States or of any State.

(e) Notwithstanding any other provision of this title or section 705 or 706 of the Communications Act of 1934, it shall not be unlawful for an officer, employee, or agent of the United States in the normal course of his official duty to conduct electronic surveillance, as defined in section 101 of the Foreign Intelligence Surveillance Act of 1978, as authorized by that Act.

(f) Nothing contained in this chapter or chapter 121 or 206 of this title, or section 705 of the Communications Act of 1934, shall be deemed to affect the acquisition by the United States Government of foreign intelligence information from international or foreign communications, or foreign intelligence activities conducted in accordance with otherwise applicable Federal law involving a foreign electronic communications system, utilizing a means other than electronic surveillance as defined in section 101 of the Foreign Intelligence Surveillance Act of 1978, and procedures in this chapter or chapter 121 and the Foreign Intelligence Surveillance Act of 1978 shall be the exclusive means by which electronic surveillance, as defined in section 101 of such Act, and the interception of domestic wire, oral, and electronic communications may be conducted.

(g) It shall not be unlawful under this chapter or chapter 121 of this title for any person—

(i) to intercept or access an electronic communication made through an electronic communication system that is configured so that such electronic communication is readily accessible to the general public;

(ii) to intercept any radio communication which is transmitted—

(I) by any station for the use of the general public, or that relates to ships, aircraft, vehicles, or persons in distress;

(II) by any governmental, law enforcement, civil defense, private land mobile, or public safety communications system, including police and fire, readily accessible to the general public;

(III) by a station operating on an authorized frequency within the bands allocated to the amateur, citizens band, or general mobile radio services; or

(IV) by any marine or aeronautical communications system;

(iii) to engage in any conduct which—

(I) is prohibited by section 633 of the Communications Act of 1934; or

(II) is excepted from the application of section 705(a) of the Communications Act of 1934 by section 705(b) of that Act;

(iv) to intercept any wire or electronic communication the transmission of which is causing harmful interference to any lawfully operating station or consumer electronic equipment, to the extent necessary to identify the source of such interference; or

(v) for other users of the same frequency to intercept any radio communication made through a system that utilizes frequencies monitored by individuals engaged in the provision or the use of such system, if such communication is not scrambled or encrypted.

(h) It shall not be unlawful under this chapter—

(i) to use a pen register or a trap and trace device (as those terms are defined for the purposes of chapter 206 (relating to pen registers and trap and trace devices) of this title); or

(ii) for a provider of electronic communication service to record the fact that a wire or electronic communication was initiated or completed in order to protect such provider, another provider furnishing service toward the completion of the wire or electronic communication, or a user of that service, from fraudulent, unlawful or abusive use of such service.

(i) It shall not be unlawful under this chapter for a person acting under color of law to intercept the wire or electronic communications of a computer trespasser transmitted to, through, or from the protected computer, if—

(I) the owner or operator of the protected computer authorizes the interception of the computer trespasser's communications on the protected computer;

(II) the person acting under color of law is lawfully engaged in an investigation;

(III) the person acting under color of law has reasonable grounds to believe that the contents of the computer trespasser's communications will be relevant to the investigation; and

(IV) such interception does not acquire communications other than those transmitted to or from the computer trespasser.

(3)(a) Except as provided in paragraph (b) of this subsection, a person or entity providing an electronic communication service to the public shall not intentionally divulge the contents of any communication (other than one to such person or entity, or an agent thereof) while in transmission on that service to any person or entity other than an addressee or intended recipient of such communication or an agent of such addressee or intended recipient.

(b) A person or entity providing electronic communication service to the public may divulge the contents of any such communication—

(i) as otherwise authorized in section 2511(2)(a) or 2517 of this title;

(ii) with the lawful consent of the originator or any addressee or intended recipient of such communication;

(iii) to a person employed or authorized, or whose facilities are used, to forward such communication to its destination; or

(iv) which were inadvertently obtained by the service provider and which appear to pertain to the commission of a crime, if such divulgence is made to a law enforcement agency.

(4)(a) Except as provided in paragraph (b) of this subsection or in subsection (5), whoever violates subsection (1) of this section shall be fined under this title or imprisoned not more than five years, or both.

(b) Conduct otherwise an offense under this subsection that consists of or relates to the interception of a satellite transmission that is not encrypted or scrambled and that is transmitted—

(i) to a broadcasting station for purposes of retransmission to the general public; or

(ii) as an audio subcarrier intended for redistribution to facilities open to the public, but not including data transmissions or telephone calls, is not an offense under this subsection unless the conduct is for the purposes of direct or indirect commercial advantage or private financial gain.

(5)(a)(i) If the communication is—

(A) a private satellite video communication that is not scrambled or encrypted and the conduct in violation of this chapter is the private viewing of that communication and is not for a tortious or illegal purpose or for purposes of direct or indirect commercial advantage or private commercial gain; or

(B) a radio communication that is transmitted on frequencies allocated under subpart D of part 74 of the rules of the Federal Communications Commission that is not scrambled or encrypted and the conduct in violation of this chapter is not for a tortious or illegal purpose or for purposes of direct or indirect commercial advantage or private commercial gain,

then the person who engages in such conduct shall be subject to suit by the Federal Government in a court of competent jurisdiction.

(ii) In an action under this subsection—

(A) if the violation of this chapter is a first offense for the person under paragraph (a) of subsection (4) and such person has not been found liable in a civil action under section 2520 of this title, the Federal Government shall be entitled to appropriate injunctive relief; and

(B) if the violation of this chapter is a second or subsequent offense under paragraph (a) of subsection (4) or such person has been found liable in any prior civil action under section 2520, the person shall be subject to a mandatory $500 civil fine.

(b) The court may use any means within its authority to enforce an injunction issued under paragraph (ii)(A), and shall impose a civil fine of not less than $500 for each violation of such an injunction.

18 U.S.C. § 2512. MANUFACTURE, DISTRIBUTION, POSSESSION, AND ADVERTISING OF WIRE, ORAL, OR ELECTRONIC COMMUNICATION INTERCEPTING DEVICES PROHIBITED

(1) Except as otherwise specifically provided in this chapter, any person who intentionally—

(a) sends through the mail, or sends or carries in interstate or foreign commerce, any electronic, mechanical, or other device, knowing or having reason to know that the design of such device renders it primarily useful for the purpose of the surreptitious interception of wire, oral, or electronic communications;

(b) manufactures, assembles, possesses, or sells any electronic, mechanical, or other device, knowing or having reason to know that the design of such device renders it primarily useful for the purpose of the surreptitious interception of wire, oral, or electronic communications, and that such device or any component thereof has been or will be sent through the mail or transported in interstate or foreign commerce; or

(c) places in any newspaper, magazine, handbill, or other publication or disseminates by electronic means any advertisement of—

(i) any electronic, mechanical, or other device knowing the content of the advertisement and knowing or having reason to know that the design of such device renders it primarily useful for the purpose of the surreptitious interception of wire, oral, or electronic communications; or

(ii) any other electronic, mechanical, or other device, where such advertisement promotes the use of such device for the purpose of the surreptitious interception of wire, oral, or electronic communications,

knowing the content of the advertisement and knowing or having reason to know that such advertisement will be sent through the mail or transported in interstate or foreign commerce,

shall be fined under this title or imprisoned not more than five years, or both.

(2) It shall not be unlawful under this section for—

(a) a provider of wire or electronic communication service or an officer, agent, or employee of, or a person under contract with, such a provider, in the normal course of the business of providing that wire or electronic communication service, or

(b) an officer, agent, or employee of, or a person under contract with, the United States, a State, or a political subdivision thereof, in the normal course of the activities of the United States, a State, or a political subdivision thereof,

to send through the mail, send or carry in interstate or foreign commerce, or manufacture, assemble, possess, or sell any electronic, mechanical, or other device knowing or having reason to know that the design of such device renders it primarily useful for the purpose of the surreptitious interception of wire, oral, or electronic communications.

(3) It shall not be unlawful under this section to advertise for sale a device described in subsection (1) of this section if the advertisement is mailed, sent, or carried in interstate or foreign commerce solely to a domestic provider of wire or electronic communication service or to an agency of the United States, a State, or a political subdivision thereof which is duly authorized to use such device.

18 U.S.C. § 2513. CONFISCATION OF WIRE, ORAL, OR ELECTRONIC COMMUNICATION INTERCEPTING DEVICES

Any electronic, mechanical, or other device used, sent, carried, manufactured, assembled, possessed, sold, or advertised in violation of section 2511 or section 2512 of this chapter may be seized and forfeited to the United States. All provisions of law relating to (1) the seizure, summary and judicial forfeiture, and condemnation of vessels, vehicles, merchandise, and baggage for violations of the customs laws contained in title 19 of the United States Code, (2) the disposition of such vessels, vehicles, merchandise, and baggage or the proceeds from the sale thereof, (3) the remission or mitigation of such forfeiture, (4) the compromise of claims, and (5) the award of compensation to informers in respect of such forfeitures, shall apply to seizures and forfeitures incurred, or alleged to have been incurred, under the provisions of this section, insofar as applicable and not inconsistent with the provisions of this section; except that such duties as are imposed upon the collector of customs or any other person with respect to the seizure and forfeiture of vessels, vehicles, merchandise, and baggage under the provisions of the customs laws contained in title 19 of the United States Code shall be performed with respect to seizure and forfeiture of electronic, mechanical, or other intercepting devices under this section by such officers, agents, or other persons as may be authorized or designated for that purpose by the Attorney General.

18 U.S.C. § 2515. PROHIBITION OF USE AS EVIDENCE OF INTERCEPTED WIRE OR ORAL COMMUNICATIONS

Whenever any wire or oral communication has been intercepted, no part of the contents of such communication and no evidence derived therefrom may be received in evidence in any trial, hearing, or other proceeding in or before any court, grand jury, department, officer, agency, regulatory body, legislative committee, or other authority of the United States, a State, or a political subdivision thereof if the disclosure of that information would be in violation of this chapter.

18 U.S.C. § 2516. AUTHORIZATION FOR INTERCEPTION OF WIRE, ORAL, OR ELECTRONIC COMMUNICATIONS

(1) The Attorney General, Deputy Attorney General, Associate Attorney General, or any Assistant Attorney General, any acting Assistant Attorney General, or any Deputy Assistant Attorney General or

acting Deputy Assistant Attorney General in the Criminal Division or National Security Division specially designated by the Attorney General, may authorize an application to a Federal judge of competent jurisdiction for, and such judge may grant in conformity with section 2518 of this chapter an order authorizing or approving the interception of wire or oral communications by the Federal Bureau of Investigation, or a Federal agency having responsibility for the investigation of the offense as to which the application is made, when such interception may provide or has provided evidence of—

(a) any offense punishable by death or by imprisonment for more than one year under sections 2122 and 2274 through 2277 of title 42 of the United States Code (relating to the enforcement of the Atomic Energy Act of 1954), section 2284 of title 42 of the United States Code (relating to sabotage of nuclear facilities or fuel), or under the following chapters of this title: chapter 10 (relating to biological weapons), chapter 37 (relating to espionage), chapter 55 (relating to kidnapping), chapter 90 (relating to protection of trade secrets), chapter 105 (relating to sabotage), chapter 115 (relating to treason), chapter 102 (relating to riots), chapter 65 (relating to malicious mischief), chapter 111 (relating to destruction of vessels), or chapter 81 (relating to piracy);

(b) a violation of section 186 or section 501(c) of title 29, United States Code (dealing with restrictions on payments and loans to labor organizations), or any offense which involves murder, kidnapping, robbery, or extortion, and which is punishable under this title;

(c) any offense which is punishable under the following sections of this title: section 37 (relating to violence at international airports), section 43 (relating to animal enterprise terrorism), section 81 (arson within special maritime and territorial jurisdiction), section 201 (bribery of public officials and witnesses), section 215 (relating to bribery of bank officials), section 224 (bribery in sporting contests), subsection (d), (e), (f), (g), (h), or (i) of section 844 (unlawful use of explosives), section 1032 (relating to concealment of assets), section 1084 (transmission of wagering information), section 751 (relating to escape), section 832 (relating to nuclear and weapons of mass destruction threats), section 842 (relating to explosive materials), section 930 (relating to possession of weapons in Federal facilities), section 1014 (relating to loans and credit applications generally; renewals and discounts), section 1114 (relating to officers and employees of the United States), section 1116 (relating to protection of foreign officials), sections 1503, 1512, and 1513 (influencing or injuring an officer, juror, or witness generally), section 1510 (obstruction of criminal investigations), section 1511 (obstruction of State or local law enforcement), section 1591 (sex trafficking of children by force, fraud, or coercion), section 1751 (Presidential and Presidential staff assassination, kidnapping, and assault), section 1951 (interference with commerce by threats or violence), section 1952 (interstate and foreign travel or transportation in aid of racketeering enterprises), section 1958 (relating to use of interstate commerce facilities in the commission of murder for hire), section 1959 (relating to violent crimes in aid of racketeering activity), section 1954 (offer, acceptance, or solicitation to influence operations of employee benefit plan), section 1955 (prohibition of business enterprises of gambling), section 1956 (laundering of monetary instruments), section 1957 (relating to engaging in monetary transactions in property derived from specified unlawful activity), section 659 (theft from interstate shipment), section 664 (embezzlement from pension and welfare funds), section 1343 (fraud by wire, radio, or television), section 1344 (relating to bank fraud), section 1992 (relating to terrorist attacks against mass transportation), sections 2251 and 2252 (sexual exploitation of children), section 2251A (selling or buying of children), section 2252A (relating to material constituting or containing child pornography), section 1466A (relating to child obscenity), section 2260 (production of sexually explicit depictions of a minor for importation into the United States), sections 2421, 2422, 2423, and 2425 (relating to transportation for illegal sexual activity and related crimes), sections 2312, 2313, 2314, and 2315 (interstate transportation of stolen property), section 2321 (relating to trafficking in certain motor vehicles or motor vehicle parts), section 2340A (relating to torture), section 1203 (relating to hostage taking), section 1029 (relating to fraud and related activity in connection with access devices), section 3146 (relating to penalty for failure to appear), section 3521(b)(3) (relating to witness relocation and assistance), section 32 (relating to destruction of aircraft or aircraft facilities), section 38 (relating to aircraft parts fraud), section 1963 (violations with respect to racketeer influenced and corrupt organizations), section 115 (relating to threatening or retaliating against a Federal official), section 1341 (relating to mail fraud), a felony violation of section 1030 (relating to computer fraud and abuse), section 351 (violations with respect to congressional, Cabinet, or Supreme Court assassinations, kidnapping, and assault), section 831 (relating to prohibited transactions involving nuclear materials), section 33 (relating to destruction of motor vehicles or motor vehicle facilities), section 175 (relating to biological weapons), section 175c (relating to variola virus), section 956 (conspiracy to harm persons or property overseas), a felony violation of section 1028 (relating to production of false identification documentation), section 1425 (relating to the procurement of citizenship or nationalization unlawfully), section

1426 (relating to the reproduction of naturalization or citizenship papers), section 1427 (relating to the sale of naturalization or citizenship papers), section 1541 (relating to passport issuance without authority), section 1542 (relating to false statements in passport applications), section 1543 (relating to forgery or false use of passports), section 1544 (relating to misuse of passports), or section 1546 (relating to fraud and misuse of visas, permits, and other documents);

(d) any offense involving counterfeiting punishable under section 471, 472, or 473 of this title;

(e) any offense involving fraud connected with a case under title 11 or the manufacture, importation, receiving, concealment, buying, selling, or otherwise dealing in narcotic drugs, marihuana, or other dangerous drugs, punishable under any law of the United States;

(f) any offense including extortionate credit transactions under sections 892, 893, or 894 of this title;

(g) a violation of section 5322 of title 31, United States Code (dealing with the reporting of currency transactions), or section 5324 of title 31, United States Code (relating to structuring transactions to evade reporting requirement prohibited);

(h) any felony violation of sections 2511 and 2512 (relating to interception and disclosure of certain communications and to certain intercepting devices) of this title;

(i) any felony violation of chapter 71 (relating to obscenity) of this title;

(j) any violation of section 60123(b) (relating to destruction of a natural gas pipeline), section 46502 (relating to aircraft piracy), the second sentence of section 46504 (relating to assault on a flight crew with dangerous weapon), or section 46505(b)(3) or (c) (relating to explosive or incendiary devices, or endangerment of human life, by means of weapons on aircraft) of title 49;

(k) any criminal violation of section 2778 of title 22 (relating to the Arms Export Control Act);

(*l*) the location of any fugitive from justice from an offense described in this section;

(m) a violation of section 274, 277, or 278 of the Immigration and Nationality Act (8 U.S.C. 1324, 1327, or 1328) (relating to the smuggling of aliens);

(n) any felony violation of sections 922 and 924 of title 18, United States Code (relating to firearms);

(*o*) any violation of section 5861 of the Internal Revenue Code of 1986 (relating to firearms);

(p) a felony violation of section 1028 (relating to production of false identification documents), section 1542 (relating to false statements in passport applications), section 1546 (relating to fraud and misuse of visas, permits, and other documents), section 1028A (relating to aggravated identity theft) of this title or a violation of section 274, 277, or 278 of the Immigration and Nationality Act (relating to the smuggling of aliens); or

(q) any criminal violation of section 229 (relating to chemical weapons) or sections 2332, 2332a, 2332b, 2332d, 2332f, 2332g, 2332h, 2339, 2339A, 2339B, 2339C, or 2339D of this title (relating to terrorism);

(r) any criminal violation of section 1 (relating to illegal restraints of trade or commerce), 2 (relating to illegal monopolizing of trade or commerce), or 3 (relating to illegal restraints of trade or commerce in territories or the District of Columbia) of the Sherman Act (15 U.S.C. 1, 2, 3); or

(s) any conspiracy to commit any offense described in any subparagraph of this paragraph.

(2) The principal prosecuting attorney of any State, or the principal prosecuting attorney of any political subdivision thereof, if such attorney is authorized by a statute of that State to make application to a State court judge of competent jurisdiction for an order authorizing or approving the interception of wire, oral, or electronic communications, may apply to such judge for, and such judge may grant in conformity with section 2518 of this chapter and with the applicable State statute an order authorizing, or approving the interception of wire, oral, or electronic communications by investigative or law enforcement officers having responsibility for the investigation of the offense as to which the application is made, when such interception may provide or has provided evidence of the commission of the offense of murder, kidnapping, gambling, robbery, bribery, extortion, or dealing in narcotic drugs, marihuana or other dangerous drugs, or other crime dangerous to life, limb, or property, and punishable by imprisonment for more than one year, designated in any applicable State statute authorizing such interception, or any conspiracy to commit any of the foregoing offenses.

(3) Any attorney for the Government (as such term is defined for the purposes of the Federal Rules of Criminal Procedure) may authorize an application to a Federal judge of competent jurisdiction for, and such judge may grant, in conformity with section 2518 of this title, an order authorizing or approving the interception of electronic communications by an investigative or law enforcement officer having responsibility for the

investigation of the offense as to which the application is made, when such interception may provide or has provided evidence of any Federal felony.

18 U.S.C. § 2517. AUTHORIZATION FOR DISCLOSURE AND USE OF INTERCEPTED WIRE, ORAL, OR ELECTRONIC COMMUNICATIONS

(1) Any investigative or law enforcement officer who, by any means authorized by this chapter, has obtained knowledge of the contents of any wire, oral, or electronic communication, or evidence derived therefrom, may disclose such contents to another investigative or law enforcement officer to the extent that such disclosure is appropriate to the proper performance of the official duties of the officer making or receiving the disclosure.

(2) Any investigative or law enforcement officer who, by any means authorized by this chapter, has obtained knowledge of the contents of any wire, oral, or electronic communication or evidence derived therefrom may use such contents to the extent such use is appropriate to the proper performance of his official duties.

(3) Any person who has received, by any means authorized by this chapter, any information concerning a wire, oral, or electronic communication, or evidence derived therefrom intercepted in accordance with the provisions of this chapter may disclose the contents of that communication or such derivative evidence while giving testimony under oath or affirmation in any proceeding held under the authority of the United States or of any State or political subdivision thereof.

(4) No otherwise privileged wire, oral, or electronic communication intercepted in accordance with, or in violation of, the provisions of this chapter shall lose its privileged character.

(5) When an investigative or law enforcement officer, while engaged in intercepting wire, oral, or electronic communications in the manner authorized herein, intercepts wire, oral, or electronic communications relating to offenses other than those specified in the order of authorization or approval, the contents thereof, and evidence derived therefrom, may be disclosed or used as provided in subsections (1) and (2) of this section. Such contents and any evidence derived therefrom may be used under subsection (3) of this section when authorized or approved by a judge of competent jurisdiction where such judge finds on subsequent application that the contents were otherwise intercepted in accordance with the provisions of this chapter. Such application shall be made as soon as practicable.

(6) Any investigative or law enforcement officer, or attorney for the Government, who by any means authorized by this chapter, has obtained knowledge of the contents of any wire, oral, or electronic communication,

or evidence derived therefrom, may disclose such contents to any other Federal law enforcement, intelligence, protective, immigration, national defense, or national security official to the extent that such contents include foreign intelligence or counterintelligence (as defined in section 3 of the National Security Act of 1947 (50 U.S.C. 401a)), or foreign intelligence information (as defined in subsection (19) of section 2510 of this title), to assist the official who is to receive that information in the performance of his official duties. Any Federal official who receives information pursuant to this provision may use that information only as necessary in the conduct of that person's official duties subject to any limitations on the unauthorized disclosure of such information.

(7) Any investigative or law enforcement officer, or other Federal official in carrying out official duties as such Federal official, who by any means authorized by this chapter, has obtained knowledge of the contents of any wire, oral, or electronic communication, or evidence derived therefrom, may disclose such contents or derivative evidence to a foreign investigative or law enforcement officer to the extent that such disclosure is appropriate to the proper performance of the official duties of the officer making or receiving the disclosure, and foreign investigative or law enforcement officers may use or disclose such contents or derivative evidence to the extent such use or disclosure is appropriate to the proper performance of their official duties.

(8) Any investigative or law enforcement officer, or other Federal official in carrying out official duties as such Federal official, who by any means authorized by this chapter, has obtained knowledge of the contents of any wire, oral, or electronic communication, or evidence derived therefrom, may disclose such contents or derivative evidence to any appropriate Federal, State, local, or foreign government official to the extent that such contents or derivative evidence reveals a threat of actual or potential attack or other grave hostile acts of a foreign power or an agent of a foreign power, domestic or international sabotage, domestic or international terrorism, or clandestine intelligence gathering activities by an intelligence service or network of a foreign power or by an agent of a foreign power, within the United States or elsewhere, for the purpose of preventing or responding to such a threat. Any official who receives information pursuant to this provision may use that information only as necessary in the conduct of that person's official duties subject to any limitations on the unauthorized disclosure of such information, and any State, local, or foreign official who receives information pursuant to this provision may use that information only consistent with such guidelines as the Attorney General and Director of Central Intelligence shall jointly issue.

18 U.S.C. § 2518. PROCEDURE FOR INTERCEPTION OF WIRE, ORAL, OR ELECTRONIC COMMUNICATIONS

(1) Each application for an order authorizing or approving the interception of a wire, oral, or electronic communication under this chapter shall be made in writing upon oath or affirmation to a judge of competent jurisdiction and shall state the applicant's authority to make such application. Each application shall include the following information:

(a) the identity of the investigative or law enforcement officer making the application, and the officer authorizing the application;

(b) a full and complete statement of the facts and circumstances relied upon by the applicant, to justify his belief that an order should be issued, including (i) details as to the particular offense that has been, is being, or is about to be committed, (ii) except as provided in subsection (11), a particular description of the nature and location of the facilities from which or the place where the communication is to be intercepted, (iii) a particular description of the type of communications sought to be intercepted, (iv) the identity of the person, if known, committing the offense and whose communications are to be intercepted;

(c) a full and complete statement as to whether or not other investigative procedures have been tried and failed or why they reasonably appear to be unlikely to succeed if tried or to be too dangerous;

(d) a statement of the period of time for which the interception is required to be maintained. If the nature of the investigation is such that the authorization for interception should not automatically terminate when the described type of communication has been first obtained, a particular description of facts establishing probable cause to believe that additional communications of the same type will occur thereafter;

(e) a full and complete statement of the facts concerning all previous applications known to the individual authorizing and making the application, made to any judge for authorization to intercept, or for approval of interceptions of, wire, oral, or electronic communications involving any of the same persons, facilities or places specified in the application, and the action taken by the judge on each such application; and

(f) where the application is for the extension of an order, a statement setting forth the results thus far obtained from the interception, or a reasonable explanation of the failure to obtain such results.

(2) The judge may require the applicant to furnish additional testimony or documentary evidence in support of the application.

(3) Upon such application the judge may enter an ex parte order, as requested or as modified, authorizing or approving interception of wire, oral, or electronic communications within the territorial jurisdiction of the court in which the judge is sitting (and outside that jurisdiction but within the United States in the case of a mobile interception device authorized by a Federal court within such jurisdiction), if the judge determines on the basis of the facts submitted by the applicant that—

(a) there is probable cause for belief that an individual is committing, has committed, or is about to commit a particular offense enumerated in section 2516 of this chapter;

(b) there is probable cause for belief that particular communications concerning that offense will be obtained through such interception;

(c) normal investigative procedures have been tried and have failed or reasonably appear to be unlikely to succeed if tried or to be too dangerous;

(d) except as provided in subsection (11), there is probable cause for belief that the facilities from which, or the place where, the wire, oral, or electronic communications are to be intercepted are being used, or are about to be used, in connection with the commission of such offense, or are leased to, listed in the name of, or commonly used by such person.

(4) Each order authorizing or approving the interception of any wire, oral, or electronic communication under this chapter shall specify—

(a) the identity of the person, if known, whose communications are to be intercepted;

(b) the nature and location of the communications facilities as to which, or the place where, authority to intercept is granted;

(c) a particular description of the type of communication sought to be intercepted, and a statement of the particular offense to which it relates;

(d) the identity of the agency authorized to intercept the communications, and of the person authorizing the application; and

(e) the period of time during which such interception is authorized, including a statement as to whether or not the interception shall automatically terminate when the described communication has been first obtained.

An order authorizing the interception of a wire, oral, or electronic communication under this chapter shall, upon request of the applicant, direct that a provider of wire or electronic communication service, landlord, custodian or other person shall furnish the applicant forthwith all information, facilities, and technical assistance necessary to accomplish the interception unobtrusively and with a minimum of interference with the services that such service provider, landlord, custodian, or person is according the person whose communications are to be intercepted. Any provider of wire or electronic communication service, landlord, custodian or other person furnishing such facilities or technical assistance shall be compensated therefor by the applicant for reasonable expenses incurred in providing such facilities or assistance. Pursuant to section 2522 of this chapter, an order may also be issued to enforce the assistance capability and capacity requirements under the Communications Assistance for Law Enforcement Act.

(5) No order entered under this section may authorize or approve the interception of any wire, oral, or electronic communication for any period longer than is necessary to achieve the objective of the authorization, nor in any event longer than thirty days. Such thirty-day period begins on the earlier of the day on which the investigative or law enforcement officer first begins to conduct an interception under the order or ten days after the order is entered. Extensions of an order may be granted, but only upon application for an extension made in accordance with subsection (1) of this section and the court making the findings required by subsection (3) of this section. The period of extension shall be no longer than the authorizing judge deems necessary to achieve the purposes for which it was granted and in no event for longer than thirty days. Every order and extension thereof shall contain a provision that the authorization to intercept shall be executed as soon as practicable, shall be conducted in such a way as to minimize the interception of communications not otherwise subject to interception under this chapter, and must terminate upon attainment of the authorized objective, or in any event in thirty days. In the event the intercepted communication is in a code or foreign language, and an expert in that foreign language or code is not reasonably available during the interception period, minimization may be accomplished as soon as practicable after such interception. An interception under this chapter may be conducted in whole or in part by Government personnel, or by an individual operating under a contract with the Government, acting under the supervision of an investigative or law enforcement officer authorized to conduct the interception.

(6) Whenever an order authorizing interception is entered pursuant to this chapter, the order may require reports to be made to the judge who issued the order showing what progress has been made toward achievement of the authorized objective and the need for continued

interception. Such reports shall be made at such intervals as the judge may require.

(7) Notwithstanding any other provision of this chapter, any investigative or law enforcement officer, specially designated by the Attorney General, the Deputy Attorney General, the Associate Attorney General, or by the principal prosecuting attorney of any State or subdivision thereof acting pursuant to a statute of that State, who reasonably determines that—

(a) an emergency situation exists that involves—

(i) immediate danger of death or serious physical injury to any person,

(ii) conspiratorial activities threatening the national security interest, or

(iii) conspiratorial activities characteristic of organized crime,

that requires a wire, oral, or electronic communication to be intercepted before an order authorizing such interception can, with due diligence, be obtained, and

(b) there are grounds upon which an order could be entered under this chapter to authorize such interception,

may intercept such wire, oral, or electronic communication if an application for an order approving the interception is made in accordance with this section within forty-eight hours after the interception has occurred, or begins to occur. In the absence of an order, such interception shall immediately terminate when the communication sought is obtained or when the application for the order is denied, whichever is earlier. In the event such application for approval is denied, or in any other case where the interception is terminated without an order having been issued, the contents of any wire, oral, or electronic communication intercepted shall be treated as having been obtained in violation of this chapter, and an inventory shall be served as provided for in subsection (d) of this section on the person named in the application.

(8)(a) The contents of any wire, oral, or electronic communication intercepted by any means authorized by this chapter shall, if possible, be recorded on tape or wire or other comparable device. The recording of the contents of any wire, oral, or electronic communication under this subsection shall be done in such a way as will protect the recording from editing or other alterations. Immediately upon the expiration of the period of the order, or extensions thereof, such recordings shall be made available to the judge issuing such order and sealed under his directions. Custody of the recordings shall be wherever the judge orders. They shall not be destroyed except upon an order of the issuing or denying judge and in any event shall be kept for ten years. Duplicate recordings may be made for use or disclosure pursuant to the provisions of subsections (1) and (2) of section 2517 of this chapter for investigations. The presence of the seal provided for by this subsection, or a satisfactory explanation for the absence thereof, shall be a prerequisite for the use or disclosure of the contents of any wire, oral, or electronic communication or evidence derived therefrom under subsection (3) of section 2517.

(b) Applications made and orders granted under this chapter shall be sealed by the judge. Custody of the applications and orders shall be wherever the judge directs. Such applications and orders shall be disclosed only upon a showing of good cause before a judge of competent jurisdiction and shall not be destroyed except on order of the issuing or denying judge, and in any event shall be kept for ten years.

(c) Any violation of the provisions of this subsection may be punished as contempt of the issuing or denying judge.

(d) Within a reasonable time but not later than ninety days after the filing of an application for an order of approval under section 2518(7)(b) which is denied or the termination of the period of an order or extensions thereof, the issuing or denying judge shall cause to be served, on the persons named in the order or the application, and such other parties to intercepted communications as the judge may determine in his discretion that is in the interest of justice, an inventory which shall include notice of—

(1) the fact of the entry of the order or the application;

(2) the date of the entry and the period of authorized, approved or disapproved interception, or the denial of the application; and

(3) the fact that during the period wire, oral, or electronic communications were or were not intercepted.

The judge, upon the filing of a motion, may in his discretion make available to such person or his counsel for inspection such portions of the intercepted communications, applications and orders as the judge determines to be in the interest of justice. On an ex parte showing of good cause to a judge of competent jurisdiction the serving of the inventory required by this subsection may be postponed.

(9) The contents of any wire, oral, or electronic communication intercepted pursuant to this chapter or evidence derived therefrom shall not be received in evidence or otherwise disclosed in any trial, hearing, or other proceeding in a Federal or State court unless each party, not less than ten days before the trial, hearing, or proceeding, has been furnished

with a copy of the court order, and accompanying application, under which the interception was authorized or approved. This ten-day period may be waived by the judge if he finds that it was not possible to furnish the party with the above information ten days before the trial, hearing, or proceeding and that the party will not be prejudiced by the delay in receiving such information.

(10)(a) Any aggrieved person in any trial, hearing, or proceeding in or before any court, department, officer, agency, regulatory body, or other authority of the United States, a State, or a political subdivision thereof, may move to suppress the contents of any wire or oral communication intercepted pursuant to this chapter, or evidence derived therefrom, on the grounds that—

> (i) the communication was unlawfully intercepted;

> (ii) the order of authorization or approval under which it was intercepted is insufficient on its face; or

> (iii) the interception was not made in conformity with the order of authorization or approval.

Such motion shall be made before the trial, hearing, or proceeding unless there was no opportunity to make such motion or the person was not aware of the grounds of the motion. If the motion is granted, the contents of the intercepted wire or oral communication, or evidence derived therefrom, shall be treated as having been obtained in violation of this chapter. The judge, upon the filing of such motion by the aggrieved person, may in his discretion make available to the aggrieved person or his counsel for inspection such portions of the intercepted communication or evidence derived therefrom as the judge determines to be in the interests of justice.

(b) In addition to any other right to appeal, the United States shall have the right to appeal from an order granting a motion to suppress made under paragraph (a) of this subsection, or the denial of an application for an order of approval, if the United States attorney shall certify to the judge or other official granting such motion or denying such application that the appeal is not taken for purposes of delay. Such appeal shall be taken within thirty days after the date the order was entered and shall be diligently prosecuted.

(c) The remedies and sanctions described in this chapter with respect to the interception of electronic communications are the only judicial remedies and sanctions for nonconstitutional violations of this chapter involving such communications.

(11) The requirements of subsections (1)(b)(ii) and (3)(d) of this section relating to the specification of the facilities from which, or the place where, the communication is to be intercepted do not apply if—

(a) in the case of an application with respect to the interception of an oral communication—

(i) the application is by a Federal investigative or law enforcement officer and is approved by the Attorney General, the Deputy Attorney General, the Associate Attorney General, an Assistant Attorney General, or an acting Assistant Attorney General;

(ii) the application contains a full and complete statement as to why such specification is not practical and identifies the person committing the offense and whose communications are to be intercepted; and

(iii) the judge finds that such specification is not practical; and

(b) in the case of an application with respect to a wire or electronic communication—

(i) the application is by a Federal investigative or law enforcement officer and is approved by the Attorney General, the Deputy Attorney General, the Associate Attorney General, an Assistant Attorney General, or an acting Assistant Attorney General;

(ii) the application identifies the person believed to be committing the offense and whose communications are to be intercepted and the applicant makes a showing that there is probable cause to believe that the person's actions could have the effect of thwarting interception from a specified facility;

(iii) the judge finds that such showing has been adequately made; and

(iv) the order authorizing or approving the interception is limited to interception only for such time as it is reasonable to presume that the person identified in the application is or was reasonably proximate to the instrument through which such communication will be or was transmitted.

(12) An interception of a communication under an order with respect to which the requirements of subsections (1)(b)(ii) and (3)(d) of this section do not apply by reason of subsection (11)(a) shall not begin until the place where the communication is to be intercepted is ascertained by the person implementing the interception order. A provider of wire or electronic communications service that has received an order as provided for in subsection (11)(b) may move the court to modify or quash the order on the ground that its assistance with respect to the interception cannot

be performed in a timely or reasonable fashion. The court, upon notice to the government, shall decide such a motion expeditiously.

18 U.S.C. § 2519. REPORTS CONCERNING INTERCEPTED WIRE, ORAL, OR ELECTRONIC COMMUNICATIONS

(1) Within thirty days after the expiration of an order (or each extension thereof) entered under section 2518, or the denial of an order approving an interception, the issuing or denying judge shall report to the Administrative Office of the United States Courts—

(a) the fact that an order or extension was applied for;

(b) the kind of order or extension applied for (including whether or not the order was an order with respect to which the requirements of sections 2518(1)(b)(ii) and 2518(3)(d) of this title did not apply by reason of section 2518(11) of this title);

(c) the fact that the order or extension was granted as applied for, was modified, or was denied;

(d) the period of interceptions authorized by the order, and the number and duration of any extensions of the order;

(e) the offense specified in the order or application, or extension of an order;

(f) the identity of the applying investigative or law enforcement officer and agency making the application and the person authorizing the application; and

(g) the nature of the facilities from which or the place where communications were to be intercepted.

(2) In January of each year the Attorney General, an Assistant Attorney General specially designated by the Attorney General, or the principal prosecuting attorney of a State, or the principal prosecuting attorney for any political subdivision of a State, shall report to the Administrative Office of the United States Courts—

(a) the information required by paragraphs (a) through (g) of subsection (1) of this section with respect to each application for an order or extension made during the preceding calendar year;

(b) a general description of the interceptions made under such order or extension, including (i) the approximate nature and frequency of incriminating communications intercepted, (ii) the approximate nature and frequency of other communications intercepted, (iii) the approximate number of persons whose communications were intercepted, (iv) the number of orders in which encryption was encountered and whether such encryption prevented law enforcement from obtaining the plain text of communications intercepted pursuant to such order, and (v) the approximate nature, amount, and cost of the manpower and other resources used in the interceptions;

(c) the number of arrests resulting from interceptions made under such order or extension, and the offenses for which arrests were made;

(d) the number of trials resulting from such interceptions;

(e) the number of motions to suppress made with respect to such interceptions, and the number granted or denied;

(f) the number of convictions resulting from such interceptions and the offenses for which the convictions were obtained and a general assessment of the importance of the interceptions; and

(g) the information required by paragraphs (b) through (f) of this subsection with respect to orders or extensions obtained in a preceding calendar year.

(3) In April of each year the Director of the Administrative Office of the United States Courts shall transmit to the Congress a full and complete report concerning the number of applications for orders authorizing or approving the interception of wire, oral, or electronic communications pursuant to this chapter and the number of orders and extensions granted or denied pursuant to this chapter during the preceding calendar year. Such report shall include a summary and analysis of the data required to be filed with the Administrative Office by subsections (1) and (2) of this section. The Director of the Administrative Office of the United States Courts is authorized to issue binding regulations dealing with the content and form of the reports required to be filed by subsections (1) and (2) of this section.

18 U.S.C. § 2520. RECOVERY OF CIVIL DAMAGES AUTHORIZED

(a) **In general.** Except as provided in section 2511(2)(a)(ii), any person whose wire, oral, or electronic communication is intercepted, disclosed, or intentionally used in violation of this chapter may in a civil action recover from the person or entity, other than the United States, which engaged in that violation such relief as may be appropriate.

(b) **Relief.** In an action under this section, appropriate relief includes—

(1) such preliminary and other equitable or declaratory relief as may be appropriate;

(2) damages under subsection (c) and punitive damages in appropriate cases; and

(3) a reasonable attorney's fee and other litigation costs reasonably incurred.

(c) **Computation of damages.**

(1) In an action under this section, if the conduct in violation of this chapter is the private viewing of a private satellite video communication that is not scrambled or encrypted or if the communication is a radio communication that is transmitted on frequencies allocated under subpart D of part 74 of the rules of the Federal Communications Commission that is not scrambled or encrypted and the conduct is not for a tortious or illegal purpose or for purposes of direct or indirect commercial advantage or private commercial gain, then the court shall assess damages as follows:

(A) If the person who engaged in that conduct has not previously been enjoined under section 2511(5) and has not been found liable in a prior civil action under this section, the court shall assess the greater of the sum of actual damages suffered by the plaintiff, or statutory damages of not less than $50 and not more than $500.

(B) If, on one prior occasion, the person who engaged in that conduct has been enjoined under section 2511(5) or has been found liable in a civil action under this section, the court shall assess the greater of the sum of actual damages suffered by the plaintiff, or statutory damages of not less than $100 and not more than $1000.

(2) In any other action under this section, the court may assess as damages whichever is the greater of—

(A) the sum of the actual damages suffered by the plaintiff and any profits made by the violator as a result of the violation; or

(B) statutory damages of whichever is the greater of $100 a day for each day of violation or $10,000.

(d) **Defense.** A good faith reliance on—

(1) a court warrant or order, a grand jury subpoena, a legislative authorization, or a statutory authorization;

(2) a request of an investigative or law enforcement officer under section 2518(7) of this title; or

(3) a good faith determination that section 2511(3) or 2511(2)(i) of this title permitted the conduct complained of;

is a complete defense against any civil or criminal action brought under this chapter or any other law.

(e) **Limitation.** A civil action under this section may not be commenced later than two years after the date upon which the claimant first has a reasonable opportunity to discover the violation.

(f) **Administrative discipline.** If a court or appropriate department or agency determines that the United States or any of its departments or agencies has violated any provision of this chapter, and the court or appropriate department or agency finds that the circumstances surrounding the violation raise serious questions about whether or not an officer or employee of the United States acted willfully or intentionally with respect to the violation, the department or agency shall, upon receipt of a true and correct copy of the decision and findings of the court or appropriate department or agency promptly initiate a proceeding to determine whether disciplinary action against the officer or employee is warranted. If the head of the department or agency involved determines that disciplinary action is not warranted, he or she shall notify the Inspector General with jurisdiction over the department or agency concerned and shall provide the Inspector General with the reasons for such determination.

(g) **Improper disclosure is violation.** Any willful disclosure or use by an investigative or law enforcement officer or governmental entity of information beyond the extent permitted by section 2517 is a violation of this chapter for purposes of section 2520(a).

18 U.S.C. § 2521. INJUNCTION AGAINST ILLEGAL INTERCEPTION

Whenever it shall appear that any person is engaged or is about to engage in any act which constitutes or will constitute a felony violation of this chapter, the Attorney General may initiate a civil action in a district court of the United States to enjoin such violation. The court shall proceed as soon as practicable to the hearing and determination of such an action, and may, at any time before final determination, enter such a restraining order or prohibition, or take such other action, as is warranted to prevent a continuing and substantial injury to the United States or to any person or class of persons for whose protection the action is brought. A proceeding under this section is governed by the Federal Rules of Civil Procedure, except that, if an indictment has been returned against the respondent, discovery is governed by the Federal Rules of Criminal Procedure.

18 U.S.C. § 2522. ENFORCEMENT OF THE COMMUNICATIONS ASSISTANCE FOR LAW ENFORCEMENT ACT

(a) **Enforcement by court issuing surveillance order.** If a court authorizing an interception under this chapter, a State statute, or the Foreign Intelligence Surveillance Act of 1978 (50 U.S.C. 1801 et seq.) or authorizing use of a pen register or a trap and trace device under chapter 206 or a State statute finds that a telecommunications carrier has failed to comply with the requirements of the Communications Assistance for Law Enforcement Act, the court may, in accordance with section 108 of such Act, direct that the carrier comply forthwith and may direct that a provider of support services to the carrier or the manufacturer of the carrier's transmission or switching equipment furnish forthwith modifications necessary for the carrier to comply.

(b) **Enforcement upon application by Attorney General.** The Attorney General may, in a civil action in the appropriate United States district court, obtain an order, in accordance with section 108 of the Communications Assistance for Law Enforcement Act, directing that a telecommunications carrier, a manufacturer of telecommunications transmission or switching equipment, or a provider of telecommunications support services comply with such Act.

(c) **Civil penalty.**—

(1) *In general.* A court issuing an order under this section against a telecommunications carrier, a manufacturer of telecommunications transmission or switching equipment, or a provider of telecommunications support services may impose a civil penalty of up to $10,000 per day for each day in violation after the issuance of the order or after such future date as the court may specify.

(2) *Considerations.* In determining whether to impose a civil penalty and in determining its amount, the court shall take into account—

(A) the nature, circumstances, and extent of the violation;

(B) the violator's ability to pay, the violator's good faith efforts to comply in a timely manner, any effect on the violator's ability to continue to do business, the degree of culpability, and the length of any delay in undertaking efforts to comply; and

(C) such other matters as justice may require.

(d) **Definitions.** As used in this section, the terms defined in section 102 of the Communications Assistance for Law Enforcement Act have the meanings provided, respectively, in such section.

18 U.S.C. § 2701. UNLAWFUL ACCESS TO STORED COMMUNICATIONS

(a) **Offense.** Except as provided in subsection (c) of this section whoever—

(1) intentionally accesses without authorization a facility through which an electronic communication service is provided; or

(2) intentionally exceeds an authorization to access that facility;

and thereby obtains, alters, or prevents authorized access to a wire or electronic communication while it is in electronic storage in such system

shall be punished as provided in subsection (b) of this section.

(b) **Punishment.** The punishment for an offense under subsection (a) of this section is—

(1) if the offense is committed for purposes of commercial advantage, malicious destruction or damage, or private commercial gain, or in furtherance of any criminal or tortious act in violation of the Constitution or laws of the United States or any State—

(A) a fine under this title or imprisonment for not more than 5 years, or both, in the case of a first offense under this subparagraph; and

(B) a fine under this title or imprisonment for not more than 10 years, or both, for any subsequent offense under this subparagraph; and

(2) in any other case—

(A) a fine under this title or imprisonment for not more than 1 year or both, in the case of a first offense under this paragraph; and

(B) a fine under this title or imprisonment for not more than 5 years, or both, in the case of an offense under this subparagraph that occurs after a conviction of another offense under this section.

(c) **Exceptions.** Subsection (a) of this section does not apply with respect to conduct authorized—

(1) by the person or entity providing a wire or electronic communications service;

(2) by a user of that service with respect to a communication of or intended for that user; or

(3) in section 2703, 2704 or 2518 of this title.

18 U.S.C. § 2702. VOLUNTARY DISCLOSURE OF CUSTOMER COMMUNICATIONS OR RECORDS

(a) **Prohibitions.** Except as provided in subsection (b) or (c)—

(1) a person or entity providing an electronic communication service to the public shall not knowingly divulge to any person or entity the contents of a communication while in electronic storage by that service; and

(2) a person or entity providing remote computing service to the public shall not knowingly divulge to any person or entity the contents of any communication which is carried or maintained on that service—

(A) on behalf of, and received by means of electronic transmission from (or created by means of computer processing of communications received by means of electronic transmission from), a subscriber or customer of such service;

(B) solely for the purpose of providing storage or computer processing services to such subscriber or customer, if the provider is not authorized to access the contents of any such communications for purposes of providing any services other than storage or computer processing; and

(3) a provider of remote computing service or electronic communication service to the public shall not knowingly divulge a record or other information pertaining to a subscriber to or customer of such service (not including the contents of communications covered by paragraph (1) or (2)) to any governmental entity.

(b) **Exceptions for disclosure of communications.** A provider described in subsection (a) may divulge the contents of a communication—

(1) to an addressee or intended recipient of such communication or an agent of such addressee or intended recipient;

(2) as otherwise authorized in section 2517, 2511(2)(a), or 2703 of this title;

(3) with the lawful consent of the originator or an addressee or intended recipient of such communication, or the subscriber in the case of remote computing service;

(4) to a person employed or authorized or whose facilities are used to forward such communication to its destination;

(5) as may be necessarily incident to the rendition of the service or to the protection of the rights or property of the provider of that service;

(6) to the National Center for Missing and Exploited Children, in connection with a report submitted thereto under section 2258A;

(7) to a law enforcement agency—

(A) if the contents—

(i) were inadvertently obtained by the service provider; and

(ii) appear to pertain to the commission of a crime; or

(8) to a governmental entity, if the provider, in good faith, believes that an emergency involving danger of death or serious physical injury to any person requires disclosure without delay of communications relating to the emergency.

(c) **Exceptions for disclosure of customer records.** A provider described in subsection (a) may divulge a record or other information pertaining to a subscriber to or customer of such service (not including the contents of communications covered by subsection (a)(1) or (a)(2))—

(1) as otherwise authorized in section 2703;

(2) with the lawful consent of the customer or subscriber;

(3) as may be necessarily incident to the rendition of the service or to the protection of the rights or property of the provider of that service;

(4) to a governmental entity, if the provider, in good faith, believes that an emergency involving danger of death or serious physical injury to any person requires disclosure without delay of information relating to the emergency;

(5) to the National Center for Missing and Exploited Children, in connection with a report submitted thereto under section 2258A; or

(6) to any person other than a governmental entity.

(d) **Reporting of emergency disclosures.** On an annual basis, the Attorney General shall submit to the Committee on the Judiciary of the House of Representatives and the Committee on the Judiciary of the Senate a report containing—

(1) the number of accounts from which the Department of Justice has received voluntary disclosures under subsection (b)(8); and

(2) a summary of the basis for disclosure in those instances where—

(A) voluntary disclosures under subsection (b)(8) were made to the Department of Justice; and

(B) the investigation pertaining to those disclosures was closed without the filing of criminal charges.

18 U.S.C. § 2703. REQUIRED DISCLOSURE OF CUSTOMER COMMUNICATIONS OR RECORDS

(a) **Contents of wire or electronic communications in electronic storage.** A governmental entity may require the disclosure by a provider of electronic communication service of the contents of a wire or electronic communication, that is in electronic storage in an electronic communications system for one hundred and eighty days or less, only pursuant to a warrant issued using the procedures described in the Federal Rules of Criminal Procedure (or, in the case of a State court, issued using State warrant procedures) by a court of competent jurisdiction. A governmental entity may require the disclosure by a provider of electronic communications services of the contents of a wire or electronic communication that has been in electronic storage in an electronic communications system for more than one hundred and eighty days by the means available under subsection (b) of this section.

(b) **Contents of wire or electronic communications in a remote computing service.**

(1) A governmental entity may require a provider of remote computing service to disclose the contents of any wire or electronic communication to which this paragraph is made applicable by paragraph (2) of this subsection—

(A) without required notice to the subscriber or customer, if the governmental entity obtains a warrant issued using the procedures described in the Federal Rules of Criminal Procedure (or, in the case of a State court, issued using State warrant procedures) by a court of competent jurisdiction; or

(B) with prior notice from the governmental entity to the subscriber or customer if the governmental entity—

(i) uses an administrative subpoena authorized by a Federal or State statute or a Federal or State grand jury or trial subpoena; or

(ii) obtains a court order for such disclosure under subsection (d) of this section;

except that delayed notice may be given pursuant to section 2705 of this title.

(2) Paragraph (1) is applicable with respect to any wire or electronic communication that is held or maintained on that service—

(A) on behalf of, and received by means of electronic transmission from (or created by means of computer processing of communications received by means of electronic transmission from), a subscriber or customer of such remote computing service; and

(B) solely for the purpose of providing storage or computer processing services to such subscriber or customer, if the provider is not authorized to access the contents of any such communications for purposes of providing any services other than storage or computer processing.

(c) **Records concerning electronic communication service or remote computing service.**

(1) A governmental entity may require a provider of electronic communication service or remote computing service to disclose a record or other information pertaining to a subscriber to or customer of such service (not including the contents of communications) only when the governmental entity—

(A) obtains a warrant issued using the procedures described in the Federal Rules of Criminal Procedure (or, in the case of a State court, issued using State warrant procedures) by a court of competent jurisdiction;

(B) obtains a court order for such disclosure under subsection (d) of this section;

(C) has the consent of the subscriber or customer to such disclosure;

(D) submits a formal written request relevant to a law enforcement investigation concerning telemarketing fraud for the name, address, and place of business of a subscriber or customer of such provider, which subscriber or customer is engaged in telemarketing (as such term is defined in section 2325 of this title); or

(E) seeks information under paragraph (2).

(2) A provider of electronic communication service or remote computing service shall disclose to a governmental entity the—

(A) name;

(B) address;

(C) local and long distance telephone connection records, or records of session times and durations;

(D) length of service (including start date) and types of service utilized;

(E) telephone or instrument number or other subscriber number or identity, including any temporarily assigned network address; and

(F) means and source of payment for such service (including any credit card or bank account number),

of a subscriber to or customer of such service when the governmental entity uses an administrative subpoena authorized by a Federal or

State statute or a Federal or State grand jury or trial subpoena or any means available under paragraph (1).

(3) A governmental entity receiving records or information under this subsection is not required to provide notice to a subscriber or customer.

(d) **Requirements for court order.** A court order for disclosure under subsection (b) or (c) may be issued by any court that is a court of competent jurisdiction and shall issue only if the governmental entity offers specific and articulable facts showing that there are reasonable grounds to believe that the contents of a wire or electronic communication, or the records or other information sought, are relevant and material to an ongoing criminal investigation. In the case of a State governmental authority, such a court order shall not issue if prohibited by the law of such State. A court issuing an order pursuant to this section, on a motion made promptly by the service provider, may quash or modify such order, if the information or records requested are unusually voluminous in nature or compliance with such order otherwise would cause an undue burden on such provider.

(e) **No cause of action against a provider disclosing information under this chapter.** No cause of action shall lie in any court against any provider of wire or electronic communication service, its officers, employees, agents, or other specified persons for providing information, facilities, or assistance in accordance with the terms of a court order, warrant, subpoena, statutory authorization, or certification under this chapter.

(f) **Requirement to preserve evidence.**

(1) *In general.* A provider of wire or electronic communication services or a remote computing service, upon the request of a governmental entity, shall take all necessary steps to preserve records and other evidence in its possession pending the issuance of a court order or other process.

(2) *Period of retention.* Records referred to in paragraph (1) shall be retained for a period of 90 days, which shall be extended for an additional 90-day period upon a renewed request by the governmental entity.

(g) **Presence of officer not required.** Notwithstanding section 3105 of this title, the presence of an officer shall not be required for service or execution of a search warrant issued in accordance with this chapter requiring disclosure by a provider of electronic communications service or remote computing service of the contents of communications or records or other information pertaining to a subscriber to or customer of such service.

18 U.S.C. § 2704. BACKUP PRESERVATION

(a) **Backup preservation.**

(1) A governmental entity acting under section 2703(b)(2) may include in its subpoena or court order a requirement that the service provider to whom the request is directed create a backup copy of the contents of the electronic communications sought in order to preserve those communications. Without notifying the subscriber or customer of such subpoena or court order, such service provider shall create such backup copy as soon as practicable consistent with its regular business practices and shall confirm to the governmental entity that such backup copy has been made. Such backup copy shall be created within two business days after receipt by the service provider of the subpoena or court order.

(2) Notice to the subscriber or customer shall be made by the governmental entity within three days after receipt of such confirmation, unless such notice is delayed pursuant to section 2705(a).

(3) The service provider shall not destroy such backup copy until the later of—

(A) the delivery of the information; or

(B) the resolution of any proceedings (including appeals of any proceeding) concerning the government's subpoena or court order.

(4) The service provider shall release such backup copy to the requesting governmental entity no sooner than fourteen days after the governmental entity's notice to the subscriber or customer if such service provider—

(A) has not received notice from the subscriber or customer that the subscriber or customer has challenged the governmental entity's request; and

(B) has not initiated proceedings to challenge the request of the governmental entity.

(5) A governmental entity may seek to require the creation of a backup copy under subsection (a)(1) of this section if in its sole discretion such entity determines that there is reason to believe that notification under section 2703 of this title of the existence of the subpoena or court order may result in destruction of or tampering with evidence. This determination is not subject to challenge by the subscriber or customer or service provider.

(b) **Customer challenges.**

(1) Within fourteen days after notice by the governmental entity to the subscriber or customer under subsection (a)(2) of this section, such subscriber or customer may file a motion to quash such subpoena or vacate such court order, with copies served upon the governmental entity and with written notice of such challenge to the service provider. A motion to vacate a court order shall be filed in the court which issued such order. A motion to quash a subpoena shall be filed in the appropriate United States district court or State court. Such motion or application shall contain an affidavit or sworn statement—

(A) stating that the applicant is a customer or subscriber to the service from which the contents of electronic communications maintained for him have been sought; and

(B) stating the applicant's reasons for believing that the records sought are not relevant to a legitimate law enforcement inquiry or that there has not been substantial compliance with the provisions of this chapter in some other respect.

(2) Service shall be made under this section upon a governmental entity by delivering or mailing by registered or certified mail a copy of the papers to the person, office, or department specified in the notice which the customer has received pursuant to this chapter. For the purposes of this section, the term "delivery" has the meaning given that term in the Federal Rules of Civil Procedure.

(3) If the court finds that the customer has complied with paragraphs (1) and (2) of this subsection, the court shall order the governmental entity to file a sworn response, which may be filed in camera if the governmental entity includes in its response the reasons which make in camera review appropriate. If the court is unable to determine the motion or application on the basis of the parties' initial allegations and response, the court may conduct such additional proceedings as it deems appropriate. All such proceedings shall be completed and the motion or application decided as soon as practicable after the filing of the governmental entity's response.

(4) If the court finds that the applicant is not the subscriber or customer for whom the communications sought by the governmental entity are maintained, or that there is a reason to believe that the law enforcement inquiry is legitimate and that the communications sought are relevant to that inquiry, it shall deny the motion or application and order such process enforced. If the court finds that the applicant is the subscriber or customer for whom the communications sought by the governmental entity are maintained, and that there is not a reason to believe that the communications

sought are relevant to a legitimate law enforcement inquiry, or that there has not been substantial compliance with the provisions of this chapter, it shall order the process quashed.

(5) A court order denying a motion or application under this section shall not be deemed a final order and no interlocutory appeal may be taken therefrom by the customer.

18 U.S.C. § 2705. DELAYED NOTICE

(a) Delay of notification.

(1) A governmental entity acting under section 2703(b) of this title may—

(A) where a court order is sought, include in the application a request, which the court shall grant, for an order delaying the notification required under section 2703(b) of this title for a period not to exceed ninety days, if the court determines that there is reason to believe that notification of the existence of the court order may have an adverse result described in paragraph (2) of this subsection; or

(B) where an administrative subpoena authorized by a Federal or State statute or a Federal or State grand jury subpoena is obtained, delay the notification required under section 2703(b) of this title for a period not to exceed ninety days upon the execution of a written certification of a supervisory official that there is reason to believe that notification of the existence of the subpoena may have an adverse result described in paragraph (2) of this subsection.

(2) An adverse result for the purposes of paragraph (1) of this subsection is—

(A) endangering the life or physical safety of an individual;

(B) flight from prosecution;

(C) destruction of or tampering with evidence;

(D) intimidation of potential witnesses; or

(E) otherwise seriously jeopardizing an investigation or unduly delaying a trial.

(3) The governmental entity shall maintain a true copy of certification under paragraph (1)(B).

(4) Extensions of the delay of notification provided in section 2703 of up to ninety days each may be granted by the court upon application, or by certification by a governmental entity, but only in accordance with subsection (b) of this section.

(5) Upon expiration of the period of delay of notification under paragraph (1) or (4) of this subsection, the governmental entity shall serve upon, or deliver by registered or first-class mail to, the customer or subscriber a copy of the process or request together with notice that—

(A) states with reasonable specificity the nature of the law enforcement inquiry; and

(B) informs such customer or subscriber—

(i) that information maintained for such customer or subscriber by the service provider named in such process or request was supplied to or requested by that governmental authority and the date on which the supplying or request took place;

(ii) that notification of such customer or subscriber was delayed;

(iii) what governmental entity or court made the certification or determination pursuant to which that delay was made; and

(iv) which provision of this chapter allowed such delay.

(6) As used in this subsection, the term "supervisory official" means the investigative agent in charge or assistant investigative agent in charge or an equivalent of an investigating agency's headquarters or regional office, or the chief prosecuting attorney or the first assistant prosecuting attorney or an equivalent of a prosecuting attorney's headquarters or regional office.

(b) **Preclusion of notice to subject of governmental access.** A governmental entity acting under section 2703, when it is not required to notify the subscriber or customer under section 2703(b)(1), or to the extent that it may delay such notice pursuant to subsection (a) of this section, may apply to a court for an order commanding a provider of electronic communications service or remote computing service to whom a warrant, subpoena, or court order is directed, for such period as the court deems appropriate, not to notify any other person of the existence of the warrant, subpoena, or court order. The court shall enter such an order if it determines that there is reason to believe that notification of the existence of the warrant, subpoena, or court order will result in—

(1) endangering the life or physical safety of an individual;

(2) flight from prosecution;

(3) destruction of or tampering with evidence;

(4) intimidation of potential witnesses; or

(5) otherwise seriously jeopardizing an investigation or unduly delaying a trial.

18 U.S.C. § 2706. COST REIMBURSEMENT

(a) **Payment.** Except as otherwise provided in subsection (c), a governmental entity obtaining the contents of communications, records, or other information under section 2702, 2703, or 2704 of this title shall pay to the person or entity assembling or providing such information a fee for reimbursement for such costs as are reasonably necessary and which have been directly incurred in searching for, assembling, reproducing, or otherwise providing such information. Such reimbursable costs shall include any costs due to necessary disruption of normal operations of any electronic communication service or remote computing service in which such information may be stored.

(b) **Amount.** The amount of the fee provided by subsection (a) shall be as mutually agreed by the governmental entity and the person or entity providing the information, or, in the absence of agreement, shall be as determined by the court which issued the order for production of such information (or the court before which a criminal prosecution relating to such information would be brought, if no court order was issued for production of the information).

(c) **Exception.** The requirement of subsection (a) of this section does not apply with respect to records or other information maintained by a communications common carrier that relate to telephone toll records and telephone listings obtained under section 2703 of this title. The court may, however, order a payment as described in subsection (a) if the court determines the information required is unusually voluminous in nature or otherwise caused an undue burden on the provider.

18 U.S.C. § 2707. CIVIL ACTION

(a) **Cause of action.** Except as provided in section 2703(e), any provider of electronic communication service, subscriber, or other person aggrieved by any violation of this chapter in which the conduct constituting the violation is engaged in with a knowing or intentional state of mind may, in a civil action, recover from the person or entity, other than the United States, which engaged in that violation such relief as may be appropriate.

(b) **Relief.** In a civil action under this section, appropriate relief includes—

(1) such preliminary and other equitable or declaratory relief as may be appropriate;

(2) damages under subsection (c); and

(3) a reasonable attorney's fee and other litigation costs reasonably incurred.

(c) **Damages.** The court may assess as damages in a civil action under this section the sum of the actual damages suffered by the plaintiff and any profits made by the violator as a result of the violation, but in no case shall a person entitled to recover receive less than the sum of $1,000. If the violation is willful or intentional, the court may assess punitive damages. In the case of a successful action to enforce liability under this section, the court may assess the costs of the action, together with reasonable attorney fees determined by the court.

(d) **Administrative discipline.** If a court or appropriate department or agency determines that the United States or any of its departments or agencies has violated any provision of this chapter, and the court or appropriate department or agency finds that the circumstances surrounding the violation raise serious questions about whether or not an officer or employee of the United States acted willfully or intentionally with respect to the violation, the department or agency shall, upon receipt of a true and correct copy of the decision and findings of the court or appropriate department or agency promptly initiate a proceeding to determine whether disciplinary action against the officer or employee is warranted. If the head of the department or agency involved determines that disciplinary action is not warranted, he or she shall notify the Inspector General with jurisdiction over the department or agency concerned and shall provide the Inspector General with the reasons for such determination.

(e) **Defense.** A good faith reliance on—

(1) a court warrant or order, a grand jury subpoena, a legislative authorization, or a statutory authorization (including a request of a governmental entity under section 2703(f) of this title);

(2) a request of an investigative or law enforcement officer under section 2518(7) of this title; or

(3) a good faith determination that section 2511(3) of this title permitted the conduct complained of;

is a complete defense to any civil or criminal action brought under this chapter or any other law.

(f) **Limitation.** A civil action under this section may not be commenced later than two years after the date upon which the claimant first discovered or had a reasonable opportunity to discover the violation.

(g) **Improper disclosure.** Any willful disclosure of a 'record', as that term is defined in section 552a(a) of title 5, United States Code, obtained by an investigative or law enforcement officer, or a governmental entity, pursuant to section 2703 of this title, or from a device installed pursuant to section 3123 or 3125 of this title, that is not a disclosure made in the proper performance of the official functions of the officer or governmental entity making the disclosure, is a violation of this chapter. This provision shall not apply to information previously lawfully disclosed (prior to the commencement of any civil or administrative proceeding under this chapter) to the public by a Federal, State, or local governmental entity or by the plaintiff in a civil action under this chapter.

18 U.S.C. § 2708. EXCLUSIVITY OF REMEDIES

The remedies and sanctions described in this chapter are the only judicial remedies and sanctions for nonconstitutional violations of this chapter.

18 U.S.C. § 2711. DEFINITIONS FOR CHAPTER

As used in this chapter—

(1) the terms defined in section 2510 of this title have, respectively, the definitions given such terms in that section;

(2) the term "remote computing service" means the provision to the public of computer storage or processing services by means of an electronic communications system;

(3) the term "court of competent jurisdiction" includes—

(A) any district court of the United States (including a magistrate judge of such a court) or any United States court of appeals that—(i) has jurisdiction over the offense being investigated; (ii) is in or for a district in which the provider of a wire or electronic communication service is located or in which the wire or electronic communications, records, or other information are stored; or (iii) is acting on a request for foreign assistance pursuant to section 3512 of this title; or

(B) a court of general criminal jurisdiction of a State authorized by the law of that State to issue search warrants; and

(4) the term "governmental entity" means a department or agency of the United States or any State or political subdivision thereof.

18 U.S.C. § 3121. GENERAL PROHIBITION ON PEN REGISTER AND TRAP AND TRACE DEVICE USE; EXCEPTION

(a) **In general.** Except as provided in this section, no person may install or use a pen register or a trap and trace device without first obtaining a court order under section 3123 of this title or under the Foreign Intelligence Surveillance Act of 1978 (50 U.S.C. 1801 et seq.).

(b) **Exception.** The prohibition of subsection (a) does not apply with respect to the use of a pen register or a trap and trace device by a provider of electronic or wire communication service—

(1) relating to the operation, maintenance, and testing of a wire or electronic communication service or to the protection of the rights or property of such provider, or to the protection of users of that service from abuse of service or unlawful use of service; or

(2) to record the fact that a wire or electronic communication was initiated or completed in order to protect such provider, another provider furnishing service toward the completion of the wire communication, or a user of that service, from fraudulent, unlawful or abusive use of service; or

(3) where the consent of the user of that service has been obtained.

(c) **Limitation.** A government agency authorized to install and use a pen register or trap and trace device under this chapter or under State law shall use technology reasonably available to it that restricts the recording or decoding of electronic or other impulses to the dialing, routing, addressing, and signaling information utilized in the processing and transmitting of wire or electronic communications so as not to include the contents of any wire or electronic communications.

(d) **Penalty.** Whoever knowingly violates subsection (a) shall be fined under this title or imprisoned not more than one year, or both.

18 U.S.C. § 3122. APPLICATION FOR AN ORDER FOR A PEN REGISTER OR A TRAP AND TRACE DEVICE

(a) **Application.**

(1) An attorney for the Government may make application for an order or an extension of an order under section 3123 of this title authorizing or approving the installation and use of a pen register or a trap and trace device under this chapter, in writing under oath or equivalent affirmation, to a court of competent jurisdiction.

(2) Unless prohibited by State law, a State investigative or law enforcement officer may make application for an order or an extension of an order under section 3123 of this title authorizing or approving the installation and use of a pen register or a trap and trace device under this chapter, in writing under oath or equivalent affirmation, to a court of competent jurisdiction of such State.

(b) **Contents of application.** An application under subsection (a) of this section shall include—

(1) the identity of the attorney for the Government or the State law enforcement or investigative officer making the application and

the identity of the law enforcement agency conducting the investigation; and

(2) a certification by the applicant that the information likely to be obtained is relevant to an ongoing criminal investigation being conducted by that agency.

18 U.S.C. § 3123. ISSUANCE OF AN ORDER FOR A PEN REGISTER OR A TRAP AND TRACE DEVICE

(a) **In general.**

(1) *Attorney for the Government.* Upon an application made under section 3122(a)(1), the court shall enter an ex parte order authorizing the installation and use of a pen register or trap and trace device anywhere within the United States, if the court finds that the attorney for the Government has certified to the court that the information likely to be obtained by such installation and use is relevant to an ongoing criminal investigation. The order, upon service of that order, shall apply to any person or entity providing wire or electronic communication service in the United States whose assistance may facilitate the execution of the order. Whenever such an order is served on any person or entity not specifically named in the order, upon request of such person or entity, the attorney for the Government or law enforcement or investigative officer that is serving the order shall provide written or electronic certification that the order applies to the person or entity being served.

(2) *State investigative or law enforcement officer.* Upon an application made under section 3122(a)(2), the court shall enter an ex parte order authorizing the installation and use of a pen register or trap and trace device within the jurisdiction of the court, if the court finds that the State law enforcement or investigative officer has certified to the court that the information likely to be obtained by such installation and use is relevant to an ongoing criminal investigation.

(3)(A) Where the law enforcement agency implementing an ex parte order under this subsection seeks to do so by installing and using its own pen register or trap and trace device on a packet-switched data network of a provider of electronic communication service to the public, the agency shall ensure that a record will be maintained which will identify—

(i) any officer or officers who installed the device and any officer or officers who accessed the device to obtain information from the network;

(ii) the date and time the device was installed, the date and time the device was uninstalled, and the date, time, and duration of each time the device is accessed to obtain information;

(iii) the configuration of the device at the time of its installation and any subsequent modification thereof; and

(iv) any information which has been collected by the device.

To the extent that the pen register or trap and trace device can be set automatically to record this information electronically, the record shall be maintained electronically throughout the installation and use of such device.

(B) The record maintained under subparagraph (A) shall be provided ex parte and under seal to the court which entered the ex parte order authorizing the installation and use of the device within 30 days after termination of the order (including any extensions thereof).

(b) **Contents of order.** An order issued under this section—

(1) shall specify—

(A) the identity, if known, of the person to whom is leased or in whose name is listed the telephone line or other facility to which the pen register or trap and trace device is to be attached or applied;

(B) the identity, if known, of the person who is the subject of the criminal investigation;

(C) the attributes of the communications to which the order applies, including the number or other identifier and, if known, the location of the telephone line or other facility to which the pen register or trap and trace device is to be attached or applied, and, in the case of an order authorizing installation and use of a trap and trace device under subsection (a)(2), the geographic limits of the order; and

(D) a statement of the offense to which the information likely to be obtained by the pen register or trap and trace device relates; and

(2) shall direct, upon the request of the applicant, the furnishing of information, facilities, and technical assistance necessary to accomplish the installation of the pen register or trap and trace device under section 3124 of this title.

(c) **Time period and extensions.**

(1) An order issued under this section shall authorize the installation and use of a pen register or a trap and trace device for a period not to exceed sixty days.

(2) Extensions of such an order may be granted, but only upon an application for an order under section 3122 of this title and upon the judicial finding required by subsection (a) of this section. The period of extension shall be for a period not to exceed sixty days.

(d) **Nondisclosure of existence of pen register or a trap and trace device.** An order authorizing or approving the installation and use of a pen register or a trap and trace device shall direct that

(1) the order be sealed until otherwise ordered by the court; and

(2) the person owning or leasing the line or other facility to which the pen register or a trap and trace device is attached, or applied, or who is obligated by the order to provide assistance to the applicant, not disclose the existence of the pen register or trap and trace device or the existence of the investigation to the listed subscriber, or to any other person, unless or until otherwise ordered by the court.

18 U.S.C. § 3124. ASSISTANCE IN INSTALLATION AND USE OF A PEN REGISTER OR A TRAP AND TRACE DEVICE

(a) **Pen registers.** Upon the request of an attorney for the Government or an officer of a law enforcement agency authorized to install and use a pen register under this chapter, a provider of wire or electronic communication service, landlord, custodian, or other person shall furnish such investigative or law enforcement officer forthwith all information, facilities, and technical assistance necessary to accomplish the installation of the pen register unobtrusively and with a minimum of interference with the services that the person so ordered by the court accords the party with respect to whom the installation and use is to take place, if such assistance is directed by a court order as provided in section 3123(b)(2) of this title.

(b) **Trap and trace device.** Upon the request of an attorney for the Government or an officer of a law enforcement agency authorized to receive the results of a trap and trace device under this chapter, a provider of a wire or electronic communication service, landlord, custodian, or other person shall install such device forthwith on the appropriate line or other facility and shall furnish such investigative or law enforcement officer all additional information, facilities and technical assistance including installation and operation of the device unobtrusively and with a minimum of interference with the services that the person so ordered by the court accords the party with respect to whom the installation and use is to take place, if such installation and assistance is directed by a court order as provided in section 3123(b)(2) of this title. Unless otherwise ordered by the court, the results of the trap and trace device shall be furnished, pursuant to section 3123(b) or section 3125 of this title, to the officer of a law enforcement agency, designated in the court order, at reasonable intervals during regular business hours for the duration of the order.

(c) **Compensation.** A provider of a wire or electronic communication service, landlord, custodian, or other person who furnishes facilities or technical assistance pursuant to this section shall be reasonably compensated for such reasonable expenses incurred in providing such facilities and assistance.

(d) **No cause of action against a provider disclosing information under this chapter.** No cause of action shall lie in any court against any provider of a wire or electronic communication service, its officers, employees, agents, or other specified persons for providing information, facilities, or assistance in accordance with a court order under this chapter or request pursuant to section 3125 of this title.

(e) **Defense.** A good faith reliance on a court order under this chapter, a request pursuant to section 3125 of this title, a legislative authorization, or a statutory authorization is a complete defense against any civil or criminal action brought under this chapter or any other law.

(f) **Communications assistance enforcement orders.** Pursuant to section 2522, an order may be issued to enforce the assistance capability and capacity requirements under the Communications Assistance for Law Enforcement Act.

18 U.S.C. § 3125. EMERGENCY PEN REGISTER AND TRAP AND TRACE DEVICE INSTALLATION

(a) Notwithstanding any other provision of this chapter, any investigative or law enforcement officer, specially designated by the Attorney General, the Deputy Attorney General, the Associate Attorney General, any Assistant Attorney General, any acting Assistant Attorney General, or any Deputy Assistant Attorney General, or by the principal prosecuting attorney of any State or subdivision thereof acting pursuant to a statute of that State, who reasonably determines that—

(1) an emergency situation exists that involves—

(A) immediate danger of death or serious bodily injury to any person;

(B) conspiratorial activities characteristic of organized crime;

(C) an immediate threat to a national security interest; or

      (D) an ongoing attack on a protected computer (as defined in section 1030) that constitutes a crime punishable by a term of imprisonment greater than one year;

that requires the installation and use of a pen register or a trap and trace device before an order authorizing such installation and use can, with due diligence, be obtained, and

      (2) there are grounds upon which an order could be entered under this chapter to authorize such installation and use;

may have installed and use a pen register or trap and trace device if, within forty-eight hours after the installation has occurred, or begins to occur, an order approving the installation or use is issued in accordance with section 3123 of this title.

      (b) In the absence of an authorizing order, such use shall immediately terminate when the information sought is obtained, when the application for the order is denied or when forty-eight hours have lapsed since the installation of the pen register or trap and trace device, whichever is earlier.

      (c) The knowing installation or use by any investigative or law enforcement officer of a pen register or trap and trace device pursuant to subsection (a) without application for the authorizing order within forty-eight hours of the installation shall constitute a violation of this chapter.

      (d) A provider of a wire or electronic service, landlord, custodian, or other person who furnished facilities or technical assistance pursuant to this section shall be reasonably compensated for such reasonable expenses incurred in providing such facilities and assistance.

18 U.S.C. § 3126. REPORTS CONCERNING PEN REGISTERS AND TRAP AND TRACE DEVICES

The Attorney General shall annually report to Congress on the number of pen register orders and orders for trap and trace devices applied for by law enforcement agencies of the Department of Justice, which report shall include information concerning—

      (1) the period of interceptions authorized by the order, and the number and duration of any extensions of the order;

      (2) the offense specified in the order or application, or extension of an order;

      (3) the number of investigations involved;

      (4) the number and nature of the facilities affected; and

      (5) the identity, including district, of the applying investigative or law enforcement agency making the application and the person authorizing the order.

18 U.S.C. § 3127. DEFINITIONS FOR CHAPTER

As used in this chapter—

(1) the terms "wire communication", "electronic communication", "electronic communication service", and "contents" have the meanings set forth for such terms in section 2510 of this title;

(2) the term "court of competent jurisdiction" means—

(A) any district court of the United States (including a magistrate judge of such a court) or any United States court of appeals that—(i) has jurisdiction over the offense being investigated; (ii) is in or for a district in which the provider of a wire or electronic communication service is located; (iii) is in or for a district in which a landlord, custodian, or other person subject to subsections (a) or (b) of section 3124 of this title is located; or (iv) is acting on a request for foreign assistance pursuant to section 3512 of this title; or

(B) a court of general criminal jurisdiction of a State authorized by the law of that State to enter orders authorizing the use of a pen register or a trap and trace device;

(3) the term "pen register" means a device or process which records or decodes dialing, routing, addressing, or signaling information transmitted by an instrument or facility from which a wire or electronic communication is transmitted, provided, however, that such information shall not include the contents of any communication, but such term does not include any device or process used by a provider or customer of a wire or electronic communication service for billing, or recording as an incident to billing, for communications services provided by such provider or any device or process used by a provider or customer of a wire communication service for cost accounting or other like purposes in the ordinary course of its business;

(4) the term "trap and trace device" means a device or process which captures the incoming electronic or other impulses which identify the originating number or other dialing, routing, addressing, and signaling information reasonably likely to identify the source of a wire or electronic communication, provided, however, that such information shall not include the contents of any communication;

(5) the term "attorney for the Government" has the meaning given such term for the purposes of the Federal Rules of Criminal Procedure; and

(6) the term "State" means a State, the District of Columbia, Puerto Rico, and any other possession or territory of the United States.

47 U.S.C. § 223. OBSCENE OR HARASSING TELEPHONE CALLS IN THE DISTRICT OF COLUMBIA OR IN INTERSTATE OR FOREIGN COMMUNICATIONS

(a) **Prohibited acts generally.** Whoever—

(1) in interstate or foreign communications—

(A) by means of a telecommunications device knowingly—

(i) makes, creates, or solicits, and

(ii) initiates the transmission of,

any comment, request, suggestion, proposal, image, or other communication which is obscene or child pornography, with intent to annoy, abuse, threaten, or harass another person;

(B) by means of a telecommunications device knowingly—

(i) makes, creates, or solicits, and

(ii) initiates the transmission of,

any comment, request, suggestion, proposal, image, or other communication which is obscene or child pornography, knowing that the recipient of the communication is under 18 years of age, regardless of whether the maker of such communication placed the call or initiated the communication;

(C) makes a telephone call or utilizes a telecommunications device, whether or not conversation or communication ensues, without disclosing his identity and with intent to annoy, abuse, threaten, or harass any person at the called number or who receives the communications;

(D) makes or causes the telephone of another repeatedly or continuously to ring, with intent to harass any person at the called number; or

(E) makes repeated telephone calls or repeatedly initiates communication with a telecommunications device, during which conversation or communication ensues, solely to harass any person at the called number or who receives the communication; or

(2) knowingly permits any telecommunications facility under his control to be used for any activity prohibited by paragraph (1) with the intent that it be used for such activity,

shall be fined under Title 18 or imprisoned not more than two years, or both.

(b) **Prohibited acts for commercial purposes; defense to prosecution.**

(1) Whoever knowingly—

(A) within the United States, by means of telephone, makes (directly or by recording device) any obscene communication for commercial purposes to any person, regardless of whether the maker of such communication placed the call; or

(B) permits any telephone facility under such person's control to be used for an activity prohibited by subparagraph (A),

shall be fined in accordance with Title 18 or imprisoned not more than two years, or both.

(2) Whoever knowingly—

(A) within the United States, by means of telephone, makes (directly or by recording device) any indecent communication for commercial purposes which is available to any person under 18 years of age or to any other person without that person's consent, regardless of whether the maker of such communication placed the call; or

(B) permits any telephone facility under such person's control to be used for an activity prohibited by subparagraph (A), shall be fined not more than $50,000 or imprisoned not more than six months, or both.

(3) It is a defense to prosecution under paragraph (2) of this subsection that the defendant restricted access to the prohibited communication to persons 18 years of age or older in accordance with subsection (c) of this section and with such procedures as the Commission may prescribe by regulation.

(4) In addition to the penalties under paragraph (1), whoever, within the United States, intentionally violates paragraph (1) or (2) shall be subject to a fine of not more than $50,000 for each violation. For purposes of this paragraph, each day of violation shall constitute a separate violation.

(5)(A) In addition to the penalties under paragraphs (1), (2), and (5), whoever, within the United States, violates paragraph (1) or (2) shall be subject to a civil fine of not more than $50,000 for each violation. For purposes of this paragraph, each day of violation shall constitute a separate violation.

(B) A fine under this paragraph may be assessed either—

(i) by a court, pursuant to civil action by the Commission or any attorney employed by the Commission who is designated by the Commission for such purposes, or

(ii) by the Commission after appropriate administrative proceedings.

(6) The Attorney General may bring a suit in the appropriate district court of the United States to enjoin any act or practice which violates paragraph (1) or (2). An injunction may be granted in accordance with the Federal Rules of Civil Procedure.

(c) **Restriction on access to subscribers by common carriers; judicial remedies respecting restrictions.**

(1) A common carrier within the District of Columbia or within any State, or in interstate or foreign commerce, shall not, to the extent technically feasible, provide access to a communication specified in subsection (b) of this section from the telephone of any subscriber who has not previously requested in writing the carrier to provide access to such communication if the carrier collects from subscribers an identifiable charge for such communication that the carrier remits, in whole or in part, to the provider of such communication.

(2) Except as provided in paragraph (3), no cause of action may be brought in any court or administrative agency against any common carrier, or any of its affiliates, including their officers, directors, employees, agents, or authorized representatives on account of—

(A) any action which the carrier demonstrates was taken in good faith to restrict access pursuant to paragraph (1) of this subsection; or

(B) any access permitted—

(i) in good faith reliance upon the lack of any representation by a provider of communications that communications provided by that provider are communications specified in subsection (b) of this section, or

(ii) because a specific representation by the provider did not allow the carrier, acting in good faith, a sufficient period to restrict access to communications described in subsection (b) of this section.

(3) Notwithstanding paragraph (2) of this subsection, a provider of communications services to which subscribers are denied access pursuant to paragraph (1) of this subsection may bring an action for

a declaratory judgment or similar action in a court. Any such action shall be limited to the question of whether the communications which the provider seeks to provide fall within the category of communications to which the carrier will provide access only to subscribers who have previously requested such access.

(d) Sending or displaying offensive material to persons under 18. Whoever—

    (1) in interstate or foreign communications knowingly—

        (A) uses an interactive computer service to send to a specific person or persons under 18 years of age, or

        (B) uses any interactive computer service to display in a manner available to a person under 18 years of age,

any comment, request, suggestion, proposal, image, or other communication that, is obscene or child pornography, regardless of whether the user of such service placed the call or initiated the communication; or

    (2) knowingly permits any telecommunications facility under such person's control to be used for an activity prohibited by paragraph (1) with the intent that it be used for such activity,

shall be fined under Title 18 or imprisoned not more than two years, or both.

(e) **Defenses.** In addition to any other defenses available by law:

    (1) No person shall be held to have violated subsection (a) or (d) of this section solely for providing access or connection to or from a facility, system, or network not under that person's control, including transmission, downloading, intermediate storage, access software, or other related capabilities that are incidental to providing such access or connection that does not include the creation of the content of the communication.

    (2) The defenses provided by paragraph (1) of this subsection shall not be applicable to a person who is a conspirator with an entity actively involved in the creation or knowing distribution of communications that violate this section, or who knowingly advertises the availability of such communications.

    (3) The defenses provided in paragraph (1) of this subsection shall not be applicable to a person who provides access or connection to a facility, system, or network engaged in the violation of this section that is owned or controlled by such person.

    (4) No employer shall be held liable under this section for the actions of an employee or agent unless the employee's or agent's

conduct is within the scope of his or her employment or agency and the employer (A) having knowledge of such conduct, authorizes or ratifies such conduct, or (B) recklessly disregards such conduct.

(5) It is a defense to a prosecution under subsection (a)(1)(B) or (d) of this section, or under subsection (a)(2) of this section with respect to the use of a facility for an activity under subsection (a)(1)(B) of this section that a person—

(A) has taken, in good faith, reasonable, effective, and appropriate actions under the circumstances to restrict or prevent access by minors to a communication specified in such subsections, which may involve any appropriate measures to restrict minors from such communications, including any method which is feasible under available technology; or

(B) has restricted access to such communication by requiring use of a verified credit card, debit account, adult access code, or adult personal identification number.

(6) The Commission may describe measures which are reasonable, effective, and appropriate to restrict access to prohibited communications under subsection (d) of this section. Nothing in this section authorizes the Commission to enforce, or is intended to provide the Commission with the authority to approve, sanction, or permit, the use of such measures. The Commission shall have no enforcement authority over the failure to utilize such measures. The Commission shall not endorse specific products relating to such measures. The use of such measures shall be admitted as evidence of good faith efforts for purposes of paragraph (5) in any action arising under subsection (d) of this section. Nothing in this section shall be construed to treat interactive computer services as common carriers or telecommunications carriers.

(f) Violations of law required; commercial entities, nonprofit libraries, or institutions of higher education.

(1) No cause of action may be brought in any court or administrative agency against any person on account of any activity that is not in violation of any law punishable by criminal or civil penalty, and that the person has taken in good faith to implement a defense authorized under this section or otherwise to restrict or prevent the transmission of, or access to, a communication specified in this section.

(2) No State or local government may impose any liability for commercial activities or actions by commercial entities, nonprofit libraries, or institutions of higher education in connection with an activity or action described in subsection (a)(2) or (d) of this section

that is inconsistent with the treatment of those activities or actions under this section: *Provided, however,* That nothing herein shall preclude any State or local government from enacting and enforcing complementary oversight, liability, and regulatory systems, procedures, and requirements, so long as such systems, procedures, and requirements govern only intrastate services and do not result in the imposition of inconsistent rights, duties or obligations on the provision of interstate services. Nothing in this subsection shall preclude any State or local government from governing conduct not covered by this section.

(g) **Application and enforcement of other Federal law.** Nothing in subsection (a), (d), (e), or (f) of this section or in the defenses to prosecution under subsection (a) or (d) of this section shall be construed to affect or limit the application or enforcement of any other Federal law.

(h) **Definitions.** For purposes of this section—

(1) The use of the term "telecommunications device" in this section—

(A) shall not impose new obligations on broadcasting station licensees and cable operators covered by obscenity and indecency provisions elsewhere in this chapter;

(B) does not include an interactive computer service; and

(C) in the case of subparagraph (C) of subsection (a)(1), includes any device or software that can be used to originate telecommunications or other types of communications that are transmitted, in whole or in part, by the Internet (as such term is defined in section 1104 of the Internet Tax Freedom Act (47 U.S.C. 151 note)).

(2) The term "interactive computer service" has the meaning provided in section 230(f)(2) of this title.

(3) The term "access software" means software (including client or server software) or enabling tools that do not create or provide the content of the communication but that allow a user to do any one or more of the following:

(A) filter, screen, allow, or disallow content;

(B) pick, choose, analyze, or digest content; or

(C) transmit, receive, display, forward, cache, search, subset, organize, reorganize, or translate content.

(4) The term "institution of higher education" has the meaning provided in section 1001 of Title 20.

(5) The term "library" means a library eligible for participation in State-based plans for funds under title III of the Library Services and Construction Act (20 U.S.C. 355e et seq.).

FEDERAL RULE OF CRIMINAL PROCEDURE 41
[Rule 41]

SEARCH AND SEIZURE

(a) **Scope and Definitions.**

(1) *Scope.* This rule does not modify any statute regulating search or seizure, or the issuance and execution of a search warrant in special circumstances.

(2) *Definitions.* The following definitions apply under this rule:

(A) "Property" includes documents, books, papers, any other tangible objects, and information.

(B) "Daytime" means the hours between 6:00 a.m. and 10:00 p.m. according to local time.

(C) "Federal law enforcement officer" means a government agent (other than an attorney for the government) who is engaged in enforcing the criminal laws and is within any category of officers authorized by the Attorney General to request a search warrant.

(D) "Domestic terrorism" and "international terrorism" have the meanings set out in 18 U.S.C. § 2331.

(E) "Tracking device" has the meaning set out in 18 U.S.C. § 3117(b).

(b) **Authority to Issue a Warrant.** At the request of a federal law enforcement officer or an attorney for the government:

(1) a magistrate judge with authority in the district—or if none is reasonably available, a judge of a state court of record in the district—has authority to issue a warrant to search for and seize a person or property located within the district;

(2) a magistrate judge with authority in the district has authority to issue a warrant for a person or property outside the district if the person or property is located within the district when the warrant is issued but might move or be moved outside the district before the warrant is executed;

(3) a magistrate judge—in an investigation of domestic terrorism or international terrorism—with authority in any district in which activities related to the terrorism may have occurred has authority to

issue a warrant for a person or property within or outside that district;

(4) a magistrate judge with authority in the district has authority to issue a warrant to install within the district a tracking device; the warrant may authorize use of the device to track the movement of a person or property located within the district, outside the district, or both; and

(5) a magistrate judge having authority in any district where activities related to the crime may have occurred, or in the District of Columbia, may issue a warrant for property that is located outside the jurisdiction of any state or district, but within any of the following:

(A) a United States territory, possession, or commonwealth;

(B) the premises—no matter who owns them—of a United States diplomatic or consular mission in a foreign state, including any appurtenant building, part of a building, or land used for the mission's purposes; or

(C) a residence and any appurtenant land owned or leased by the United States and used by United States personnel assigned to a United States diplomatic or consular mission in a foreign state.

(c) **Persons or Property Subject to Search or Seizure.** A warrant may be issued for any of the following:

(1) evidence of a crime;

(2) contraband, fruits of crime, or other items illegally possessed;

(3) property designed for use, intended for use, or used in committing a crime; or

(4) a person to be arrested or a person who is unlawfully restrained.

(d) **Obtaining a Warrant.**

(1) *In General.* After receiving an affidavit or other information, a magistrate judge—or if authorized by Rule 41(b), a judge of a state court of record—must issue the warrant if there is probable cause to search for and seize a person or property or to install and use a tracking device.

(2) *Requesting a Warrant in the Presence of a Judge.*

(A) *Warrant on an Affidavit.* When a federal law enforcement officer or an attorney for the government presents an affidavit in support of a warrant, the judge may require the affiant to appear personally and may examine under oath the affiant and any witness the affiant produces.

(B) *Warrant on Sworn Testimony.* The judge may wholly or partially dispense with a written affidavit and base a warrant on sworn testimony if doing so is reasonable under the circumstances.

(C) *Recording Testimony.* Testimony taken in support of a warrant must be recorded by a court reporter or by a suitable recording device, and the judge must file the transcript or recording with the clerk, along with any affidavit.

(3) *Requesting a Warrant by Telephonic or Other Means.*

(A) *In General.* A magistrate judge may issue a warrant based on information communicated by telephone or other reliable electronic means.

(B) *Recording Testimony.* Upon learning that an applicant is requesting a warrant under Rule 41(d)(3)(A), a magistrate judge must:

(i) place under oath the applicant and any person on whose testimony the application is based; and

(ii) make a verbatim record of the conversation with a suitable recording device, if available, or by a court reporter, or in writing.

(C) *Certifying Testimony.* The magistrate judge must have any recording or court reporter's notes transcribed, certify the transcription's accuracy, and file a copy of the record and the transcription with the clerk. Any written verbatim record must be signed by the magistrate judge and filed with the clerk.

(D) *Suppression Limited.* Absent a finding of bad faith, evidence obtained from a warrant issued under Rule 41(d)(3)(A) is not subject to suppression on the ground that issuing the warrant in that manner was unreasonable under the circumstances.

(e) **Issuing the Warrant.**

(1) *In General.* The magistrate judge or a judge of a state court of record must issue the warrant to an officer authorized to execute it.

(2) *Contents of the Warrant.*

(A) *Warrant to Search for and Seize a Person or Property.* Except for a tracking-device warrant, the warrant must identify the person or property to be searched, identify any person or property to be seized, and designate the magistrate judge to whom it must be returned. The warrant must command the officer to:

(i) execute the warrant within a specified time no longer than 14 days;

(ii) execute the warrant during the daytime, unless the judge for good cause expressly authorizes execution at another time; and

(iii) return the warrant to the magistrate judge designated in the warrant.

(B) *Warrant Seeking Electronically Stored Information.* A warrant under Rule 41(e)(2)(A) may authorize the seizure of electronic storage media or the seizure or copying of electronically stored information. Unless otherwise specified, the warrant authorizes a later review of the media or information consistent with the warrant. The time for executing the warrant in Rule 41(e)(2)(A) and (f)(1)(A) refers to the seizure or on-site copying of the media or information, and not to any later off-site copying or review.

(C) *Warrant for a Tracking Device.* A tracking-device warrant must identify the person or property to be tracked, designate the magistrate judge to whom it must be returned, and specify a reasonable length of time that the device may be used. The time must not exceed 45 days from the date the warrant was issued. The court may, for good cause, grant one or more extensions for a reasonable period not to exceed 45 days each. The warrant must command the officer to:

(i) complete any installation authorized by the warrant within a specified time no longer than 10 calendar days;

(ii) perform any installation authorized by the warrant during the daytime, unless the judge for good cause expressly authorizes installation at another time; and

(iii) return the warrant to the judge designated in the warrant.

(3) *Warrant by Telephonic or Other Means.* If a magistrate judge decides to proceed under Rule 41(d)(3)(A), the following additional procedures apply:

(A) *Preparing a Proposed Duplicate Original Warrant.* The applicant must prepare a "proposed duplicate original warrant" and must read or otherwise transmit the contents of that document verbatim to the magistrate judge.

(B) *Preparing an Original Warrant.* If the applicant reads the contents of the proposed duplicate original warrant, the magistrate judge must enter those contents into an original warrant. If the applicant transmits the contents by reliable electronic means, that transmission may serve as the original warrant.

(C) *Modification.* The magistrate judge may modify the original warrant. The judge must transmit any modified warrant to the applicant by reliable electronic means under Rule 41(e)(3)(D) or direct the applicant to modify the proposed duplicate original warrant accordingly.

(D) *Signing the Warrant.* Upon determining to issue the warrant, the magistrate judge must immediately sign the original warrant, enter on its face the exact date and time it is issued, and transmit it by reliable electronic means to the applicant or direct the applicant to sign the judge's name on the duplicate original warrant.

(f) **Executing and Returning the Warrant.**

(1) *Warrant to Search for and Seize a Person or Property.*

(A) *Noting the Time.* The officer executing the warrant must enter on it the exact date and time it was executed.

(B) *Inventory.* An officer present during the execution of the warrant must prepare and verify an inventory of any property seized. The officer must do so in the presence of another officer and the person from whom, or from whose premises, the property was taken. If either one is not present, the officer must prepare and verify the inventory in the presence of at least one other credible person. In a case involving the seizure of electronic storage media or the seizure or copying of electronically stored information, the inventory may be limited to describing the physical storage media that were seized or copied. The officer may retain a copy of the electronically stored information that was seized or copied.

(C) *Receipt.* The officer executing the warrant must give a copy of the warrant and a receipt for the property taken to the person from whom, or from whose premises, the property was taken or leave a copy of the warrant and receipt at the place where the officer took the property.

(D) *Return.* The officer executing the warrant must promptly return it—together with a copy of the inventory—to the magistrate judge designated on the warrant. The judge must, on request, give a copy of the inventory to the person from whom, or from whose premises, the property was taken and to the applicant for the warrant.

(2) *Warrant for a Tracking Device.*

(A) *Noting the Time.* The officer executing a tracking-device warrant must enter on it the exact date and time the device was installed and the period during which it was used.

(B) *Return.* Within 10 calendar days after the use of the tracking device has ended, the officer executing the warrant must return it to the judge designated in the warrant.

(C) *Service.* Within 10 calendar days after the use of the tracking device has ended, the officer executing a tracking-device warrant must serve a copy of the warrant on the person who was tracked or whose property was tracked. Service may be accomplished by delivering a copy to the person who, or whose property, was tracked; or by leaving a copy at the person's residence or usual place of abode with an individual of suitable age and discretion who resides at that location and by mailing a copy to the person's last known address. Upon request of the government, the judge may delay notice as provided in Rule 41(f)(3).

(3) *Delayed Notice.* Upon the government's request, a magistrate judge—or if authorized by Rule 41(b), a judge of a state court of record—may delay any notice required by this rule if the delay is authorized by statute.

(g) **Motion to Return Property.** A person aggrieved by an unlawful search and seizure of property or by the deprivation of property may move for the property's return. The motion must be filed in the district where the property was seized. The court must receive evidence on any factual issue necessary to decide the motion. If it grants the motion, the court must return the property to the movant, but may impose reasonable conditions to protect access to the property and its use in later proceedings.

(h) **Motion to Suppress.** A defendant may move to suppress evidence in the court where the trial will occur, as Rule 12 provides.

(i) **Forwarding Papers to the Clerk.** The magistrate judge to whom the warrant is returned must attach to the warrant a copy of the return, of the inventory, and of all other related papers and must deliver them to the clerk in the district where the property was seized.

PART B

CASELAW SUPPLEMENT

■ ■ ■

CHAPTER 2

COMPUTER MISUSE CRIMES

■ ■ ■

C. UNAUTHORIZED ACCESS STATUTES

3. WHAT IS AUTHORIZATION? THE CASE OF CODE-BASED RESTRICTIONS

On page 51, in the middle of the page, add the following new Notes 6–8:

6.   Consider the facts of *United States v. Auernheimer*, 748 F.3d 525 (3d Cir. 2014). In January 2010, Apple Computer introduced the iPad portable tablet computer. The iPad allowed users to connect to the Internet through either a wireless internet connection, commonly known as "wifi," or through a cellular connection, commonly referred to at the time as "3G" service. The telecommunications company AT&T established an exclusive contract with Apple to provide 3G access to iPad users.

AT&T created a website to allow its customers to access their AT&T accounts using the combination of an e-mail address and a password. The AT&T website was available at the Internet address *https://dcp2.att.com*, and it contained a login prompt that appeared whenever a user visited the website. When iPad users registered with AT&T and created an account, they also provided AT&T with an e-mail address. AT&T registered each iPad using a serial number found on the part of the iPad used to send and receive communications. The serial numbers were known as "integrated circuit card identifiers," or ICC-IDs. Each ICC-ID is a nineteen or twenty digit number.

To make it easier for iPad owners to access their AT&T accounts, AT&T programmed its website to automatically pre-populate the login prompt with the e-mail address associated with that particular iPad computer. From the user's perspective, an iPad owner with an AT&T account who visited the website found that the "e-mail" part of the login prompt was automatically filled in with the user's e-mail address. This feature was designed to save users time. Because the e-mail address would appear automatically, the user only needed to manually enter in his password to log in to the AT&T website. AT&T implemented this feature by directing the iPad to a specific Internet address. When an iPad user with an ICC-ID visited the AT&T website, it would automatically be directed to the following website, with "X" standing for the specific ICC-ID number: *https://dcp2.att.com/OEPClient/openPage? ICCID=X&IMEI=0.*

When any computer using the correct browser setting visited that particular webpage, the AT&T website would return the e-mail address associated with that specific ICC-ID number. iPads registered with AT&T would visit the page associated with that address automatically. However, AT&T configured its website so that it would share an e-mail address with anyone—not just the account holder—who entered the correct website address.

A computer hacker by the name of Daniel Spitler identified this feature when he attempted to sign up for service with AT&T using a network card he had purchased from AT&T. Spitler wanted to obtain the 3G Internet service that was available only to iPad users, so he purchased a network card and configured a program to make it seem like it was an iPad. After studying the iPad operating system, Spitler realized the AT&T website was configured to include a space in the Internet address for ICC-IDs. When Spitler entered his own ICC-ID number in that space, he was surprised to see that the AT&T login page already had his e-mail address filled out.

Curious about how AT&T's website could return his e-mail address, Spitler changed the ICC-ID number of the website by one digit and the website "pre-populated" the login page with a different e-mail address. Spitler realized that AT&T had stored the e-mail addresses associated with different iPads on AT&T's servers. He concluded that he could collect many e-mail addresses using an automated computer program that he called the "account slurper." Spitler configured his program so it would visit the AT&T website many times using web addresses with different ICC-ID numbers. When the website address contained an ICC-ID number that matched that of a registered iPad user, AT&T's website would send back that user's e-mail address.

Spitler shared his discovery with notorious Internet "troll" and hacker Andrew Auernheimer, who helped Spitler brainstorm ways to improve the program. Ultimately, the program collected approximately 114,000 e-mail addresses before AT&T discovered its customers' e-mail addresses were public. AT&T quickly disabled the feature that pre-populated a customer's e-mail address.

In an effort to draw attention to the computer skills of both Spitler and himself—the goal being to make a big splash in the news and bring attention and business to their computer security company—Auernheimer contacted various media members and reporters to persuade them to write about how the e-mails were collected. One of those reporters was Ryan Tate of the online publication *Gawker*. Auernheimer explained to Tate how the e-mail addresses had been collected. To confirm the collection, he shared the list of e-mail addresses with Tate.

On June 9, 2010, *Gawker* ran a story written by Tate titled "Apple's Worst Security Breach: 114,000 iPad Owners Exposed." The story included a thorough discussion of how the e-mail addresses were collected, and it credited Spitler and Auernheimer with their collection. The popular website *Drudge Report* prominently linked to the story.

Both Spitler and Auernheimer were charged in New Jersey with conspiracy to violate the felony provisions of the CFAA. Spitler pled guilty and testified against Auernheimer. According to the indictment, Spitler and Auernheimer had conspired to commit an unauthorized access in violation of 18 U.S.C. § 1030(a)(2)(C) in furtherance of the New Jersey state unauthorized access law. Under federal law, Auernheimer was responsible for the acts of Spitler that were in furtherance of the goal of the conspiracy. At trial, Auernheimer was convicted of conspiracy to violate the felony provisions of the CFAA.

On appeal, Auernheimer argued that there was no unauthorized access as a matter of law because Spitler's "account slurper" program merely visited a public website to see information that AT&T had published on the web. The government responded that Spitler's program had accessed AT&T's website without authorization because Spitler and Auernheimer had used their computer expertise to breach a code-based barrier and collect information from AT&T's website that AT&T had never intended to be collected. The Third Circuit vacated Auernheimer's conviction for reasons of improper venue without reaching the question of whether the conduct violated the CFAA.

Do you think Auernheimer and Spitler's conduct constituted an unauthorized access under the CFAA? Although the Third Circuit did not answer this question, the court did add a footnote about liability under New Jersey's unauthorized access law that may have hinted at the court's likely answer for liability under the CFAA:

> We also note that in order to be guilty of accessing "without authorization, or in excess of authorization" under New Jersey law, the Government needed to prove that Auernheimer or Spitler circumvented a code-or password-based barrier to access. See State v. Riley, 412 N.J.Super. 162, 988 A.2d 1252, 1267 (N.J.Super.Ct.Law Div.2009). Although we need not resolve whether Auernheimer's conduct involved such a breach, no evidence was advanced at trial that the account slurper ever breached any password gate or other code-based barrier. The account slurper simply accessed the publicly facing portion of the login screen and scraped information that AT&T unintentionally published.

United States v. Auernheimer, 748 F.3d 525, 534 n.5 (3d Cir. 2014).

7. *United States v. Aaron Swartz.* In 2011 and 2012, the United States Department of Justice prosecuted an Internet activist named Aaron Swartz for violating the CFAA. Tragically, Swartz committed suicide before the case went to trial. As a result, no legal decision was handed down in his case. But consider the facts of the case against Swartz, and ask whether you think Swartz violated the CFAA.

JSTOR is an organization that sells universities, libraries, and publishers access to a database of over 1,000 academic journals. For a large research university, JSTOR charges as much as $50,000 a year for an annual subscription fee, at least parts of which go to pay copyright fees to the owners of the articles in the databases. The JSTOR database is not freely available: Normally, a username and password are required to access it. But if you access the site from a computer network owned by a university that has purchased a subscription, you can access the site without a username and password from their network. Users of the service then have to agree to use JSTOR in a particular way when they log in to the site. They generally can download one article at a time, but the JSTOR software is configured to block efforts to download large groups of articles.

Internet activist Aaron Swartz decided to "liberate" the entire JSTOR database. His apparent plan was to allow everyone access to all of the journals in the database, so he came up with a plan to gain access to the database and copy it so he could make it publicly available to everyone via filesharing networks. Swartz lived in the Boston area, and he had legitimate access to the JSTOR database using Harvard's network, where he was a fellow at an academic center on ethics. But Swartz decided not to use Harvard's network. Instead, he used MIT's network across town. Swartz did not have an account or formal relationship with MIT, but MIT is known for having relatively open account practices.

Swartz purchased a laptop, went into a building at MIT, and used the MIT wireless network to create a guest account on MIT's network. He then accessed JSTOR and executed a program called "keepgrabbing" that circumvented JSTOR's limits on how many articles a person could download—thus enabling Swartz to start to download a massive number of articles. MIT and JSTOR eventually caught on to what was happening, and they blocked Swartz's computer from being able to access the MIT network by banning the IP address that he had been assigned.

Swartz responded by changing his IP address, and it took a few hours before JSTOR noticed and blocked his new IP address. To try to stop Swartz from just changing IP addresses again, JSTOR then blocked a range of IP addresses from MIT and contacted MIT for more help. MIT responded by canceling the new account and blocking Swartz' computer from accessing the MIT address by banning his MAC address, a unique identifier associated with his laptop.

Swartz bought a new laptop and also spoofed the MAC address from his old one to circumvent the ban. Using the two laptops and the program designed to circumvent JSTOR's limits on downloading articles, he started to download a significant chunk of JSTOR's database. A day or two later, JSTOR responded by blocking all of MIT's access to JSTOR for a few days.

Instead of trying to connect to the MIT network wirelessly, Swartz next entered a closet in the basement of a building at MIT and connected his computer directly to the network—hiding his computer under a box so no one would see it. The closet was normally locked and Swartz did not have the key, although the lock to the door apparently was broken and the door could be pushed open without the key. Over several weeks, he succeeded in downloading a major portion of JSTOR's database.

Investigators were on to Swartz at this point, however. They installed a video camera in the closet to catch Swartz when he accessed the closet to swap out storage devices or retrieve his computer. Swartz was caught on camera, and he even seems to have realized that he was being filmed; at one point he was filmed entering the closet using his bicycle helmet as a mask to avoid being identified. Swartz was spotted on MIT's campus soon after by the police and tried to run away, but he was then caught and arrested. Federal charges followed.

Because Swartz committed suicide before his case went to trial, neither the court nor the jury passed judgment on whether Swartz's conduct violated the CFAA. In your view, did Swartz access a computer without authorization or exceed his authorized access?

8. In *Craigslist v. 3Taps*, 2013 WL 4447520 (N.D. Cal. August 16, 2013), a company named 3Taps aggregated and republished ads from the popular Craigslist website by scraping data from Craigslist. Craigslist responded by sending 3Taps a cease-and-desist letter and by blocking the IP addresses associated with 3Taps's computers. 3Taps continued to access Craigslist by changing the IP addresses by which its computers accessed Craigslist's servers. Craigslist then sued 3Taps, alleging claims including copyright, state law violations, and the CFAA. For its CFAA claims, Craigslist argued that 3Taps violated the CFAA by circumventing the IP address block after receiving a cease-and-desist letter. The District Court agreed:

> Here, under the plain language of the statute, 3Taps was "without authorization" when it continued to pull data off of Craigslist's website after Craigslist revoked its authorization to access the website. As the "ordinary, contemporary, common meaning" of the word indicates, "authorization" turns on the decision of the "authority" that grants—or prohibits—access. Craigslist gave the world permission (i.e., "authorization") to access the public information on its public website. Then, it rescinded that permission for 3Taps. Further access by 3Taps after that rescission was "without authorization."

> Craigslist made a complete access restriction when it told 3Taps that it could not access Craigslist's website "for any reason," and then put in place a technological barrier designed to completely cut off 3Taps' ability to view the site.

> IP blocking may be an imperfect barrier to screening out a human being who can change his IP address, but it is a real barrier, and a

clear signal from the computer owner to the person using the IP address that he is no longer authorized to access the website.

Is the District Court correct?

D. 18 U.S.C. § 1030(a)(2) AND ITS FELONY ENHANCEMENTS

2. 18 U.S.C. § 1030(a)(2) FELONY LIABILITY

On page 88, at the end of Note 2, add the following:

United States v. Auernheimer, 2012 WL 5389142 (D.N.J. 2012), *vacated on other grounds*, 748 F.3d 525 (3d Cir. 2014), raised an interesting variation on *Cioni*. In *Auernheimer*, the government argued that a misdemeanor violation of § 1030(a)(2) becomes a felony under § 1030(c)(2)(B)(ii) if the act also violates a state unauthorized access statute. In that instance, the government argued, the offense becomes a federal unauthorized access crime in furtherance of a state unauthorized access crime. The district court agreed, at least when the state unauthorized access includes an extra element that 1030(a)(2) does not have:

> Although there is an overlap of facts for the first two elements of each offense, N.J.S.A. 2C:20–31(a) requires the additional component that defendant "knowingly or recklessly discloses or causes to be disclosed any data . . . or personal identifying information." Hence, an essential N.J.S.A. 2C:20–31(a) element requires proof of conduct not required for a CFAA offense

2012 WL 5389142 at *4.

On appeal, the defendant argued that the district court had misapplied *Cioni*. According to the defendant, the key question under *Cioni* was whether the government had charged two different acts, not two different statutes. Otherwise, mere overlap with analogous state unauthorized access statutes would transform every § 1030(a)(2) misdemeanor into a felony. The Third Circuit vacated the defendant's conviction on venue grounds without reaching the felony enhancement issue. If the Third Circuit had reached the issue, how should it have ruled?

CHAPTER 3

TRADITIONAL CRIMES

■ ■ ■

A. ECONOMIC CRIMES

1. PROPERTY CRIMES

At the bottom of page 150, add the following new Note 6:

6. In *United States v. Agrawal*, 726 F.3d 235 (2d Cir. 2013), a quantitative analyst named Agrawal was working at a high-frequency trading group at a company named SocGen in New York City. Agrawal decided to seek employment opportunities elsewhere. In effort to impress prospective employers, Agrawal came into his regular office one day, "printed out more than a thousand pages of [SocGen's trading] code, put the printed pages into a backpack, and physically transported the papers to his apartment in New Jersey." During subsequent interviews, Agrawal promised prospective employers that he could replicate the valuable code for them to use to compete against SocGen. As in *Aleynikov*, Agrawal was charged with violating 18 U.S.C. § 2314 and the EEA.

Under the deferential standard of plain error review (applied because Agrawal did not challenge the issue at trial), the Second Circuit the affirmed the conviction for violating 18 U.S.C. § 2314 because Agrawal stole a physical copy of the code:

> Relying on *Aleynikov,* Agrawal challenges the legal sufficiency of his NSPA charge, complaining that he too is accused of stealing computer code constituting only intangible property. The argument fails because it ignores *Aleynikov's* emphasis on the format in which intellectual property is taken. In *Aleynikov,* the defendant stole computer code in an intangible form, electronically downloading the code to a server in Germany and then from that server to his own computer. By contrast, Agrawal stole computer code in the tangible form of thousands of sheets of paper, which paper he then transported to his home in New Jersey. This makes all the difference. As *Aleynikov* explained, a defendant who transfers code electronically never assumes "physical control" over anything tangible. *Id.* By contrast, a defendant such as Agrawal, who steals papers on which intangible intellectual property is reproduced, *does* assume physical control over something tangible as is necessary for the item to be a 'good' for purposes of the NSPA.

Here, Agrawal produced paper copies of SocGen's computer code in the company's office, on its paper and with its equipment. The fact that the code had been in an intangible form before Agrawal, a SocGen employee, himself reproduced it on company paper is irrelevant. The papers belonged to SocGen, not Agrawal. When Agrawal removed this tangible property from SocGen's offices without authorization, and transported it to his home in New Jersey, he was engaged in the theft or conversion of a "good" in violation of the NSPA.

2. THE ECONOMIC ESPIONAGE ACT

On page 160, at the middle of the page, add the following new Note 4:

4.   The significance of *Aleynikov* was significantly undercut by the Second Circuit's subsequent decision in *United States v. Agrawal*, 726 F.3d 235 (2d Cir. 2013). Agrawal was working at a high-frequency trading group at SocGen when he decided to seek employment opportunities elsewhere. Agrawal came into his SocGen office, "printed out more than a thousand pages of [SocGen's trading] code, put the printed pages into a backpack, and physically transported the papers to his apartment in New Jersey." Agrawal then promised prospective employers that he could replicate the valuable SocGen code he had taken for them to use. Somewhat surprisingly, at least in light of *Aleynikov*, the Second Circuit held that this conduct violated the EEA and was distinguishable from *Aleynikov*:

> As to the EEA charge, in this case, neither the indictment nor the prosecution's arguments or the court's charge identified SocGen's confidential HFT systems as the "product" relied on to satisfy the crime's jurisdictional element. Rather, the record indicates that the relevant product was the publicly traded *securities* bought and sold by SocGen using its HFT systems.

> In *United States v. Aleynikov,* this court construed the phrase "a product that is produced for or placed in interstate or foreign commerce" as a "limitation" on the scope of the EEA, signaling that Congress did not intend to invoke its full Commerce Clause power to criminalize the theft of trade secrets. *Aleynikov* explained that for a product to be "placed in" commerce, it must have "already been introduced into the stream of commerce and have reached the marketplace." Products "being developed or readied for the marketplace" qualified "as being 'produced for,' if not yet actually 'placed in,' commerce." But a "product" could not be deemed "produced for" commerce simply because its "purpose is to facilitate or engage in such commerce"; such a construction of the EEA's product requirement would deprive the statutory language of any limiting effect.

Aleynikov's construction of the phrase "a product that is produced for or placed in interstate commerce" controls on this appeal. We note, however, that the reversal of Aleynikov's EEA conviction was based on the application of that phrase to the particular "product" that was the basis of the jurisdictional allegation in his case. As we explain below, the present case was submitted to the jury on a very different product theory than that relied on in *Aleynikov.* Thus, the same construction that prompted reversal in *Aleynikov* leads to affirmance here.

In *Aleynikov,* the EEA charge was submitted to the jury on the theory that the trade secret converted by the defendant, *i.e.,* the proprietary computer code, was "included in" a single product: Goldman Sachs's confidential trading system. The jury instructions in *Aleynikov* unambiguously stated that "[t]he indictment [in that case] charges that the Goldman Sachs high-frequency *trading platform* is a product," and that the jury's responsibility was to "determin[e] whether the trading platform was produced for or placed in interstate or foreign commerce." This had been the court's and the parties' understanding of the *Aleynikov* indictment from the start. In its opinion denying the defendant's motion to dismiss the indictment, the court noted the parties' agreement "that the trade secret at issue in [the EEA Count] is the source code, and that the relevant 'product' is the Trading System." *United States v. Aleynikov,* 737 F.Supp.2d 173, 178 (S.D.N.Y.2010).

It was on this understanding that this court held the *Aleynikov* indictment legally insufficient. As *Aleynikov* construed the phrase "a product that is produced for or placed in interstate or foreign commerce," Goldman Sachs's trading system could not constitute such a product because Goldman Sachs "had no intention of selling its HFT system or licensing it to anyone." *United States v. Aleynikov,* 676 F.3d at 82. To the contrary, the value of the system depended entirely on preserving its secrecy. *See id.*

Agrawal submits that *Aleynikov* mandates the same conclusion here because the computer code at issue, like the code in *Aleynikov,* was included in a confidential HFT system. But this case differs from *Aleynikov* in an important respect. Here, neither the prosecution nor the district court presented the case to the jury on the theory that SocGen's *trading system* was the "product" placed in interstate commerce. Nor did they suggest that the EEA's jurisdictional nexus was satisfied by computer code (the stolen trade secret) being "included in" that "product."

Rather, the record reveals that EEA jurisdiction was here put to the jury on a more obvious, convincing—and legally sufficient—theory that was not pursued and, therefore, not addressed in *Aleynikov:* that the *securities* traded by SocGen using its HFT systems, rather than the systems themselves, were the "products placed in" interstate commerce. Under that theory, the jurisdictional nexus was satisfied because SocGen's stolen computer code "related to" the securities (the product) it identified for purchase and sale.

In contrast to *Aleynikov,* the court here made no mention of the confidential HFT system. Of course, the EEA further requires a nexus between the converted trade secret and the product produced for or placed in interstate commerce. *See* 18 U.S.C. § 1832(a) (requiring that trade secret "relate[ ] to" or be "included in" product). In *Aleynikov,* where the employer's HFT system was the sole product at issue, the prosecution contended that the stolen computer code was included in that product. Where, as here, the relevant product is publicly traded securities, the statute's "related to" provision comes into play: Was the stolen code related to traded securities? We answer that question "yes."

In a footnote, the Second Circuit noted that Congress had amended the EEA in light of *Aleynikov,* but that the amendment was irrelevant to the *Agrawal* case because it occurred after the events at issue in *Agrawal*:

Aleynikov's identification of a congressional intent to limit the reach of the EEA has since been disavowed by Congress itself, which quickly amended the EEA to remove the purportedly limiting language and to clarify its intent to reach broadly in protecting against the theft of trade secrets. See Theft of Trade Secrets Clarification Act of 2012, Pub.L. No. 112–236, 126 Stat. 1627 (providing for EEA to be amended to strike phrase "or included in a product that is produced for or placed in" and to insert phrase "a product or service used in or intended for use in," so that relevant language now reads: "Whoever, with intent to convert a trade secret, that is related to a product or service used in or intended for use in interstate or foreign commerce."); 158 Cong. Rec. S6978–03 (daily ed. Nov. 27, 2012) (statement of Sen. Leahy) (observing that *Aleynikov* decision "cast doubt on the reach" of EEA, and that "clarifying legislation that the Senate will pass today corrects the court's narrow reading to ensure that our federal criminal laws adequately address the theft of trade secrets" (emphasis added)).

On this appeal, we have no occasion to construe the revised EEA. Rather, we are obliged to apply the EEA as it existed at the time of Agrawal's conviction and as construed in *Aleynikov*.

B. CRIMES AGAINST PERSONS

1. THREATS AND HARASSMENT

A) Statutory Issues

On page 212, in the middle of the page, add the following new Note 5:

5.   In June 2014, the United States Supreme Court agreed to rule on the proper interpretation of 18 U.S.C. § 875 in *Elonis v. United States*, No. 13–983. The first question presented in *Elonis* is the following:

> Whether, as a matter of statutory interpretation, conviction of threatening another person under 18 U.S.C. § 875(c) requires proof of the defendant's subjective intent to threaten.

The defendant in *Elonis* posted a series of threatening-sounding Facebook updates about his estranged wife. According to Elonis, he never intended his updates to be serious: Rather, he considered his updates to be a therapeutic fantasy emulating rappers such as Eminem. The first question presented in *Elonis* is whether this should be a defense as a matter of statutory interpretation: Is a communication that sounds threatening but was actually never intended as an expression of harm a "threat" for purposes of § 875(c)?

Oral argument in the case is scheduled for December 1, 2014, and a decision is expected before July 2015.

B) Constitutional Limits

On page 223, at the bottom of the page, add the following new Note 5:

5.   In June 2014, the United States Supreme Court agreed to consider the First Amendment limits of threat liability in *Elonis v. United States*, No. 13–983. The second question presented in *Elonis* is the following:

> Whether, consistent with the First Amendment . . . , conviction of threatening another person requires proof of the defendant's subjective intent to threaten; or whether it is enough to show that a "reasonable person" would regard the statement as threatening.

According to the defendant, the First Amendment does not allow a person to be published for speech that is reasonably understood as threatening if the defendant did not subjectively intend the speech as a threat. The defendant claims that a contrary result would amount to "criminal liability for negligently failing to anticipate that remarks would be seen as threats," which the First Amendment does not allow. Brief for Petitioner in Elonis v. United States, No. 13–983, at 4.

The government in *Elonis* responds that the subjective intent of the speaker is irrelevant to what is a threat:

> A speaker's subjective intention that his statement not be interpreted as a threat, if not made manifest to a reasonable person with knowledge of the context and circumstances, neither increases the expressive value of the statement nor decreases the statement's propensity to cause disruption and harm. A bomb threat that appears to be serious is equally harmful regardless of the speaker's private state of mind.

Brief for the United States in Elonis v. United States, No. 13–983, at 16.

Oral argument in the case is scheduled for December 1, 2014, and a decision is expected before July 2015.

On page 226, add the following material before the *Notes and Questions* begin:

On appeal, the Seventh Circuit unanimously reversed the district court and reinstated the conviction. *See United States v. White*, 698 F.3d 1005 (7th Cir. 2012). Here is the Seventh Circuit's rationale:

> A reasonable jury could have found that the government met [its] burden. Whether White's post was a criminal solicitation depended on context, and the government provided ample evidence of such context from which a rational jury could have concluded that the post was an invitation for others to harm Juror A, though fortunately no one accepted the invitation. The post attributed to Juror A characteristics intended to make the target loathed by readers of White's neo-Nazi website: a Jew, a homosexual with a black lover, and above all the foreman of the jury that had convicted Overthrow.com's hero, Matthew Hale— an anti-Semitic white supremacist—of soliciting the murder of a federal judge. And whereas White previously refrained from "republishing the personal information" of others involved in the Hale trial because, as White acknowledged, "there was so great a potential for action linked to such posting," White expressly published Juror A's personal information, including Juror A's photograph, home address, and telephone numbers.

> The post has a context created by previous posts on the website that had solicited the murder of Barack Obama, Richard Warman (a Canadian civil rights lawyer and the bane of hate groups), Elie Wiesel, and six black teenagers known as the "Jena 6." Other posts had congratulated murderers or urged the murder of enemies defined in terms that would embrace Juror A. All that was missing was an explicit solicitation to murder Juror A. But the description summarized above would have made

Juror A seem to loyal readers of Overthrow.com as being at least as worthy of assassination as Richard Warman, who had been described in a post, published only a few months before the Juror A post, as "Richard, the sometimes Jewish, sometimes not, attorney behind the abuses of Canada's Human Rights Tribunal," who "should be drug out into the street and shot, after appropriate trial by a revolutionary tribunal of Canada's white activists. It won't be hard to do, he can be found, easily, at his home, at [address]." And Juror A could be found at home just as easily because White posted Juror A's personal contact information along with the denunciation.

The "abuses" of the Canadian Human Rights Tribunal had been left unspecified in the denunciation of Warman, whereas Juror A was identified as instrumental in the conviction of the hero Hale: If "all [Juror A] was . . . was another anonymous voice in a dirty Jewish mob, screaming for blood and for the further impoverishment of the white worker . . . [he/she] would hardly be of note. But [Juror A] is something more. [He/She] was not only a juror at the nationally publicized trial of Matt Hale, but the jury foreman, and the architect of both Hale's conviction and his extreme and lengthy 40-year sentence." If Warman should be killed, then *a fortiori* Juror A should be killed, or at least injured. White didn't have to *say* harm Juror A. All he had to do and did do to invite violence was to sketch the characteristics that made Juror A a mortal enemy of White's neo-Nazi movement and to publish Juror A's personal contact information.

The fact that White made an effort to discourage assassination attempts against Juror A when law enforcement moved against his website shows at a minimum that he knew he was playing with fire. But a reasonable jury could have also interpreted such evidence as intent to solicit violence against Juror A followed by a change of mind when he realized that if someone harmed Juror A he could get in trouble. There was enough evidence of White's intent to solicit the murder of, or other physical violence against, Juror A, to justify a reasonable jury in convicting him.

It's true that the posts that establish the context that makes the solicitation to violence unmistakable were not links to the posts on Overthrow.com about Juror A. That is, they were not words or phrases in blue in the posts that if clicked on by the reader would appear on the reader's computer screen. Some of the explicit solicitations to murder had been published on Overthrow.com months, even years, earlier, though others were recent. The Juror A posts had appeared between September 11 and October 3, 2008, the postings regarding Wiesel and the Jena

6 between February 3 and September 20, 2007. But the Warman and Obama death threats were recent—March 26, 2008 and September 9, 2008 respectively—the latter threat having been posted two days before the first threat against Juror A.

Regardless of when these other still-accessible posts were technically created, a reasonable jury cannot be expected to ignore the audience, who may not have been as concerned about such chronological specifics. Readers of Overthrow.com were not casual Web browsers, but extremists molded into a community by the internet—loyal and avid readers who, whether or not they remember every specific solicitation to assassination, knew that Overthrow.com identified hateful enemies who should be assassinated. A reasonable jury could infer that members of the Party were regular readers of the Overthrow website, which prominently displayed links to the Party's own website, to its streaming radio, and to its hotline. One witness testified that he learned of the Party through Overthrow.com. White identified one reader in a post on the website as a "loyal soldier" and "fan of this website," and there is similar language in other posts. Two members of the party who testified made clear their familiarity with the contents of the website over a period of years. Though these members specifically denied interpreting White's post as an invitation to harm Juror A, a reasonable jury could have thought, based on White's reaching out to them for support following the search of White's home, that they were biased in White's favor and therefore skewed their testimony in order to protect a fellow supremacist.

White rightfully emphasizes that the First Amendment protects even speech that is loathsome. But criminal solicitations are simply not protected by the First Amendment. A reasonable jury could have found that White's posts constituted a proposal to engage in illegal activity and not merely the abstract advocacy of illegality. Accordingly, the First Amendment provides no shelter for White's criminal behavior.

United States v. White, 698 F.3d 1005, 1014–16 (7th Cir. 2012).

On page 228, at the end of Note 1, add the following:

The Hal Turner case was heard on appeal before a panel of judges of the Second Circuit because all of the Seventh Circuit judges were recused. The Second Circuit affirmed the conviction by a 2–1 vote. *See United States v. Turner*, 720 F.3d 411 (2d Cir. 2013). Writing for the majority, Judge Livingston ruled that the evidence was sufficient to constitute a true threat:

The full context of Turner's remarks reveals a gravity readily distinguishable from mere hyperbole or common public discourse. In his blog post, Turner not only wrote that these three judges should be killed, but also explained how Judge Lefkow had ruled against Matt Hale and how, "[s]hortly thereafter, a gunman entered the home of that lower court Judge and slaughtered the Judge's mother and husband. Apparently, the 7th U.S. Circuit court didn't get the hint after those killings. It appears another lesson is needed." Judges Easterbrook, Bauer, and Posner were of course familiar with those murders, with Judge Lefkow, and with Matt Hale's subsequent prosecution for soliciting someone to kill Judge Lefkow. Such serious references to actual acts of violence carried out in apparent retribution for a judge's decision would clearly allow a reasonable juror to conclude that Turner's statements were a true threat.

The evidence of a threat in this case is even stronger [than that in *United States v. White*]. Turner posted on his website that "Judge Lefkow made a ruling in court that I opined made her 'worthy of death,' and after I said that, someone went out and murdered her husband and mother inside the Judges Chicago house." Given that Turner's statements publicly implied a causal connection between Turner's calls for judges' deaths and actual murders, his statements about Judges Easterbrook, Bauer, and Posner, were quite reasonably interpreted by the jury as the serious expression of intent that these judges, too, come to harm. The seriousness of the threat, moreover, was further shown by Turner's posting of the judges' photographs and work addresses. Coupled with Turner's admission in an email a few weeks earlier that releasing addresses was an "effective way to cause otherwise immune public servants to seriously rethink how they use their power," the jury had abundant evidence from which to conclude that Turner was threatening the judges in retaliation for their ruling, rather than engaging in mere political hyperbole.

Judge Pooler dissented. According to Judge Pooler, Turner's speech may have constituted incitement of others under the *Brandenburg* test. However, because Turner was charged only with making a threat and not with incitement, Judge Pooler reasoned that there was insufficient evidence that he had made a threat:

> I would hold that Turner's communications were advocacy of the use of force and not a threat. It is clear that Turner wished for the deaths of Judges Easterbrook, Posner, and Bauer. But I read his statements, made in the passive voice, as an exhortation toward "free men willing to walk up to them and kill them" and not as a warning of planned violence directed toward the intended victims. This reading is furthered by the fact that Turner's words were posted on a blog on a publicly accessible website, and had the

trappings of political discourse, invoking Thomas Jefferson's famous quotation that "the tree of liberty must be replenished from time to time with the blood of tyrants and patriots." Although vituperative, there is no doubt that this was public political discourse. His speech might be subject to a different interpretation if, for example, the statements were sent to the Judges in a letter or email. However, Turner's public statements of political disagreement are different from a threat.

On page 231, at the middle of the page before the break for Section 2, add the following new Note 6:

6. *"Revenge porn" laws.* In the last two years, thirteen states have enacted new criminal laws on so-called "revenge porn." Broadly speaking, there are two kinds of revenge porn laws. The narrower type prohibits distributing nude images of another without the other person's consent and with the intent to harm. The name "revenge porn" captures this narrower type of offense, as it would punish one who seeks revenge against a former lover by posting on the Internet nude images that the individual obtained during the period of their intimacy. Importantly, revenge porn laws apply regardless of whether the image was originally taken with the subject's consent. Thus, the crime is the nonconsensual distribution of the consensually-created image.

The broader type of revenge porn law prohibits distributing nude images of another without the other person's consent even if not done with intent to harm. In the broader form, the law recognizes a right to control one's own private images; distribution without consent violates that right, even if done without intent to harm. *See generally* Danielle Keats Citron & Mary Anne Franks, *Criminalizing Revenge Porn*, 49 Wake Forest L. Rev. 345 (2014). For a summary of existing state laws prohibiting revenge porn, see http://www.ncsl.org/research/telecommunications-and-information-technology/state-revenge-porn-legislation.aspx.

Perhaps the broadest revenge porn law is Arizona's new statute, Ariz. Rev. Stat. 13–1425:

Unlawful distribution of images; state of nudity; classification; definitions

A. It is unlawful to intentionally disclose, display, distribute, publish, advertise or offer a photograph, videotape, film or digital recording of another person in a state of nudity or engaged in specific sexual activities if the person knows or should have known that the depicted person has not consented to the disclosure.

B. This section does not apply to any of the following: 1. Lawful and common practices of law enforcement, reporting unlawful activity, or when permitted or required by law or rule in legal proceedings. 2. Lawful and common practices of medical treatment. 3. Images involving voluntary exposure in a public or commercial setting. 4. An interactive computer service, as defined in 47 United States Code section 230(f)(2), or an information service, as defined in 47 United States Code section 153, with regard to content provided by another person.

C. A violation of this section is a class 5 felony, except that a violation of this section is a class 4 felony if the depicted person is recognizable.

D. For the purposes of this section, "state of nudity" and "specific sexual activities" have the same meanings prescribed in section 11– 811.

In September 2014, a coalition of bookstores, newspapers, photographers, publishers, and librarians filed suit against Arizona's broad revenge porn law on First Amendment grounds. An ACLU press release about the lawsuit gives a flavor of the some of the acts that the challengers claim the law prohibits but that the First Amendment protects:

> A bookseller who sells a history book containing an iconic image such as the Pulitzer Prize-winning photograph "Napalm Girl"—the unclothed Vietnamese girl running from a napalm attack—could be prosecuted under the law. A library lending a photo book about breast feeding to a new mother, a newspaper publishing pictures of abuse at the Abu Ghraib prison, or a newsweekly running a story about a local art show could all be convicted of a felony.

https://www.aclu.org/free-speech/first-amendment-lawsuit-challenges-arizona-criminal-law-banning-nude-images.

Should states or the federal government enact revenge porn statutes? If so, how broadly should such laws extend?

D. CHILD EXPLOITATION CRIMES

1. CHILD PORNOGRAPHY

E) Statutory Elements of 18 U.S.C. §§ 2252 and 2252A

On page 276, replace Note 1 with the following new Note 1:

1.   Imagine Shaffer had placed the files in the shared folder of his computer intending that other Kazaa users could access them, but that no users had actually done so. Is Shaffer still guilty of distributing the images?

The Third Circuit answered that question "no" in United States v. Husmann, 765 F.3d 169 (3d Cir. 2014). By a vote of 2 to 1, the court concluded that the word "distribute" requires a transfer of possession from one person to another. Because that does not occur when a file is merely placed in the shared folder, the defendant is not guilty of distribution:

Black's Law Dictionary defines "distribute" as: "to apportion; to divide among several" and "to deliver." *Black's Law Dictionary* 487 (9th ed.2009). Merriam-Webster provides the following definitions, among others, for the term "distribute": "to divide among several or many" and "to give out or deliver especially to members of a group." *See Distribute Definition,* Merriam-Webster Dictionary. We find additional guidance in the definition of "distribute" set forth in the controlled substances context. Under the Model Criminal Jury Instructions for the Third Circuit, to distribute a controlled substance means "(*to deliver or to transfer*) possession or control of a controlled substance from one person to another." Model Criminal Jury Instructions for the Third Circuit § 6.21.841–2 (2014); *see also* 21 U.S.C. § 802(11) (providing that " 'distribute' means to deliver" for purposes of drug offenses).

The statutory context confirms that "distribute" in § 2252(a)(2) means to apportion, give out, or deliver and that distribution necessarily involves the transfer of materials to another person. Significantly, Congress legislated specific prohibitions against offering and promoting child pornography within the same statutory scheme as it prohibited distributing child pornography. *See* 18 U.S.C. § 2251(d)(1)(A) (prohibiting offers to distribute child pornography); 18 U.S.C. § 2252A(a)(3)(B) (prohibiting the advertisement and promotion of child pornography); *see also United States v. Sewell,* 513 F.3d 820, 822 (8th Cir.2008) (holding that placing images of child pornography in a shared folder on a peer-to-peer file sharing program was "clearly an offer to distribute the file," in violation of 18 U.S.C. § 2251(d)(1)(A)).

Congress also penalized the attempted distribution of child pornography through specific statutory provisions. *See* 18 U.S.C. §§ 2252(b)(1), 2252A(b)(1). Because Congress has separately criminalized offering, promoting, and attempting to distribute child pornography, a broad definition of the term "distribute" would create unnecessary surplusage. To give effect to the entire statutory scheme, "distribute" must require the transfer of possession of child pornography to another person.

We hold that the term "distribute" in § 2252(a)(2) requires evidence that a defendant's child pornography materials were completely transferred to or downloaded by another person. Of course, knowingly placing child pornography in a shared folder on a file sharing network remains a criminal offense. *See, e.g.,* 18 U.S.C. § 2251(d)(1)(A) (prohibiting offers to distribute child pornography); 18 U.S.C. § 2252(b)(1) (prohibiting attempted distribution). It just isn't distribution. In the end, our interpretation of "distribute" in § 2252(a)(2) might affect the government's charging decisions, but it does not handicap the government's ability to prosecute child pornography offenses.

Id. at 174, 176. Judge Van Antwerpen dissented:

> Husmann placed images of child pornography into a shared folder accessible to *all global users* of the peer-to-peer file sharing program 360 Share Pro. Once in the shared folder, a search term and a click of a mouse allowed access to these images by any user on the system. My colleagues' definition of "distribution," under 18 U.S.C. § 2252, would create a system in which a person who intentionally posted child pornography on the Internet, knowing it is accessible to hundreds, if not millions, of individuals, is not "distribution." This is certainly not what Congress had in mind and following the majority's approach, the crime of distribution would not be complete until a police officer downloaded the image. This is a distinction without merit.

> Given the plain meaning of the term, the intent of Congress, and the advancement of technology, the placing of child pornography into a shared file accessible over a peer-to-peer file sharing network *alone* should constitute "distribution." Husmann took all the necessary steps to make a product available to the public in a publicly accessible location, and whether or not a party took that product is irrelevant to both the purpose of § 2252 and to his role as distributor. For that reason, the conviction of Appellant George Husmann for "distribution" under 18 U.S.C. § 2252 should be upheld.

> The ease, anonymity, and virtual untraceability with which Husmann made child pornography globally available is the engine behind § 2252, and the reason that "distribute" should be given a broader interpretation than the majority gives it. In analyzing the plain meaning of the statute, we need not define the outer boundaries of the term "distribution"; rather, we need only answer the specific question of whether placing an image of child pornography into a modern day "shared" folder as part of a peer-to-peer network is "distribution," as the District Court found.

> Looking both to Black's and Merriam-Webster's dictionaries, we find the plain meaning of "distribute" to be: "1. To apportion; to divide among several. 2. To arrange by class or order. 3. To deliver. 4. To spread out; to disperse." *Black's Law Dictionary* 487 (9th ed. 2009). Clearly the actions undertaken by Husmann, placing the images in a folder shared globally, dispersed and apportioned these images to third parties within the plain meaning of the statute.

> Determining that placing an image of child pornography into a shared folder constitutes "distribution" would, in light of the technological advances, encompass the plain meaning and the purpose of § 2252.

Id. at 177–78 (Van Antwerpen, J., dissenting). Which reading of the statute is more persuasive?

The majority opinion in *Husmann* suggests that placing an image of child pornography in a shared folder might (absent downloading) violate the crime of *attempting* to distribute child pornography in violation of 18 U.S.C. § 2252(b)(1). Under federal attempt law, proving attempt requires the government to show both that the accused intended to commit the underlying substantive offense and that he took a substantial step toward committing that crime. *See* United States v. Gobbi, 471 F.3d 302, 309 (1st Cir. 2006).

In your view, does placing an image in the shared folder of a peer-to-peer network necessarily establish attempted distribution of that image? What facts would you want to know to determine when placement of a file in a shared folder constitutes attempted distribution?

CHAPTER 4

SENTENCING

■ ■ ■

C. SENTENCING IN COMPUTER MISUSE CASES

On pages 357–63, replace United States v. Dinh with the following new case:

UNITED STATES V. STRATMAN

United States District Court for the District of Nebraska, 2014.
2014 WL 3109805.

JOHN M. GERRARD, DISTRICT JUDGE.

This case is before the Court with respect to the loss calculation for purposes of sentencing. The defendant pleaded guilty to one count of violating the Computer Fraud and Abuse Act (CFAA)—specifically, 18 U.S.C. § 1030(a)(5)(A)—based on an intrusion into a protected computer system or systems that began in approximately May 2012. As directed by the Court in its Amended Order on Sentencing Schedule, the parties submitted a statement of uncontroverted facts, and a hearing was held at which evidence was adduced and submitted of losses allegedly incurred by the two primary victims in this case: the University of Nebraska and the Nebraska State College System.

The burden is on the government to prove the factual basis for a sentencing enhancement by a preponderance of the evidence. For violations of the CFAA, the victim's "loss" may include "any reasonable cost to any victim, including the cost of responding to an offense, conducting a damage assessment, and restoring the data, program, system, or information to its condition prior to the offense, and any revenue lost, cost incurred, or other consequential damages incurred because of interruption of service."18 U.S.C. § 1030(e)(11).

The losses at issue in this case involve the costs of investigating the defendant's intrusion into the victims' computer systems. There is, for instance, no evidence that the victims incurred meaningful costs *repairing* damage to their systems. Instead, the evidence relates to the substantial time and expense that the victims incurred investigating the breach after it was discovered, and in attempting to ascertain the scope of their exposure. The bulk of the costs are in four categories: hours worked by University information technology (IT) department workers in response to the breach; similar hours worked by State Colleges IT workers; the cost of investigative services provided by Fishnet Services, Inc., a third-party IT consultant hired by the University; and the cost of investigative services provided by Kroll Advisory Solutions, a third-party consultant hired by the State Colleges' insurance company.

The Court accepts, as a general proposition, that the costs of investigating the scope of an intrusion into a computer system may be losses for purposes of sentencing and restitution. Such costs may be included when incurred by a private investigation conducted by the victim or consultants hired by the victim. Such losses may also, in principle, include the expense of notifying those whose personal information was compromised by the breach.

But the costs incurred must be reasonable. The CFAA defines "loss" in terms of "reasonable cost," and it cannot be said that unreasonable expenses are either caused by the offense of conviction for purposes of restitution, or reasonably foreseeable within the meaning of § 2B1.1.

The Court agrees with the defendant that part of the government's burden of proving loss for purposes of sentencing and restitution is showing that the costs incurred by the victims were *reasonably* incurred.

The Court begins with the easy part: the defendant has not objected to the University's Fishnet bills, with the exception of some reservations about whether some of those bills involved double counting. The Court has reviewed Fishnet's invoices carefully and found that each line item was unique, and that the total matched that represented by the University. The Court therefore finds that the Fishnet bills represent losses for purposes of sentencing and restitution, totaling $107,722.58.[4]

The same cannot be said of the Kroll invoices. The government's witnesses—primarily University employees—were clear about why Fishnet was hired and what Fishnet's services eventually produced for the University. Kroll was initially retained to help the State Colleges, but soon they and their insurer agreed to share the Fishnet forensic analysis with the University. The lion's share of Kroll's billing—over $308,000, as set forth in Exhibit 24—is attributed to notification services, *i.e.,* informing people whose personal information might have been compromised. But the Court cannot determine why that was so expensive for the State Colleges, or how it was determined that approximately 185,000 people needed to be notified.

The government has provided affidavits from two Kroll employees, and one employee of the insurer that hired Kroll, which generally describe the contents of Kroll's invoices and conclude that the services and expenses

---

[4] To be clear—the Court also finds based on the evidence that Fishnet's costs, while substantial, were reasonable given the services performed, and that it was reasonable for the University to retain those services when it did, shortly after the breach, when the scope of the intrusion was still unclear.

were fair and reasonable. But the Court does not find those conclusory opinions persuasive. Kroll's forensic analysis (which was presumably cut short when Fishnet became the primary investigator) essentially concludes that there was no evidence of exfiltration or access to personal information from the PeopleSoft database, but it was hard to be sure.

The only apparent source for the number of people to be notified, 185,000+, is also in Exhibit 28—an "audit" that was conducted by Kroll "to re-mail any records that mailed in error."(Whatever that means.) The import of the audit, as the Court understands it after puzzling over it for a bit, seems to be that some of the 185,000+ client records were duplicated, and only 117,845 were actually unique. So in Exhibit 31, Kroll's employee witness talks about Kroll's services including "the facilitation of mailing letters to each of approximately 185,000 potential victims of the breach," but the only substantiation in the record for that number is an audit that contradicts it. In sum, the Court is left with considerable uncertainty about how many people the State Colleges actually needed to notify, how many actually were notified, and how the costs for doing so were determined. Given that uncertainty, the Court finds that the reasonability of those expenses has not been proven.

The Court has similar questions about the employee hours devoted to the intrusion by employees of the University and the State Colleges. No doubt an appropriate response was necessary—and in the immediate wake of the breach, "all hands on deck" might well have been warranted. But at some point, after the defendant was locked out (and quickly indicted), the actual depth of the intrusion would have been clear, and an all-out effort would no longer have been necessary. The record, as it stands, does not permit the Court to determine what the victims knew and when they knew it, nor does it permit the Court to compare the victims' knowledge with the intensity of their ongoing efforts related to the breach. The record also contains very little from which the Court could determine that the victims' employees performed with reasonable efficiency and were compensated at a reasonable rate.[6]

The victims' calculations for costs attributed to employee hours consist of the time spent on tasks associated with the breach, multiplied by that employee's hourly wage. But, for instance, if the Court was awarding attorney fees, the Court would have to ask what tasks were performed, whether the number of hours spent on each task was appropriate, and whether the attorney's billing rate for performing the task was fair and reasonable. The Court does not see why similar questions should not be asked under these circumstances—and the Court cannot find the answer in the record.

---

[6]   To be clear—the Court is not criticizing the victims' employees, or suggesting that they are inefficient or overpaid. The Court would prefer to assume that they are all capable, and compensated appropriately. But the Court needs evidence, not assumptions.

It is also not entirely clear whether all those hours are attributable to the *defendant* for purposes of sentencing and restitution. For instance, the University's former information security officer testified that some of that time was spent implementing recommendations from the Fishnet report, and "cleaning up some of the incidents." He did testify that all the activities reflected in the government's evidence were "related to" the defendant's intrusion. But that may or may not be the same as "caused by" the defendant's intrusion.

A simple example will illustrate the point. A homeowner has a broken lock on her front door. A thief finds out and uses the vulnerability to enter the home and steal property. The losses from that crime include the value of the stolen property. They might even include investigating the crime. But they would not include repairing the lock, which was broken before the thief ever came along. The repair might be "related to" the theft, because the theft called attention to the vulnerability. But the thief didn't break the lock, and wouldn't have to pay to fix it.

Similarly, the victims no doubt learned, from the defendant's intrusion, about vulnerabilities in their computer systems. But the defendant is not responsible for creating those vulnerabilities, and he isn't liable for the cost of fixing them—or, more to the point, those costs are not the result of the offense of conviction. It is hard for the Court to conclude, on the evidence presented, that over 3,600 hours of employee time was a foreseeable consequence of the crime. And from the evidence presented, the Court cannot parse out how much time the victims' employees spent securing the system from the defendant specifically, and how much time they spent addressing the vulnerabilities he had called to their attention. The victims' exhibits reflect dozens of employees spending thousands of hours on tasks that are mostly unclear from the record. The only evidence to connect most of those hours to the defendant is that they were recorded with a project billing code that was created in response to the breach, and that the employees were verbally instructed to use for "anything related" to the defendant's intrusion.

For instance, one of the government's primary witnesses—the University's former information security officer—was listed in the government's exhibits as having spent 351 hours on the project initiated by the defendant's breach. But he was unable to say specifically how long he continued to log time on the project, other than that his "best guess" was that he was working on the project through October. And there is even less evidence with respect to other employees and how they were spending their time—the summaries provided by the victims, and adduced by the government, simply total the hours worked by each employee between May 20, 2012, and June 4, 2013. The breach was detected by the University on May 23–24, 2012, and even if the Court was willing to presume that the hours spent on the project in the immediate wake of the breach were sufficiently connected to the defendant's crime (a fair presumption), there is no way for the Court to determine from the evidence how many hours were worked during that timeframe. That, the Court finds, is insufficient evidence to prove *which* hours represent losses that can be causally connected to the defendant's crime for purposes of sentencing and restitution. The Court has no basis to estimate, or even guess, at how many hours would be attributable to the defendant—any attempt to pick a number would be unsatisfactorily arbitrary.

Finally, there is some evidence of other expenses—for example, the EnCase forensic analysis tool that the University purchased to help investigate the breach. While the Court has no particular reason to doubt those expenses, there is also little to establish that they were reasonable or necessary. It is also unclear whether the victims' purchases are of ongoing utility to them, which would preclude characterizing the entirety of those costs as "losses" for purposes of sentencing and restitution.

In sum, the Court finds that except for the Fishnet invoices, the evidence is not sufficient to prove that the victims' costs were "losses" for purposes of sentencing and restitution. The Court finds that based on the evidence before the Court, the appropriate loss calculation figure, for purposes of sentencing and restitution, is $107,722.58.

NOTES AND QUESTIONS

1.   The court states that "it is hard for the Court to conclude, on the evidence presented, that over 3,600 hours of employee time was a foreseeable consequence of the crime." Notably, however, § 2B1.1 does not require that costs be foreseeable in § 1030 offenses. Does this error influence the court's analysis, and if so, how?

2.   In United States v. Auernheimer, 748 F.3d 525 (3d Cir. 2014), the district court at sentencing held that the defendant's intrusion caused $78,000 of loss based on the costs of notifying victims of the crime. The defendant had helped collect more than 100,000 customer e-mail addresses of AT&T customers from AT&T's website. Initially, AT&T had sent out an e-mail to its customers notifying them that their e-mail addresses had been collected. Next, AT&T spent $78,000 in printing and mailing costs following up the e-mail notification with postal letter notification. The district court held that the printing and mailing costs of the postal letter were caused by the intrusion and were reasonable costs for purposes of calculating loss. The defendant was sentenced to 41 months in prison in significant part based on the district court's finding that he had caused $78,000 in loss.

The defendant challenged that ruling on appeal, but the Third Circuit vacated the conviction without ruling on the question. If the Third Circuit had reached the issue, should it have allowed the higher sentence based on $78,000 in loss?

CHAPTER 5

THE FOURTH AMENDMENT

▪ ▪ ▪

A. THE REQUIREMENT OF GOVERNMENT ACTION

At the bottom of page 386, add the following new Note 6:

6.   In United States v. Keith, 980 F.Supp.2d 33 (D.Mass. 2013), AOL's automated software detected an illegal image in an e-mail based on its hash value. AOL forwarded the e-mail electronically to NCMEC. At NCMEC, an analyst opened the file and examined it and concluded that it constituted child pornography. The NCMEC analyst created a report that was then forwarded on to law enforcement and led to a warrant and then charges against the defendant.

When the defendant moved to suppress the fruits of the warrant based on the legality of discovering the initial image, the district court held (a) that AOL was a private actor, but (b) that NCMEC was a state actor and that the NCMEC analyst's viewing of the image was not merely a reenactment of AOL's private search:

> NCMEC's examination of the file uploaded by AOL to the NCMEC CyberTipline was a search conducted for the sole purpose of assisting the prosecution of child pornography crimes. NCMEC's goal in operating the CyberTipline is a worthy and laudable one, but it is one that it pursues in "partnership," 42 U.S.C. § 5771(9)(B), with the government. Unlike AOL, which monitors its email traffic to serve its own business interest, NCMEC's operation of the CyberTipline is intended to, and does, serve the public interest in crime prevention and prosecution, rather than a private interest.

> Through congressional authorization and funding of the CyberTipline, the government "instigates" such searches. A statutory provision requires NCMEC to report discovered child pornography to federal law enforcement, and another encourages similar reporting to state and foreign law enforcement agencies. 18 U.S.C. § 2258A(c)(1, 2). This requirement addresses the "control" factor identified by the First Circuit. Finally, the CyberTipline serves no private purpose for NCMEC separate from assisting law enforcement.

The "partnership" between NCMEC and law enforcement with respect to the operation of the CyberTipline is not just rhetorical but real. Members of law enforcement serve on various NCMEC boards, and U.S. Marshals and other law enforcement personnel provide on-site support and referral assistance for NCMEC's Exploited Child Division. As noted above, NCMEC makes the results of its examination of suspected files available exclusively to federal and state law enforcement officials by means of a dedicated V PN, accessible only to law enforcement personnel. It is clear that NCMEC's CyberTipline is, and is intended by Congress to be, an integral part of the governmental effort to detect and prosecute child pornography crimes.

If AOL had sent the file directly to the FBI or the State Police instead of to NCMEC's CyberTipline, it could not seriously be contended that the law enforcement agency could open and inspect the contents of the file without regard to the Fourth Amendment's warrant requirement. *See* Walter v. United States, 447 U.S. 649 (1980). In *Walter,* a package containing boxes of film was mistakenly delivered to a private company. The company's employees opened the package and saw that the individual boxes bore outside labeling suggesting that they contained obscene material. They notified FBI agents, who took custody of the boxes, opened them, and viewed the films, confirming what the outside labeling suggested. The Court held that the opening and viewing of the films by the FBI was an expansion of the private search that required a warrant.

Although the media in which criminally obscene material was stored are different in *Walter* and this case, the pattern is the same. A label (here, hash value) that is examined without opening the film or file suggested the nature of the contents. For that reason, concerned private parties provided the film or file to the government without first reviewing the contents themselves. Government personnel then examined the contents of the film or file by opening and viewing it. *Walter* holds that the examination should not have been done without due compliance with the warrant requirement imposed by the Fourth Amendment. The only possibly significant difference between the circumstances in *Walter* and here is that instead of a direct employee of the FBI or State Police performing the examination, an outside contractor performed the examination for the benefit of the law enforcement agency. There is nothing wrong with the government outsourcing part of its investigative work to a private cooperating partner, but doing so does not avoid the obligation to abide by the requirements of the Fourth Amendment.

The government weakly argues that a NCMEC analyst's viewing of the contents of the file was not an expansion of AOL's private search, citing United States v. Jacobsen, 466 U.S. 109 (1984). In that case, FedEx employees opened a damaged box for private, non-governmental reasons, discovered what appeared to be cocaine, and contacted the Drug Enforcement Administration. The FedEx employees put the contents back in the box. When DEA agents arrived, they reopened the package and removed the cocaine. In these circumstances, the Supreme Court held there had been no separate search by the police to which the Fourth Amendment applied.

An argument that *Jacobsen* is factually similar to this case is untenable in light of the testimony given at the evidentiary hearing. It is indisputable that AOL forwarded the suspect file only because its hash value matched a stored hash value, not because some AOL employee had opened the file and viewed the contents. The NCMEC analyst expanded the review by opening the file and viewing (and evaluating) its contents. *Walter,* and not *Jacobsen,* is the better analog.

In this regard it is worth noting that matching the hash value of a file to a stored hash value is not the virtual equivalent of viewing the contents of the file. What the match says is that the two files are identical; it does not itself convey any information about the contents of the file. It does say that the suspect file is identical to a file that someone, sometime, identified as containing child pornography, but the provenance of that designation is unknown. So a match alone indicts a file as contraband but cannot alone convict it. That is surely why a CyberTipline analyst opens the file to view it, because the actual viewing of the contents provides information additional to the information provided by the hash match. This is unlike what the Court found the case to be in Jacobsen, where the subsequent DEA search provided no more information than had already been exposed by the initial FedEx search. *Jacobsen* is inapposite.

Id. at 41–43.

B. DEFINING SEARCHES AND SEIZURES

2. SEIZURES

On page 409, in the middle, add the following new Note 6:

6.   The Second Circuit considered the meaning of "seizures" in the context of digital copying in United States v. Ganias, 755 F.3d 125 (2d Cir. 2014). In *Ganias*, the government executed a search warrant for digital evidence by making electronic copies of all of the defendant's files on his computer hard drives without physically removing any of the hard drives from the defendant's home. The government then held the copies in law

enforcement custody, including the files that were not responsive to the warrant, for over two years.

The Second Circuit ruled that copying the files and retaining the copies was a continuing Fourth Amendment seizure. "The Government's retention of copies of Ganias's personal computer records for two-and-a-half years deprived him of exclusive control over those files," the court noted. "This was a meaningful interference with Ganias's possessory rights in those files and constituted a seizure within the meaning of the Fourth Amendment." *Id.* at 137.

C. EXCEPTIONS TO THE WARRANT REQUIREMENT

3. Search Incident to Arrest

Replace all of this section, pages 445–52 with the following new decision and notes:

RILEY v. CALIFORNIA
Supreme Court of the United States, 2014.
134 S.Ct. 2473.

CHIEF JUSTICE ROBERTS delivered the opinion of the Court.

These two cases raise a common question: whether the police may, without a warrant, search digital information on a cell phone seized from an individual who has been arrested.

I

A

In the first case, petitioner David Riley was stopped by a police officer for driving with expired registration tags. In the course of the stop, the officer also learned that Riley's license had been suspended. The officer impounded Riley's car, pursuant to department policy, and another officer conducted an inventory search of the car. Riley was arrested for possession of concealed and loaded firearms when that search turned up two handguns under the car's hood.

An officer searched Riley incident to the arrest and found items associated with the "Bloods" street gang. He also seized a cell phone from Riley's pants pocket. According to Riley's uncontradicted assertion, the phone was a "smart phone," a cell phone with a broad range of other functions based on advanced computing capability, large storage capacity, and Internet connectivity. The officer accessed information on the phone and noticed that some words (presumably in text messages or a contacts list) were preceded by the letters "CK"—a label that, he believed, stood for "Crip Killers," a slang term for members of the Bloods gang.

At the police station about two hours after the arrest, a detective specializing in gangs further examined the contents of the phone. The detective testified that he went through Riley's phone looking for evidence, "because gang members will often video themselves with guns or take pictures of themselves with the guns." Although there was "a lot of stuff" on the phone, particular files that caught the detective's eye included videos of young men sparring while someone yelled encouragement using the moniker "Blood." The police also found photographs of Riley standing in front of a car they suspected had been involved in a shooting a few weeks earlier.

Riley was ultimately charged, in connection with that earlier shooting, with firing at an occupied vehicle, assault with a semiautomatic firearm, and attempted murder. The State alleged that Riley had committed those crimes for the benefit of a criminal street gang, an aggravating factor that carries an enhanced sentence. Prior to trial, Riley moved to suppress all evidence that the police had obtained from his cell phone. He contended that the searches of his phone violated the Fourth Amendment, because they had been performed without a warrant and were not otherwise justified by exigent circumstances. The trial court rejected that argument. At Riley's trial, police officers testified about the photographs and videos found on the phone, and some of the photographs were admitted into evidence. Riley was convicted on all three counts and received an enhanced sentence of 15 years to life in prison.

The California Court of Appeal affirmed. The court relied on the California Supreme Court's decision in *People v. Diaz,* 51 Cal.4th 84, 119 Cal.Rptr.3d 105 (2011), which held that the Fourth Amendment permits a warrantless search of cell phone data incident to an arrest, so long as the cell phone was immediately associated with the arrestee's person.

B

In the second case, a police officer performing routine surveillance observed respondent Brima Wurie make an apparent drug sale from a car. Officers subsequently arrested Wurie and took him to the police station. At the station, the officers seized two cell phones from Wurie's person. The one at issue here was a "flip phone," a kind of phone that is flipped open for use and that generally has a smaller range of features than a smart phone. Five to ten minutes after arriving at the station, the officers noticed that the phone was repeatedly receiving calls from a source identified as "my house" on the phone's external screen. A few minutes later, they opened the phone and saw a photograph of a woman and a baby set as the phone's wallpaper. They pressed one button on the phone to access its call log, then another button to determine the phone number associated with the "my house" label. They next used an online phone directory to trace that phone number to an apartment building.

When the officers went to the building, they saw Wurie's name on a mailbox and observed through a window a woman who resembled the woman in the photograph on Wurie's phone. They secured the apartment while obtaining a search warrant and, upon later executing the warrant, found and seized 215 grams of crack cocaine, marijuana, drug paraphernalia, a firearm and ammunition, and cash.

Wurie was charged with distributing crack cocaine, possessing crack cocaine with intent to distribute, and being a felon in possession of a firearm and ammunition. He moved to suppress the evidence obtained from the search of the apartment, arguing that it was the fruit of an unconstitutional search of his cell phone. The District Court denied the motion. Wurie was convicted on all three counts and sentenced to 262 months in prison.

A divided panel of the First Circuit reversed the denial of Wurie's motion to suppress and vacated Wurie's convictions for possession with intent to distribute and possession of a firearm as a felon. The court held that cell phones are distinct from other physical possessions that may be searched incident to arrest without a warrant, because of the amount of personal data cell phones contain and the negligible threat they pose to law enforcement interests.

II

The two cases before us concern the reasonableness of a warrantless search incident to a lawful arrest. In 1914, this Court first acknowledged in dictum "the right on the part of the Government, always recognized under English and American law, to search the person of the accused when legally arrested to discover and seize the fruits or evidences of crime." *Weeks v. United States,* 232 U.S. 383, 392 (1914). Since that time, it has been well accepted that such a search constitutes an exception to the warrant requirement. Indeed, the label "exception" is something of a misnomer in this context, as warrantless searches incident to arrest occur with far greater frequency than searches conducted pursuant to a warrant. See 3 W. LaFave, Search and Seizure § 5.2(b), p. 132, and n. 15 (5th ed. 2012).

Although the existence of the exception for such searches has been recognized for a century, its scope has been debated for nearly as long. That debate has focused on the extent to which officers may search property found on or near the arrestee. Three related precedents set forth the rules governing such searches:

The first, *Chimel v. California,* 395 U.S. 752 (1969), laid the groundwork for most of the existing search incident to arrest doctrine.

Police officers in that case arrested Chimel inside his home and proceeded to search his entire three-bedroom house, including the attic and garage. In particular rooms, they also looked through the contents of drawers.

The Court crafted the following rule for assessing the reasonableness of a search incident to arrest:

> When an arrest is made, it is reasonable for the arresting officer to search the person arrested in order to remove any weapons that the latter might seek to use in order to resist arrest or effect his escape. Otherwise, the officer's safety might well be endangered, and the arrest itself frustrated. In addition, it is entirely reasonable for the arresting officer to search for and seize any evidence on the arrestee's person in order to prevent its concealment or destruction. There is ample justification, therefore, for a search of the arrestee's person and the area 'within his immediate control'—construing that phrase to mean the area from within which he might gain possession of a weapon or destructible evidence.

The extensive warrantless search of Chimel's home did not fit within this exception, because it was not needed to protect officer safety or to preserve evidence.

Four years later, in *United States v. Robinson,* 414 U.S. 218 (1973), the Court applied the *Chimel* analysis in the context of a search of the arrestee's person. A police officer had arrested Robinson for driving with a revoked license. The officer conducted a patdown search and felt an object that he could not identify in Robinson's coat pocket. He removed the object, which turned out to be a crumpled cigarette package, and opened it. Inside were 14 capsules of heroin.

The Court of Appeals concluded that the search was unreasonable because Robinson was unlikely to have evidence of the crime of arrest on his person, and because it believed that extracting the cigarette package and opening it could not be justified as part of a protective search for weapons. This Court reversed, rejecting the notion that "case-by-case adjudication" was required to determine "whether or not there was present one of the reasons supporting the authority for a search of the person incident to a lawful arrest." *Id.* at 235. As the Court explained,

> the authority to search the person incident to a lawful custodial arrest, while based upon the need to disarm and to discover evidence, does not depend on what a court may later decide was the probability in a particular arrest situation that weapons or evidence would in fact be found upon the person of the suspect. Instead, a custodial arrest of a suspect based on probable cause is a reasonable intrusion under the Fourth Amendment; that

intrusion being lawful, a search incident to the arrest requires
no additional justification.

The Court thus concluded that the search of Robinson was reasonable
even though there was no concern about the loss of evidence, and the
arresting officer had no specific concern that Robinson might be armed. In
doing so, the Court did not draw a line between a search of Robinson's
person and a further examination of the cigarette pack found during that
search. It merely noted that, "having in the course of a lawful search come
upon the crumpled package of cigarettes, the officer was entitled to
inspect it." A few years later, the Court clarified that this exception was
limited to "personal property immediately associated with the person of
the arrestee." *United States v. Chadwick,* 433 U.S. 1, 15 (1977) (200-
pound, locked footlocker could not be searched incident to arrest),
abrogated on other grounds by *California v. Acevedo,* 500 U.S. 565 (1991).

The search incident to arrest trilogy concludes with *Arizona v. Gant,*
556 U.S. 332 (2009), which analyzed searches of an arrestee's vehicle.
Gant, like *Robinson,* recognized that the *Chimel* concerns for officer
safety and evidence preservation underlie the search incident to arrest
exception. As a result, the Court concluded that *Chimel* could authorize
police to search a vehicle "only when the arrestee is unsecured and within
reaching distance of the passenger compartment at the time of the
search." *Gant* added, however, an independent exception for a
warrantless search of a vehicle's passenger compartment "when it is
'reasonable to believe evidence relevant to the crime of arrest might be
found in the vehicle.'" That exception stems not from *Chimel,* the Court
explained, but from "circumstances unique to the vehicle context."

III

These cases require us to decide how the search incident to arrest
doctrine applies to modern cell phones, which are now such a pervasive
and insistent part of daily life that the proverbial visitor from Mars might
conclude they were an important feature of human anatomy. A smart
phone of the sort taken from Riley was unheard of ten years ago; a
significant majority of American adults now own such phones. See A.
Smith, Pew Research Center, Smartphone Ownership—2013 Update
(June 5, 2013). Even less sophisticated phones like Wurie's, which have
already faded in popularity since Wurie was arrested in 2007, have been
around for less than 15 years. Both phones are based on technology
nearly inconceivable just a few decades ago, when *Chimel* and *Robinson*
were decided.

Absent more precise guidance from the founding era, we generally
determine whether to exempt a given type of search from the warrant
requirement by assessing, on the one hand, the degree to which it
intrudes upon an individual's privacy and, on the other, the degree to

which it is needed for the promotion of legitimate governmental interests. Such a balancing of interests supported the search incident to arrest exception in *Robinson,* and a mechanical application of *Robinson* might well support the warrantless searches at issue here.

But while *Robinson*'s categorical rule strikes the appropriate balance in the context of physical objects, neither of its rationales has much force with respect to digital content on cell phones. On the government interest side, *Robinson* concluded that the two risks identified in *Chimel*—harm to officers and destruction of evidence—are present in all custodial arrests. There are no comparable risks when the search is of digital data. In addition, *Robinson* regarded any privacy interests retained by an individual after arrest as significantly diminished by the fact of the arrest itself. Cell phones, however, place vast quantities of personal information literally in the hands of individuals. A search of the information on a cell phone bears little resemblance to the type of brief physical search considered in *Robinson.*

We therefore decline to extend *Robinson* to searches of data on cell phones, and hold instead that officers must generally secure a warrant before conducting such a search.

A

We first consider each *Chimel* concern in turn. In doing so, we do not overlook *Robinson*'s admonition that searches of a person incident to arrest, "while based upon the need to disarm and to discover evidence," are reasonable regardless of "the probability in a particular arrest situation that weapons or evidence would in fact be found." Rather than requiring the "case-by-case adjudication" that *Robinson* rejected, we ask instead whether application of the search incident to arrest doctrine to this particular category of effects would untether the rule from the justifications underlying the *Chimel* exception.

1

Digital data stored on a cell phone cannot itself be used as a weapon to harm an arresting officer or to effectuate the arrestee's escape. Law enforcement officers remain free to examine the physical aspects of a phone to ensure that it will not be used as a weapon—say, to determine whether there is a razor blade hidden between the phone and its case. Once an officer has secured a phone and eliminated any potential physical threats, however, data on the phone can endanger no one.

Perhaps the same might have been said of the cigarette pack seized from Robinson's pocket. Once an officer gained control of the pack, it was unlikely that Robinson could have accessed the pack's contents. But unknown physical objects may always pose risks, no matter how slight, during the tense atmosphere of a custodial arrest. The officer in *Robinson* testified that he could not identify the objects in the cigarette pack but knew they were not cigarettes. Given that, a further search was a reasonable protective measure. No such unknowns exist with respect to digital data. As the First Circuit explained, the officers who searched Wurie's cell phone knew exactly what they would find therein: data. They also knew that the data could not harm them.

The United States and California both suggest that a search of cell phone data might help ensure officer safety in more indirect ways, for example by alerting officers that confederates of the arrestee are headed to the scene. There is undoubtedly a strong government interest in warning officers about such possibilities, but neither the United States nor California offers evidence to suggest that their concerns are based on actual experience. The proposed consideration would also represent a broadening of *Chimel*'s concern that an *arrestee himself* might grab a weapon and use it against an officer "to resist arrest or effect his escape." And any such threats from outside the arrest scene do not "lurk in all custodial arrests." *Chadwick,* 433 U.S., at 14–15. Accordingly, the interest in protecting officer safety does not justify dispensing with the warrant requirement across the board. To the extent dangers to arresting officers may be implicated in a particular way in a particular case, they are better addressed through consideration of case-specific exceptions to the warrant requirement, such as the one for exigent circumstances.

2

The United States and California focus primarily on the second *Chimel* rationale: preventing the destruction of evidence.

Both Riley and Wurie concede that officers could have seized and secured their cell phones to prevent destruction of evidence while seeking a warrant. And once law enforcement officers have secured a cell phone, there is no longer any risk that the arrestee himself will be able to delete incriminating data from the phone.

The United States and California argue that information on a cell phone may nevertheless be vulnerable to two types of evidence destruction unique to digital data—remote wiping and data encryption. Remote wiping occurs when a phone, connected to a wireless network, receives a signal that erases stored data. This can happen when a third party sends a remote signal or when a phone is preprogrammed to delete data upon entering or leaving certain geographic areas (so-called "geofencing"). See Dept. of Commerce, National Institute of Standards and Technology, R. Ayers, S. Brothers, & W. Jansen, Guidelines on Mobile Device Forensics (Draft) 29, 31 (SP 800–101 Rev. 1, Sept. 2013). Encryption is a security feature that some modern cell phones use in addition to password protection. When such phones lock, data becomes protected by sophisticated encryption that renders a phone all but "unbreakable" unless police know the password.

As an initial matter, these broader concerns about the loss of evidence are distinct from *Chimel's* focus on a defendant who responds to arrest by trying to conceal or destroy evidence within his reach. With respect to remote wiping, the Government's primary concern turns on the actions of third parties who are not present at the scene of arrest. And data encryption is even further afield. There, the Government focuses on the ordinary operation of a phone's security features, apart from *any* active attempt by a defendant or his associates to conceal or destroy evidence upon arrest.

We have also been given little reason to believe that either problem is prevalent. The briefing reveals only a couple of anecdotal examples of remote wiping triggered by an arrest. Similarly, the opportunities for officers to search a password-protected phone before data becomes encrypted are quite limited. Law enforcement officers are very unlikely to come upon such a phone in an unlocked state because most phones lock at the touch of a button or, as a default, after some very short period of inactivity. See, *e.g.,* iPhone User Guide for iOS 7.1 Software 10 (2014) (default lock after about one minute). This may explain why the encryption argument was not made until the merits stage in this Court, and has never been considered by the Courts of Appeals.

Moreover, in situations in which an arrest might trigger a remote-wipe attempt or an officer discovers an unlocked phone, it is not clear that the ability to conduct a warrantless search would make much of a difference. The need to effect the arrest, secure the scene, and tend to other pressing matters means that law enforcement officers may well not be able to turn their attention to a cell phone right away. Cell phone data would be vulnerable to remote wiping from the time an individual anticipates arrest to the time any eventual search of the phone is completed, which might be at the station house hours later. Likewise, an officer who seizes a phone in an unlocked state might not be able to begin his search in the short time remaining before the phone locks and data becomes encrypted.

In any event, as to remote wiping, law enforcement is not without specific means to address the threat. Remote wiping can be fully prevented by disconnecting a phone from the network. There are at least two simple ways to do this: First, law enforcement officers can turn the phone off or remove its battery. Second, if they are concerned about encryption or other potential problems, they can leave a phone powered on and place it in an enclosure that isolates the phone from radio waves. Such devices are commonly called "Faraday bags," after the English scientist Michael Faraday. They are essentially sandwich bags made of aluminum foil: cheap, lightweight, and easy to use. They may not be a complete answer to the problem, but at least for now they provide a reasonable response. In fact, a number of law enforcement agencies around the country already encourage the use of Faraday bags. See, *e.g.,* Dept. of Justice, National Institute of Justice, Electronic Crime Scene Investigation: A Guide for First Responders 14, 32 (2d ed. Apr. 2008).

To the extent that law enforcement still has specific concerns about the potential loss of evidence in a particular case, there remain more targeted ways to address those concerns. If the police are truly confronted with a 'now or never' situation—for example, circumstances suggesting that a defendant's phone will be the target of an imminent remote-wipe attempt—they may be able to rely on exigent circumstances to search the phone immediately. Or, if officers happen to seize a phone in an unlocked state, they may be able to disable a phone's automatic-lock feature in order to prevent the phone from locking and encrypting data.

B

The search incident to arrest exception rests not only on the heightened government interests at stake in a volatile arrest situation, but also on an arrestee's reduced privacy interests upon being taken into police custody. Put simply, a patdown of Robinson's clothing and an inspection of the cigarette pack found in his pocket constituted only minor additional intrusions compared to the substantial government authority exercised in taking Robinson into custody.

The United States asserts that a search of all data stored on a cell phone is "materially indistinguishable" from searches of physical items. That is like saying a ride on horseback is materially indistinguishable from a flight to the moon. Both are ways of getting from point A to point B, but little else justifies lumping them together. Modern cell phones, as a category, implicate privacy concerns far beyond those implicated by the search of a cigarette pack, a wallet, or a purse. A conclusion that inspecting the contents of an arrestee's pockets works no substantial additional intrusion on privacy beyond the arrest itself may make sense as applied to physical items, but any extension of that reasoning to digital data has to rest on its own bottom.

1

Cell phones differ in both a quantitative and a qualitative sense from other objects that might be kept on an arrestee's person. The term "cell phone" is itself misleading shorthand; many of these devices are in fact minicomputers that also happen to have the capacity to be used as a telephone. They could just as easily be called cameras, video players, rolodexes, calendars, tape recorders, libraries, diaries, albums, televisions, maps, or newspapers.

One of the most notable distinguishing features of modern cell phones is their immense storage capacity. Before cell phones, a search of a person was limited by physical realities and tended as a general matter to constitute only a narrow intrusion on privacy. Most people cannot lug around every piece of mail they have received for the past several months, every picture they have taken, or every book or article they have read— nor would they have any reason to attempt to do so. And if they did, they would have to drag behind them a trunk of the sort held to require a search warrant in *Chadwick, supra,* rather than a container the size of the cigarette package in *Robinson.*

But the possible intrusion on privacy is not physically limited in the same way when it comes to cell phones. The current top-selling smart phone has a standard capacity of 16 gigabytes (and is available with up to 64 gigabytes). Sixteen gigabytes translates to millions of pages of text, thousands of pictures, or hundreds of videos. Cell phones couple that capacity with the ability to store many different types of information: Even the most basic phones that sell for less than $20 might hold photographs, picture messages, text messages, Internet browsing history, a calendar, a thousand-entry phone book, and so on. We expect that the gulf between physical practicability and digital capacity will only continue to widen in the future.

The storage capacity of cell phones has several interrelated consequences for privacy. First, a cell phone collects in one place many distinct types of information—an address, a note, a prescription, a bank statement, a video—that reveal much more in combination than any isolated record. Second, a cell phone's capacity allows even just one type of information to convey far more than previously possible. The sum of an individual's private life can be reconstructed through a thousand photographs labeled with dates, locations, and descriptions; the same cannot be said of a photograph or two of loved ones tucked into a wallet. Third, the data on a phone can date back to the purchase of the phone, or even earlier. A person might carry in his pocket a slip of paper reminding him to call Mr. Jones; he would not carry a record of all his communications with Mr. Jones for the past several months, as would routinely be kept on a phone.

Finally, there is an element of pervasiveness that characterizes cell phones but not physical records. Prior to the digital age, people did not typically carry a cache of sensitive personal information with them as they went about their day. Now it is the person who is not carrying a cell phone, with all that it contains, who is the exception. According to one poll, nearly three-quarters of smart phone users report being within five feet of their phones most of the time, with 12% admitting that they even use their phones in the shower. See Harris Interactive, 2013 Mobile Consumer Habits Study (June 2013). A decade ago police officers searching an arrestee might have occasionally stumbled across a highly personal item such as a diary. But those discoveries were likely to be few and far between. Today, by contrast, it is no exaggeration to say that many of the more than 90% of American adults who own a cell phone keep on their person a digital record of nearly every aspect of their lives— from the mundane to the intimate. Allowing the police to scrutinize such records on a routine basis is quite different from allowing them to search a personal item or two in the occasional case.

Although the data stored on a cell phone is distinguished from physical records by quantity alone, certain types of data are also qualitatively different. An Internet search and browsing history, for example, can be found on an Internet-enabled phone and could reveal an individual's private interests or concerns—perhaps a search for certain symptoms of disease, coupled with frequent visits to WebMD. Data on a cell phone can also reveal where a person has been. Historic location information is a standard feature on many smart phones and can reconstruct someone's specific movements down to the minute, not only around town but also within a particular building.

Mobile application software on a cell phone, or "apps," offer a range of tools for managing detailed information about all aspects of a person's life. There are apps for Democratic Party news and Republican Party news; apps for alcohol, drug, and gambling addictions; apps for sharing prayer requests; apps for tracking pregnancy symptoms; apps for planning your budget; apps for every conceivable hobby or pastime; apps for improving your romantic life. There are popular apps for buying or selling just about anything, and the records of such transactions may be accessible on the phone indefinitely. There are over a million apps available in each of the two major app stores; the phrase "there's an app for that" is now part of the popular lexicon. The average smart phone user has installed 33 apps, which together can form a revealing montage of the user's life. See Brief for Electronic Privacy Information Center as *Amicus Curiae* in No. 13–132, p. 9.

In 1926, Learned Hand observed (in an opinion later quoted in *Chimel*) that it is "a totally different thing to search a man's pockets and use against him what they contain, from ransacking his house for everything which may incriminate him." *United States v. Kirschenblatt,* 16 F.2d 202, 203 (C.A.2). If his pockets contain a cell phone, however, that is no longer true. Indeed, a cell phone search would typically expose to the government far *more* than the most exhaustive search of a house: A phone not only contains in digital form many sensitive records previously found in the home; it also contains a broad array of private information never found in a home in any form—unless the phone is.

2

To further complicate the scope of the privacy interests at stake, the data a user views on many modern cell phones may not in fact be stored on the device itself. Treating a cell phone as a container whose contents may be searched incident to an arrest is a bit strained as an initial matter. But the analogy crumbles entirely when a cell phone is used to access data located elsewhere, at the tap of a screen. That is what cell phones, with increasing frequency, are designed to do by taking advantage of "cloud computing." Cloud computing is the capacity of Internet-connected devices to display data stored on remote servers rather than on the device itself. Cell phone users often may not know whether particular information is stored on the device or in the cloud, and it generally makes little difference. Moreover, the same type of data may be stored locally on the device for one user and in the cloud for another.

The United States concedes that the search incident to arrest exception may not be stretched to cover a search of files accessed remotely—that is, a search of files stored in the cloud. Such a search would be like finding a key in a suspect's pocket and arguing that it allowed law enforcement to unlock and search a house. But officers searching a phone's data would not typically know whether the information they are viewing was stored locally at the time of the arrest or has been pulled from the cloud.

Although the Government recognizes the problem, its proposed solutions are unclear. It suggests that officers could disconnect a phone from the network before searching the device—the very solution whose feasibility it contested with respect to the threat of remote wiping. Alternatively, the Government proposes that law enforcement agencies "develop protocols to address" concerns raised by cloud computing. Reply Probably a good idea, but the Founders did not fight a revolution to gain the right to government agency protocols. The possibility that a search might extend well beyond papers and effects in the physical proximity of an arrestee is yet another reason that the privacy interests here dwarf those in *Robinson*.

IV

We cannot deny that our decision today will have an impact on the ability of law enforcement to combat crime. Cell phones have become important tools in facilitating coordination and communication among members of criminal enterprises, and can provide valuable incriminating information about dangerous criminals. Privacy comes at a cost.

Our holding, of course, is not that the information on a cell phone is immune from search; it is instead that a warrant is generally required before such a search, even when a cell phone is seized incident to arrest.

Moreover, even though the search incident to arrest exception does not apply to cell phones, other case-specific exceptions may still justify a warrantless search of a particular phone.

In light of the availability of the exigent circumstances exception, there is no reason to believe that law enforcement officers will not be able to address some of the more extreme hypotheticals that have been suggested: a suspect texting an accomplice who, it is feared, is preparing to detonate a bomb, or a child abductor who may have information about the child's location on his cell phone. The defendants here recognize—indeed, they stress—that such fact-specific threats may justify a warrantless search of cell phone data. The critical point is that, unlike the search incident to arrest exception, the exigent circumstances exception requires a court to examine whether an emergency justified a warrantless search in each particular case.

Modern cell phones are not just another technological convenience. With all they contain and all they may reveal, they hold for many Americans the privacies of life. The fact that technology now allows an individual to carry such information in his hand does not make the information any less worthy of the protection for which the Founders fought. Our answer to the question of what police must do before searching a cell phone seized incident to an arrest is accordingly simple—get a warrant.

NOTES AND QUESTIONS

1.   Although *Riley* speaks of cell phones, its reasoning presumably applies to all digital storage devices. If a suspect has a thumb drive on his key chain, for example, *Riley* would block a warrantless search incident to arrest of the thumb drive. Under *Riley*, then, the search-incident-to-arrest exception applies to physical storage devices but not electronic storage devices.

2.   In September 2014, just a few months after *Riley*, Apple announced that its new operating system, iOS8, no longer included a means to allow the decryption of an encrypted cell phone pursuant to a warrant. Under earlier Apple operating systems, law enforcement could obtain a warrant and send the phone to Apple for decryption. Apple could then decrypt at least parts of the phone under the warrant. Under the new operating system, however, Apple has no way to decrypt an encrypted iPhone. As the *Washington Post* explains:

> The move, announced with the publication of a new privacy policy tied to the release of Apple's latest mobile operating system, iOS 8, amounts to an engineering solution to a legal quandary: Rather than comply with binding court orders, Apple has reworked its latest encryption in a way that prevents the company—or anyone

but the device's owner—from gaining access to the vast troves of user data typically stored on smartphones or tablet computers.

Craig Timberg, *Apple Will No Longer Unlock Most iPhones and iPads For Police, Even With Search Warrants*, available at http://www.washington post.com/business/technology/2014/09/17/2612af58-3ed2-11e4-b03f-de718edeb92f_story.html.

If an officer makes an arrest and the search incident to arrest recovers an iPhone that is not locked, can the officer now search the phone under the exigent circumstances exception without a warrant on the theory that the evidence will be entirely lost to law enforcement as soon as the phone locks? *Riley* indicates that "if officers happen to seize a phone in an unlocked state, they may be able to disable a phone's automatic-lock feature in order to prevent the phone from locking and encrypting data." But what if disabling the automatic lock feature requires the password that the agent does not have? Does use of Apple's new operating system allow the officer to search without a warrant on the ground that the data on the phone will not be available pursuant to a warrant?

4. BORDER SEARCHES

Replace *United States v. Arnold* (pages 452–57) with the following new decision:

UNITED STATES V. COTTERMAN

United States Court of Appeals for the Ninth Circuit (en banc), 2013.
709 F.3d 952.

MCKEOWN, CIRCUIT JUDGE:

Every day more than a million people cross American borders, from the physical borders with Mexico and Canada to functional borders at airports such as Los Angeles (LAX), Honolulu (HNL), New York (JFK, LGA), and Chicago (ORD, MDW). As denizens of a digital world, they carry with them laptop computers, iPhones, iPads, iPods, Kindles, Nooks, Surfaces, tablets, Blackberries, cell phones, digital cameras, and more. These devices often contain private and sensitive information ranging from personal, financial, and medical data to corporate trade secrets. And, in the case of Howard Cotterman, child pornography.

Agents seized Cotterman's laptop at the U.S.-Mexico border in response to an alert based in part on a fifteen-year-old conviction for child molestation. The initial search at the border turned up no incriminating material. Only after Cotterman's laptop was shipped almost 170 miles away and subjected to a comprehensive forensic examination were images of child pornography discovered.

This watershed case implicates both the scope of the narrow border search exception to the Fourth Amendment's warrant requirement and privacy rights in commonly used electronic devices. Specifically, we consider the reasonableness of a computer search that began as a cursory review at the border but transformed into a forensic examination of Cotterman's hard drive.

Computer forensic examination is a powerful tool capable of unlocking password-protected files, restoring deleted material, and retrieving images viewed on web sites. But while technology may have changed the expectation of privacy to some degree, it has not eviscerated it, and certainly not with respect to the gigabytes of data regularly maintained as private and confidential on digital devices. Our Founders were indeed prescient in specifically incorporating "papers" within the Fourth Amendment's guarantee of "the right of the people to be secure in their persons, houses, papers, and effects." U.S. Const. amend. IV. The papers we create and maintain not only in physical but also in digital form reflect our most private thoughts and activities.

Although courts have long recognized that border searches constitute a "historically recognized exception to the Fourth Amendment's general principle that a warrant be obtained," *United States v. Ramsey,* 431 U.S. 606, 621 (1977), reasonableness remains the touchstone for a warrantless search. Even at the border, we have rejected an "anything goes" approach. *See United States v. Seljan,* 547 F.3d 993, 1000 (9th Cir.2008) (en banc).

Mindful of the heavy burden on law enforcement to protect our borders juxtaposed with individual privacy interests in data on portable digital devices, we conclude that, under the circumstances here, reasonable suspicion was required for the forensic examination of Cotterman's laptop. Because border agents had such a reasonable suspicion, we reverse the district court's order granting Cotterman's motion to suppress the evidence of child pornography obtained from his laptop.

I.   FACTUAL BACKGROUND AND PROCEDURAL HISTORY

Howard Cotterman and his wife were driving home to the United States from a vacation in Mexico on Friday morning, April 6, 2007, when they reached the Lukeville, Arizona, Port of Entry. During primary inspection by a border agent, the Treasury Enforcement Communication System ("TECS") returned a hit for Cotterman. The TECS hit indicated that Cotterman was a sex offender—he had a 1992 conviction for two counts of use of a minor in sexual conduct, two counts of lewd and lascivious conduct upon a child, and three counts of child molestation— and that he was potentially involved in child sex tourism. Because of the hit, Cotterman and his wife were referred to secondary inspection, where they were instructed to exit their vehicle and leave all their belongings in the car. The border agents called the contact person listed in the TECS entry and, following that conversation, believed the hit to reflect

Cotterman's involvement "in some type of child pornography." The agents searched the vehicle and retrieved two laptop computers and three digital cameras. Officer Antonio Alvarado inspected the electronic devices and found what appeared to be family and other personal photos, along with several password-protected files.

Border agents contacted Group Supervisor Craig Brisbine at the Immigration and Customs Enforcement ("ICE") office in Sells, Arizona, and informed him about Cotterman's entry and the fact that he was a sex offender potentially involved in child sex tourism. The Sells Duty Agent, Mina Riley, also spoke with Officer Alvarado and then contacted the ICE Pacific Field Intelligence Unit, the office listed on the TECS hit, to get more information. That unit informed Riley that the alert was part of Operation Angel Watch, which was aimed at combating child sex tourism by identifying registered sex offenders in California, particularly those who travel frequently outside the United States. She was advised to review any media equipment, such as computers, cameras, or other electronic devices, for potential evidence of child pornography. Riley then spoke again to Alvarado, who told her that he had been able to review some of the photographs on the Cottermans' computers but had encountered password-protected files that he was unable to access.

Agents Brisbine and Riley departed Sells for Lukeville at about 1:30 p.m. and decided en route to detain the Cottermans' laptops for forensic examination. Upon their arrival, they gave Cotterman and his wife *Miranda* warnings and interviewed them separately. The interviews revealed nothing incriminating. During the interview, Cotterman offered to help the agents access his computer. The agents declined the offer out of concern that Cotterman might be able to delete files surreptitiously or that the laptop might be "booby trapped."

The agents allowed the Cottermans to leave the border crossing around 6 p.m., but retained the Cottermans' laptops and a digital camera. Agent Brisbine drove almost 170 miles from Lukeville to the ICE office in Tucson, Arizona, where he delivered both laptops and one of the three digital cameras to ICE Senior Special Agent & Computer Forensic Examiner John Owen. Agent Owen began his examination on Saturday, the following day. He used a forensic program to copy the hard drives of the electronic devices. He determined that the digital camera did not contain any contraband and released the camera that day to the Cottermans, who had traveled to Tucson from Lukeville and planned to stay there a few days. Agent Owen then used forensic software that often must run for several hours to examine copies of the laptop hard drives. He began his personal examination of the laptops on Sunday. That evening, Agent Owen found seventy-five images of child pornography within the unallocated space of Cotterman's laptop.[5]

On April 11, Agent Owen finally managed to open twenty-three password-protected files on Cotterman's laptop. The files revealed approximately 378 images of child pornography. Over the next few months, Agent Owen discovered hundreds more pornographic images, stories, and videos depicting children.

A grand jury indicted Cotterman for a host of offenses related to child pornography. Cotterman moved to suppress the evidence gathered from his laptop and the fruits of that evidence. The magistrate judge filed a Report and Recommendation finding that the forensic examination was an "extended border search" that required reasonable suspicion. He found that the TECS hit and the existence of password-protected files on Cotterman's laptop were suspicious, but concluded that those facts did not suffice to give rise to reasonable suspicion of criminal activity. The district judge adopted the Report and Recommendation and granted Cotterman's motion to suppress.

In its interlocutory appeal of that order, the government characterized the issue as follows: "Whether the authority to search a laptop computer *without reasonable suspicion* at a border point of entry permits law enforcement to take it to another location to be forensically examined, when it has remained in the continuous custody of the government." A divided panel of this court answered that question in the affirmative and reversed. *United States v. Cotterman,* 637 F.3d 1068 (9th Cir.2011). The panel concluded that reasonable suspicion was not required for the search and that the district court erred in suppressing the evidence lawfully obtained under border search authority.

II.   THE BORDER SEARCH

The broad contours of the scope of searches at our international borders are rooted in "the long-standing right of the sovereign to protect itself by stopping and examining persons and property crossing into this country." *Ramsey,* 431 U.S. at 616. Thus, border searches form a narrow exception to the Fourth Amendment prohibition against warrantless searches without probable cause. Because "the Government's interest in preventing the entry of unwanted persons and effects is at its zenith at the international border," *United States v. Flores-Montano,* 541 U.S. 149, 152 (2004), border searches are generally deemed reasonable simply by virtue of the fact that they occur at the border.

---

[5]   "Unallocated space is space on a hard drive that contains deleted data, usually emptied from the operating system's trash or recycle bin folder, that cannot be seen or accessed by the user without the use of forensic software. Such space is available to be written over to store new information." *United States v. Flyer,* 633 F.3d 911, 918 (9th Cir.2011).

This does not mean, however, that at the border anything goes. Even at the border, individual privacy rights are not abandoned but balanced against the sovereign's interests. That balance is qualitatively different than in the interior and is struck much more favorably to the Government. Nonetheless, the touchstone of the Fourth Amendment analysis remains reasonableness. The reasonableness of a search or seizure depends on the totality of the circumstances, including the scope and duration of the deprivation.

In view of these principles, the legitimacy of the initial search of Cotterman's electronic devices at the border is not in doubt. Officer Alvarado turned on the devices and opened and viewed image files while the Cottermans waited to enter the country. It was, in principle, akin to the search in *Seljan,* where we concluded that a suspicionless cursory scan of a package in international transit was not unreasonable. Similarly, we have approved a quick look and unintrusive search of laptops. *United States v. Arnold,* 533 F.3d 1003, 1009 (9th Cir. 2008) (holding border search reasonable where CBP officers simply had traveler boot the laptop up, and looked at what he had inside). Had the search of Cotterman's laptop ended with Officer Alvarado, we would be inclined to conclude it was reasonable even without particularized suspicion. But the search here transformed into something far different. The difficult question we confront is the reasonableness, without a warrant, of the forensic examination that comprehensively analyzed the hard drive of the computer.

A. The Forensic Examination Was Not An Extended Border Search

Cotterman urges us to treat the examination as an extended border search that requires particularized suspicion. Although the semantic moniker "extended border search" may at first blush seem applicable here, our jurisprudence does not support such a claim. We have defined an extended border search as any search away from the border where entry is not apparent, but where the dual requirements of reasonable certainty of a recent border crossing and reasonable suspicion of criminal activity are satisfied. The key feature of an extended border search is that an individual can be assumed to have cleared the border and thus regained an expectation of privacy in accompanying belongings.

Cotterman's case is different. Cotterman was stopped and searched at the border. Although he was allowed to depart the border inspection station after the initial search, some of his belongings, including his laptop, were not. The follow-on forensic examination was not an "extended border search." A border search of a computer is not transformed into an extended border search simply because the device is transported and examined beyond the border.

B. Forensic Examination At The Border Requires Reasonable Suspicion

It is the comprehensive and intrusive nature of a forensic examination—not the location of the examination—that is the key factor triggering the requirement of reasonable suspicion here. The search would have been every bit as intrusive had Agent Owen traveled to the border with his forensic equipment. Indeed, Agent Owen had a laptop with forensic software that he could have used to conduct an examination at the port of entry itself, although he testified it would have been a more time-consuming effort. To carry out the examination of Cotterman's laptop, Agent Owen used computer forensic software to copy the hard drive and then analyze it in its entirety, including data that ostensibly had been deleted. This painstaking analysis is akin to reading a diary line by line looking for mention of criminal activity—plus looking at everything the writer may have erased.[9]

Notwithstanding a traveler's diminished expectation of privacy at the border, the search is still measured against the Fourth Amendment's reasonableness requirement, which considers the nature and scope of the search. Significantly, the Supreme Court has recognized that the dignity and privacy interests of the person being searched" at the border will on occasion demand "some level of suspicion in the case of highly intrusive searches of the person. Likewise, the Court has explained that some searches of property are so destructive, particularly offensive, or overly intrusive in the manner in which they are carried out as to require particularized suspicion. The Court has never defined the precise dimensions of a reasonable border search, instead pointing to the necessity of a case-by-case analysis. As we have emphasized, reasonableness, when used in the context of a border search, is incapable of comprehensive definition or of mechanical application.

We are now presented with a case directly implicating substantial personal privacy interests. The private information individuals store on digital devices—their personal "papers" in the words of the Constitution— stands in stark contrast to the generic and impersonal contents of a gas tank [that can be searched without reasonable suspicion]. We rest our analysis on the reasonableness of this search, paying particular heed to the nature of the electronic devices and the attendant expectation of privacy.

The amount of private information carried by international travelers was traditionally circumscribed by the size of the traveler's luggage or automobile. That is no longer the case. Electronic devices are capable of

---

[9] Agent Owen used a software program called EnCase that exhibited the distinctive features of computer forensic examination. The program copied, analyzed, and preserved the data stored on the hard drive and gave the examiner access to far more data, including password-protected, hidden or encrypted, and deleted files, than a manual user could access.

storing warehouses full of information. The average 400-gigabyte laptop hard drive can store over 200 million pages—the equivalent of five floors of a typical academic library. Even a car full of packed suitcases with sensitive documents cannot hold a candle to the sheer, and ever-increasing, capacity of digital storage.

The nature of the contents of electronic devices differs from that of luggage as well. Laptop computers, iPads and the like are simultaneously offices and personal diaries. They contain the most intimate details of our lives: financial records, confidential business documents, medical records and private emails. This type of material implicates the Fourth Amendment's specific guarantee of the people's right to be secure in their "papers." U.S. Const. amend. IV. The express listing of papers reflects the Founders' deep concern with safeguarding the privacy of thoughts and ideas—what we might call freedom of conscience—from invasion by the government. These records are expected to be kept private and this expectation is one that society is prepared to recognize as 'reasonable.'

Electronic devices often retain sensitive and confidential information far beyond the perceived point of erasure, notably in the form of browsing histories and records of deleted files. This quality makes it impractical, if not impossible, for individuals to make meaningful decisions regarding what digital content to expose to the scrutiny that accompanies international travel. A person's digital life ought not be hijacked simply by crossing a border. When packing traditional luggage, one is accustomed to deciding what papers to take and what to leave behind. When carrying a laptop, tablet or other device, however, removing files unnecessary to an impending trip is an impractical solution given the volume and often intermingled nature of the files. It is also a time-consuming task that may not even effectively erase the files.

The present case illustrates this unique aspect of electronic data. Agents found incriminating files in the unallocated space of Cotterman's laptop, the space where the computer stores files that the user ostensibly deleted and maintains other "deleted" files retrieved from web sites the user has visited. Notwithstanding the attempted erasure of material or the transient nature of a visit to a web site, computer forensic examination was able to restore the files. It is as if a search of a person's suitcase could reveal not only what the bag contained on the current trip, but everything it had ever carried.

This is not to say that simply because electronic devices house sensitive, private information they are off limits at the border. The relevant inquiry, as always, is one of reasonableness. But that reasonableness determination must account for differences in property. Unlike searches involving a reassembled gas tank, or small hole in the bed of a pickup truck, which have minimal or no impact beyond the search itself—and little implication for an individual's dignity and privacy interests—the exposure of confidential and personal information has permanence. It cannot be undone. Accordingly, the uniquely sensitive nature of data on electronic devices carries with it a significant expectation of privacy and thus renders an exhaustive exploratory search more intrusive than with other forms of property.

After their initial search at the border, customs agents made copies of the hard drives and performed forensic evaluations of the computers that took days to turn up contraband. It was essentially a computer strip search. An exhaustive forensic search of a copied laptop hard drive intrudes upon privacy and dignity interests to a far greater degree than a cursory search at the border. It is little comfort to assume that the government—for now—does not have the time or resources to seize and search the millions of devices that accompany the millions of travelers who cross our borders. It is the potential unfettered dragnet effect that is troublesome.

The effort to interdict child pornography is also a legitimate one. But legitimate concerns about child pornography do not justify unfettered crime-fighting searches or an unregulated assault on citizens' private information. Reasonable suspicion is a modest, workable standard that is already applied in the extended border search, *Terry* stop, and other contexts. Its application to the forensic examination here will not impede law enforcement's ability to monitor and secure our borders or to conduct appropriate searches of electronic devices.

We have confidence in the ability of law enforcement to distinguish a review of computer files from a forensic examination. We do not share the alarm expressed by the concurrence and the dissent that the standard we announce will prove unmanageable or give border agents a "Sophie's choice" between thorough searches and *Bivens* actions. Determining whether reasonable suspicion is required does not necessitate a complex legal determination to be made on a moment-by-moment basis. Rather, it requires that officers make a commonsense differentiation between a manual review of files on an electronic device and application of computer software to analyze a hard drive, and utilize the latter only when they possess a particularized and objective basis for suspecting the person stopped of criminal activity.

International travelers certainly expect that their property will be searched at the border. What they do not expect is that, absent some particularized suspicion, agents will mine every last piece of data on their devices or deprive them of their most personal property for days (or perhaps weeks or even months, depending on how long the search takes). Such a thorough and detailed search of the most intimate details of one's life is a substantial intrusion upon personal privacy and dignity. We therefore hold that the forensic examination of Cotterman's computer required a showing of reasonable suspicion, a modest requirement in light of the Fourth Amendment.

III. REASONABLE SUSPICION

Reasonable suspicion is defined as a particularized and objective basis for suspecting the particular person stopped of criminal activity. This assessment is to be made in light of the totality of the circumstances. Even when factors considered in isolation from each other are susceptible to an innocent explanation, they may collectively amount to a reasonable suspicion. We review reasonable suspicion determinations de novo, reviewing findings of historical fact for clear error and giving due weight to inferences drawn from those facts by resident judges and local law enforcement officers.

In the district court and in supplemental briefing, the government argued that the border agents had reasonable suspicion to conduct the initial search and the forensic examination of Cotterman's computer. We agree.

The objective facts reflect that both the agents at the border and the agents who arrived later from Sells based their decision to search Cotterman's belongings on the TECS hit. Officer Alvarado was told by those in charge of administering the TECS database that he should search Cotterman's property because the TECS hit indicated "that Cotterman appeared to have been involved in some type of child pornography." Agent Riley also looked up Cotterman's criminal record and understood that he had a prior conviction for child pornography. As it turned out, Cotterman's previous conviction was not for pornography, but for child molestation. Nonetheless, the agents' *understanding* of the objective facts, albeit mistaken, is the baseline for determining reasonable suspicion.

By itself, Cotterman's 1992 conviction for child molestation does not support reasonable suspicion to conduct an extensive forensic search of his electronic devices. The TECS alert was not based merely on Cotterman's conviction—the agents were aware that the alert targeted Cotterman because he was a sex offender "who traveled frequently out of the country" and who was "possibly involved in child sex tourism." Further, Agent Riley testified that an examination of Cotterman's passport confirmed that he had traveled in and out of the country frequently since his conviction in 1992.

In further support of reasonable suspicion, the government asserts that Mexico, from which the Cottermans were returning, is a country associated with sex tourism. Cotterman's TECS alert, prior child-related conviction, frequent travels, crossing from a country known for sex tourism, and collection of electronic equipment, plus the parameters of the Operation Angel Watch program, taken collectively, gave rise to reasonable suspicion of criminal activity.

To these factors, the government adds another—the existence of password-protected files on Cotterman's computer. We are reluctant to place much weight on this factor because it is commonplace for business travelers, casual computer users, students and others to password protect their files. Law enforcement cannot rely solely on factors that would apply to many law-abiding citizens, and password protection is ubiquitous. National standards require that users of mobile electronic devices password protect their files. Computer users are routinely advised—and in some cases, required by employers—to protect their files when traveling overseas.

Although password protection of files, in isolation, will not give rise to reasonable suspicion, where, as here, there are other indicia of criminal activity, password protection of files may be considered in the totality of the circumstances. To contribute to reasonable suspicion, encryption or password protection of files must have some relationship to the suspected criminal activity. Here, making illegal files difficult to access makes perfect sense for a suspected holder of child pornography. When combined with the other circumstances, the fact that Officer Alvarado encountered at least one password protected file on Cotterman's computer contributed to the basis for reasonable suspicion to conduct a forensic examination.

For the above reasons, we conclude that the examination of Cotterman's electronic devices was supported by reasonable suspicion and that the scope and manner of the search were reasonable under the Fourth Amendment. Cotterman's motion to suppress therefore was erroneously granted.

REVERSED.

CALLAHAN, CIRCUIT JUDGE, concurring in part, dissenting in part, and concurring in the judgment:

Whether it is drugs, bombs, or child pornography, we charge our government with finding and excluding any and all illegal and unwanted articles and people before they cross our international borders. Accomplishing that Herculean task requires that the government be mostly free from the Fourth Amendment's usual restraints on searches of people and their property. Today the majority ignores that reality by erecting a new rule requiring reasonable suspicion for any thorough search of electronic devices entering the United States. This rule flouts more than a century of Supreme Court precedent, is unworkable and unnecessary, and will severely hamstring the government's ability to protect our borders.

The majority's opinion turns primarily on the notion that electronic devices deserve special consideration because they are ubiquitous and can store vast quantities of personal information. That idea is fallacious and has no place in the border search context.

The two courts of appeals—including this court—that have had occasion to address whether electronic devices deserve special consideration have correctly concluded that they do not. In *United States v. Arnold,* 533 F.3d 1003, 1008–10 (9th Cir. 2008), we held that laptops are like other property. Similarly, in *United States v. Ickes,* 393 F.3d 501, 503–07 (4th Cir. 2005), the Fourth Circuit upheld an extensive border search of the defendant's laptop that revealed child pornography. Notably, the court held that the border agents had reasonable suspicion to search the defendant's laptop, but explained why that did not matter:

> The agents did not inspect the contents of Ickes's computer until they had already discovered marijuana paraphernalia, photo albums of child pornography, a disturbing video focused on a young ball boy, and an outstanding warrant for Ickes's arrest. As a practical matter, computer searches are most likely to occur where—as here—the traveler's conduct or the presence of other items in his possession suggest the need to search further. However, to state the probability that reasonable suspicions will give rise to more intrusive searches is a far cry from enthroning this notion as a matter of constitutional law. The essence of border search doctrine is a reliance upon the trained observations and judgments of customs officials, rather than upon constitutional requirements applied to the inapposite context of this sort of search.

Id. at 507. Thus, the Fourth Circuit has recognized what the majority does not: electronic devices are like any other container that the Supreme Court has held may be searched at the border without reasonable suspicion. Though we are not bound by *Arnold* nor *Ickes* in this en banc proceeding, we *are* bound by what the Supreme Court has said: in the unique context of border searches, property is property and we may not chip away at the government's authority to search it by adopting a sliding scale of intrusiveness. It's the border, not the technology, that "matters."

The court erects a new bright-line rule: "forensic examination" of electronic devices "at the border requires reasonable suspicion. The majority never defines "forensic," leaving border agents to wonder exactly what types of searches are off-limits. Even if the majority means to require reasonable suspicion for any type of digital forensic border search, no court has ever erected so categorical a rule, based on so general a type of search or category of property, and the Supreme Court has rightly slapped down anything remotely similar. The majority invites—indeed, requires—the Court to do so again.

The border search exception to the Fourth Amendment may be just that—an exception—but it is, and must be, a mighty one. The government's right and duty to protect our nation's territorial integrity demand that the government have clear authority to exclude—*and thus to find*—those people and things we have decided are offensive, threatening, or otherwise unwanted. Recognizing this, the Supreme Court has only once required reasonable suspicion for border searches in the 125 years it has been reviewing them. In the remaining cases, the Court has eschewed bright-line rules, balancing tests, and sliding intrusiveness scales, alluding to the possibility of, but never finding, a "particularly offensive" search. The fact that electronic devices can store large amounts of private information, or that the government can search them forensically, does not make a thorough search of such devices "particularly offensive." Rather, the Supreme Court and this court have wisely avoided making the reasonableness of a search turn on the nature of the property being searched, for the many reasons discussed above. The result has been a clear, well-understood, efficient, and effective rule that border searches are *per se* reasonable.

Regrettably the majority, dispensing with these well-settled, sensible, and *binding* principles, lifts our anchor and charts a course for muddy waters. Now border agents, instead of knowing that they may search any and all property that crosses the border for illegal articles, must ponder whether their searches are sufficiently "comprehensive and intrusive," to require reasonable suspicion, and whether they have such suspicion. In most cases the answer is going to be as clear as, well, mud. We're due for another course correction.

D. SEARCHING AND SEIZING COMPUTERS WITH A WARRANT

2. THE PHYSICAL SEARCH STAGE

On page 504, add the following new Note 5:

5.   *Access to files possessed because of an earlier overseizure.* Judicial approval of overseizing digital evidence at the physical search stage means that the government will have additional files in its possession that are outside the scope of the warrant. Can the government maintain possession of those non-responsive files? What happens if the government later develops probable cause to believe that the non-responsive files in its possession are evidence of a second crime? Can investigators obtain a second warrant to search the files in its possession—files that it possesses only because of the

overseizure allowed by the first warrant? Or are the overseized files somehow exempt from later government access with a second warrant?

The Second Circuit addressed these questions in an important ruling in United States v. Ganias, 755 F.3d 125 (2d Cir. 2014). Officers executed a first search warrant in 2003 for customer files stored by Ganias as part of his accounting business in an investigation into crimes by Ganias's customers. When agents executed the warrant in 2003, they made electronic copies of all three of Ganias's computer hard drives. Those copies were then stored by law enforcement. More than two years later, agents came to suspect that Ganias himself had committed different crimes and that the evidence for the different crimes would be found on the copies of Ganias's files that were already in the government's possession from the first warrant.

In 2006, agent obtained a second warrant allowing the agents to search the copies of Ganias's files in the government's possession for evidence of the second crime. A search pursuant to the 2006 warrant revealed evidence used to convict Ganias of the second crime. Further, it turned out that the evidence found in the copies stored by law enforcement for over two years were the only existing copies. In the intervening two-plus years, before the government obtained the second warrant, Ganias had deleted his own copies. As a result, the only reason the government was able to obtain the evidence sought by the 2006 warrant was because of the overseizure in carrying out the 2003 warrant.

The Second Circuit held that this procedure violated the Fourth Amendment. According to the Second Circuit, the Fourth Amendment does not permit officials who "execut[e] a warrant for the seizure of particular data on a computer to seize and indefinitely retain every file on that computer for use in future criminal investigations." *Id.* at 137. According to the court, retaining copies of non-responsive files indefinitely was an unreasonable seizure:

> If the 2003 warrant authorized the Government to retain all the data on Ganias's computers on the off-chance the information would become relevant to a subsequent criminal investigation, it would be the equivalent of a general warrant. The Government's retention of copies of Ganias's personal computer records for two-and-a-half years deprived him of exclusive control over those files for an unreasonable amount of time. This combination of circumstances enabled the Government to possess indefinitely personal records of Ganias that were beyond the scope of the warrant while it looked for other evidence to give it probable cause to search the files. This was a meaningful interference with Ganias's possessory rights in those files and constituted a seizure within the meaning of the Fourth Amendment.

> We conclude that the unauthorized seizure and retention of these documents was unreasonable. The Government had no warrant authorizing the seizure of Ganias's personal records in 2003. By

December 2004, these documents had been separated from those relevant to the investigation of [Ganias's clients]. Nevertheless, the Government continued to retain them for another year-and-a-half until it finally developed probable cause to search and seize them in 2006. Without some independent basis for its retention of those documents in the interim, the Government clearly violated Ganias's Fourth Amendment rights by retaining the files for a prolonged period of time and then using them in a future criminal investigation.

The Government offers several arguments to justify its actions, but none provides any legal authorization for its continued and prolonged possession of the non-responsive files. First, it argues that it must be allowed to make the mirror image copies as a matter of practical necessity and, according to the Government's investigators, those mirror images were "the government's property." As explained above, practical considerations may well justify a reasonable accommodation in the manner of executing a search warrant, such as making mirror images of hard drives and permitting off-site review, but these considerations do not justify the indefinite retention of non-responsive documents. Without a warrant authorizing seizure of Ganias's personal financial records, the copies of those documents could not become *ipso facto* "the government's property" without running afoul of the Fourth Amendment.

Second, the Government asserts that by obtaining the 2006 search warrant, it cured any defect in its search of the wrongfully retained files. But this argument reduces the Fourth Amendment to a form of words. The essence of a provision forbidding the acquisition of evidence in a certain way is that not merely evidence so acquired shall not be used before the Court but that it shall not be used at all unless some exception applies. If the Government could seize and retain non-responsive electronic records indefinitely, so it could search them whenever it later developed probable cause, every warrant to search for particular electronic data would become, in essence, a general warrant.

Third, the Government argues that it must be permitted to search the mirror images in its possession because the evidence no longer existed on Ganias's computers. But the ends, however, do not justify the means. The loss of the personal records is irrelevant in this case because the Government concedes that it never considered performing a new search of Ganias's computers and did not know that the files no longer existed when it searched the mirror images in its possession. And even if it were relevant, the Fourth Amendment clearly embodies a judgment that some evidence of criminal activity may be lost for the sake of protecting property and privacy rights.

Fourth, the Government contends that returning or destroying the non-responsive files is "entirely impractical" because doing so would compromise the remaining data that was responsive to the warrant, making it impossible to authenticate or use it in a criminal prosecution. We are not convinced that there is no other way to preserve the evidentiary chain of custody. But even if we assumed it were necessary to maintain a complete copy of the hard drive solely to authenticate evidence responsive to the original warrant, that does not provide a basis for using the mirror image for any other purpose.

Because the Government has demonstrated no legal basis for retaining the non-responsive documents, its retention and subsequent search of those documents were unconstitutional. The Fourth Amendment was intended to prevent the Government from entering individuals' homes and indiscriminately seizing all their papers in the hopes of discovering evidence about previously unknown crimes. Yet this is exactly what the Government claims it may do when it executes a warrant calling for the seizure of particular electronic data relevant to a different crime. Perhaps the "wholesale removal" of intermingled computer records is permissible where off-site sorting is necessary and reasonable, but this accommodation does not somehow authorize the Government to retain all non-responsive documents indefinitely, for possible use in future criminal investigations.

Id. at 137–40.

Do you read *Ganias* as imposing an affirmative duty on the government to delete all non-responsive files after a warrant for digital evidence is collected? If so, when is this "right to delete" triggered? Alternatively, do you read *Ganias* as imposing a use restriction, so that if such non-responsive files must be collected they cannot be used in a different criminal case even with a second warrant?

4.   EX ANTE RESTRICTIONS ON COMPUTER WARRANTS

On page 528, add the following new Note 9:

9.   In *In re Search Warrant*, 71 A.3d 1158 (Vt. 2012), the Vermont Supreme Court considered whether the Fourth Amendment permits magistrates to impose ex ante search restrictions on computer warrants. Vermont investigators had applied for a search warrant to search the home of a suspect for evidence of credit card fraud. The warrant requested permission to seize any computers that might be found at the home and to search the computers off-site. The magistrate signed the warrant but imposed ten ex ante restrictions with the following conditions:

(1) restricting the police from relying on the plain view doctrine to seize any incriminatory electronic record not authorized by the warrant—that is, "any digital evidence relating to criminal matters other than identity theft offenses";

(2) requiring third parties or specially trained computer personnel to conduct the search behind a "firewall" and provide to State investigatory agents only "digital evidence relating to identity theft offenses";

(3) requiring digital evidence relating to the offenses to be segregated and redacted from surrounding nonevidentiary data before being delivered to the case investigators, "no matter how intermingled it is";

(4) precluding State police personnel who are involved in conducting the search under condition (2) from disclosing their work to prosecutors or investigators;

(5) limiting the search protocol to methods designed to uncover only information for which the State has probable cause;

(6) precluding the use of specialized "hashing tools" and "similar search tools" without specific authorization of the court;

(7) allowing only evidence "relevant to the targeted alleged activities" to be copied to provide to State agents;

(8) requiring the State to return "non-responsive data" and to inform the court of this action;

(9) directing police to destroy remaining copies of electronic data absent judicial authorization otherwise; and

(10) requiring the State to file a return within the time limit of the warrant to indicate precisely what data were obtained, returned, and destroyed.

Id. at 1162–63. The police executed the warrant and seized a computer and an iPad but did not search it. Instead, the police asked the court to strike the ex ante restrictions to enable them to search the computer and iPad without complying with the restrictions. The government argued that magistrates lack the constitutional authority to impose ex ante restrictions because the constitutionality of a search pursuant to a warrant must be reviewed ex post after the search occurs, when all the facts are known.

Reviewing the magistrate's decision under an abuse of discretion standard, as dictated by Vermont law, the Vermont Supreme Court ruled that ex ante search restrictions are "sometimes acceptable" because they can be a way to ensure that searches are executed in a narrow way. The court then reviewed each of the ten restrictions to determine if they were acceptable, striking the first restriction as an abuse of discretion but upholding the remaining restrictions.

The court invalidated the first restriction—the one requiring the government to forswear the plain view exception—on the ground that it was "unnecessary for privacy protection and inappropriate." It was unnecessary because the other restrictions in the warrant made it unlikely that the government would be in a position to rely on evidence in plain view. The first restriction also was inappropriate because it amounted to an effort to overturn Supreme Court precedent:

> It is beyond the authority of a judicial officer issuing a warrant to abrogate a legal doctrine in this way. Judicial supervision of the administration of criminal justice in the courts implies the duty of establishing and maintaining civilized standards of procedure and evidence. This supervisory power does not, however, go so far as to allow a judicial officer to alter what legal principles will or will not apply in a particular case.

> This proposition was established in *United States v. Payner*, 447 U.S. 727(1980), in which the trial court attempted to use its supervisory authority to suppress items seized in violation of a third party's constitutional rights, thereby avoiding the established rules for Fourth Amendment standing. In reversing, the Supreme Court concluded that, if it accepted such use of the supervisory power, it "would confer on the judiciary discretionary power to disregard the considered limitations of the law it is charged with enforcing." In this case, allowing instruction (1) would confer on a judicial officer the authority to pick and choose what legal doctrines would apply to a particular police search. Because we do not believe that a judicial officer holds such authority, we conclude that the State's [request to invalidate the search restrictions] must be granted with regard to instruction (1).

Id. at 1174.

The court upheld the remaining restrictions. The second set of restrictions—requiring the computer to be searched by non-investigative personnel who would then set up a "wall" and not give any evidence to the investigators that was not, in their view, related to the crime under investigation—were allowed because they were efforts to try to restore particularity. "In lieu of a particular description of the files" that would ordinarily be required under the Fourth Amendment, this provisions allowed a substitute of "a procedure for identifying the relevant files and exposing them only to police investigators." According to the court, exposure of "embarrassing information to a detached third party constitutes a lesser injury" to privacy interest than does exposure to the police, so this procedure minimizes the invasiveness of a computer search and is therefore "not so wholly without basis as to constitute an abuse of discretion." (Two Justices dissented on this part of the opinion: They argued that these search restrictions were a procedure designed to frustrate the plain view exception, and thus were not permitted for the same reason that it was impermissible to force the government to forswear reliance on the plain view exception.)

The third set of restrictions was a requirement of special search protocols and a ban on using "sophisticated hashing tools" and "similar tools" without special permission. The court permitted these restrictions because they were ways to limit the scope of the search that could limit the privacy invasion. If the government searches the computer and investigators believe that there may be more evidence on the machine, the court reasoned, investigators can always apply for a second warrant to use "sophisticated" tools. The magistrate might reject the government's application, but at least the government was allowed to request permission.

The fourth set of restrictions required only responsive data to be copied, non-responsive data to be destroyed, and the search to be completed in a particular period of time. The court permitted these restrictions on the ground that they were similar to the kind of restrictions traditionally imposed by statutory rules governing warrants.

In dicta, the court expressed the view that the search restrictions "generally" are binding on law enforcement when issued, although the government can try to argue that circumstances changed and that therefore the restrictions need not be followed. The court also suggests that the fact that the restrictions are always optional and not always binding when issued means that there can still be ex post litigation to figure out what kind of search rules are constitutional as a matter of law.

E.   THE FOURTH AMENDMENT AND COMPUTER NETWORKS

2.   NON-CONTENT INFORMATION

On page 559, add the following new case and Notes:

UNITED STATES V. SKINNER

United States Court of Appeals for the Sixth Circuit, 2012.
690 F.3d 772.

ROGERS, CIRCUIT JUDGE.

When criminals use modern technological devices to carry out criminal acts and to reduce the possibility of detection, they can hardly complain when the police take advantage of the inherent characteristics of those very devices to catch them. This is not a case in which the government secretly placed a tracking device in someone's car. The drug runners in this case used pay-as-you-go (and thus presumably more difficult to trace) cell phones to communicate during the cross-country shipment of drugs. Unfortunately for the drug runners, the phones were trackable in a way they may not have suspected. The Constitution, however, does not protect their erroneous expectations regarding the undetectability of their modern tools.

The government used data emanating from Melvin Skinner's pay-as-you-go cell phone to determine its real-time location. This information was used to establish Skinner's location as he transported drugs along public thoroughfares between Arizona and Tennessee. As a result of tracking the cell phone, DEA agents located Skinner and his son at a rest stop near Abilene, Texas, with a motorhome filled with over 1,100 pounds of marijuana. The district court denied Skinner's motion to suppress all evidence obtained as a result of the search of his vehicle, and Skinner was later convicted of two counts related to drug trafficking and one count of conspiracy to commit money laundering. The convictions must be upheld as there was no Fourth Amendment violation, and Skinner's other arguments on appeal lack merit. In short, Skinner did not have a reasonable expectation of privacy in the data emanating from his cell phone that showed its location.

I.

Melvin Skinner was convicted by a jury on two counts related to drug trafficking and one count of conspiracy to commit money laundering in connection with his role as a courier in a large-scale drug-trafficking operation led by James Michael West.

The events leading up to Skinner's arrest and conviction began in January 2006, when Christopher S. Shearer, a participant in West's marijuana-trafficking conspiracy, was stopped in Flagstaff, Arizona with $362,000. Police stopped Shearer on his way to deliver money to West's marijuana supplier, Philip Apodaca, who lived in Tucson, Arizona.

Drug Enforcement Administration ("DEA") authorities learned from Shearer how West operated his drug conspiracy. Between 2001 and 2006, Apodaca would send marijuana that he obtained from Mexico to West in Tennessee via couriers. Apodaca purchased pay-as-you-go cell phones that he programmed with contact information and then gave to the couriers to maintain communication. When buying the phones, Apodaca provided false names and addresses for the phone subscriber information. After some time, West and his affiliates would discard their pay-as-you-go phones and get new ones with different telephone numbers and fictitious names. Apodaca was unaware that these phones were equipped with GPS technology.

In May and June 2006, authorities obtained orders authorizing the interception of wire communications from two phones that were not pay-as-you-go, but rather phones subscribed in West's name. Through these calls between West and Shearer, agents learned that West used as a courier an over-the-road truck driver referred to as "Big Foot" (later identified as the defendant in this case, Melvin Skinner). From Shearer and the phone calls, agents determined that, on many occasions beginning in 2001, Big Foot delivered money to Apodaca in Arizona and then returned to Tennessee with hundreds of pounds of marijuana for West. Big Foot's courier activities temporarily ceased between 2002–2004, but thereafter he resumed transporting drugs and money for West. In late 2005, West advanced Big Foot money to purchase a pickup truck for transporting drugs.

In June 2006, authorities determined that West was using one secret phone to communicate with Apodaca and a second secret phone to communicate with Big Foot. Authorities thought that Big Foot was using a phone with the number (520) 869–6447 ("6447 phone").

Based on calls intercepted in late June and early July 2006, authorities learned that Big Foot had recently delivered between $150,000 and $300,000 to Apodaca to pay off existing drug debt and purchase additional drugs. In later calls between West and Apodaca, the agents also determined that Big Foot would meet Apodaca in Tucson, Arizona on July 11, 2006, to pick up approximately 900 pounds of marijuana. Big Foot would be driving a "nice [RV] with a diesel engine," while Big Foot's son would be driving an F-250 pickup truck, both with Southern license plates. Big Foot would then leave for West's home in Mooresburg, Tennessee, on or about Thursday, July 13, 2006. Believing that Big Foot was carrying the 6447 phone, authorities obtained an order from a federal magistrate judge on July 12, 2006, authorizing the phone company to release subscriber information, cell site information, GPS real-time location, and "ping" data for the 6447 phone in order to learn Big Foot's location while he was en route to deliver the drugs.

That same day, agents "pinged" the 6447 phone and discovered that it was currently located in Candler, North Carolina, the location of West's primary residence. Based upon intercepted calls as well as the 6447 phone's records, agents determined that West was using the 6447 phone to communicate with Big Foot on a phone with a (520) 869-6820 number ("6820 phone"). Authorities then obtained a second order from the magistrate judge authorizing release of the same information for the 6820 phone, which revealed that the phone was located near Flagstaff, Arizona.

By continuously "pinging" the 6820 phone, authorities learned that Big Foot left Tucson, Arizona on Friday, July 14, 2006, and was traveling on Interstate 40 across Texas. At no point did agents follow the vehicle or conduct any type of visual surveillance. At around 2:00 a.m. on Sunday, July 16, 2006, the GPS indicated that the 6820 phone had stopped somewhere near Abilene, Texas. Authorities coordinated with agents in the Lubbock, Texas office of the DEA, who were quickly dispatched to a truck stop. At the truck stop, agents discovered a motorhome and a truck with Georgia license plates. An officer approached the motorhome, knocked on the door, and introduced himself to the man, later identified as Skinner, who answered the door. After Skinner denied the officer's request to search the vehicle, a K-9 officer and his dog who were at the scene conducted a perimeter dog sniff around the motorhome that alerted officers to the presence of narcotics. The officers then entered the motorhome, where they discovered sixty-one bales of marijuana, over 1,100 pounds, as well as two cellular phones and two semi-automatic handguns. Skinner and his son, Samuel, were placed under arrest.

Skinner was charged with conspiracy to distribute and possess with intent to distribute in excess of 1,000 kilograms of marijuana, in violation of 21 U.S.C. §§ 846, 841(a)(1), and 841(b)(1)(A), conspiracy to commit money laundering, in violation of 18 U.S.C. § 1956(h), and aiding and abetting the attempt to distribute in excess of 100 kilograms of marijuana, in violation of 21 U.S.C. §§ 846, 841(a)(1), 841(b)(1)(B), and 18 U.S.C. § 2.

Prior to trial, Skinner sought to suppress the search of the motorhome, alleging that the agents' use of GPS location information emitted from his cell phone was a warrantless search that violated the Fourth Amendment. After an evidentiary hearing, the magistrate judge determined that, "[b]ased on the thrust of Fourth Amendment precedent and the facts of this case," Skinner lacked standing to assert a Fourth Amendment protected interest because the cell phone was not subscribed to him and was used as part of a criminal scheme. The magistrate judge further opined that because the cell phone was utilized on public thoroughfares and was "bought by a drug supplier and provided to Skinner as part and parcel of his drug trafficking enterprise," Skinner did not have a legitimate expectation of privacy in the phone or in the motorhome that was driven on public roads. In addition, the magistrate judge determined that, "even if the search was found unconstitutional, the good faith exception would apply." The district court fully adopted the magistrate judge's Report and Recommendation, and denied Skinner's motion to suppress.

Skinner's case proceeded to a ten-day trial, and the jury found Skinner guilty on all counts. Skinner was sentenced to 235 months' imprisonment as to each of Counts One, Two, and Three, with the terms to run concurrently. This term of imprisonment was at the low end of the advisory guideline range of 235–239 months.

Skinner now appeals, arguing that the use of the GPS location information emitted from his cell phone was a warrantless search that violated the Fourth Amendment.

II.

There is no Fourth Amendment violation because Skinner did not have a reasonable expectation of privacy in the data given off by his voluntarily procured pay-as-you-go cell phone. If a tool used to transport contraband gives off a signal that can be tracked for location, certainly the police can track the signal. The law cannot be that a criminal is entitled to rely on the expected untrackability of his tools. Otherwise, dogs could not be used to track a fugitive if the fugitive did not know that the dog hounds had his scent. A getaway car could not be identified and followed based on the license plate number if the driver reasonably thought he had gotten away unseen. The recent nature of cell phone location technology does not change this. If it did, then technology would help criminals but not the police. It follows that Skinner had no expectation of privacy in the context of this case, just as the driver of a getaway car has no expectation of privacy in the particular combination of colors of the car's paint.

This conclusion is directly supported by *United States v. Knotts,* 460 U.S. 276 (1983). In *Knotts,* the police, with the consent of a chemical company, placed a beeper in a five-gallon drum of chloroform in order to track the movements of a defendant and discover the location of a clandestine drug laboratory. Using visual surveillance, as well as the signal emitted from the beeper when police lost visual contact, law enforcement officials traced the car to a secluded cabin, where the defendant and others had been manufacturing illicit drugs. The Supreme Court held that this monitoring did not violate the Constitution because "the governmental surveillance conducted by means of the beeper in this case amounted principally to the following of an automobile on public streets and highways. A person traveling in an automobile on public thoroughfares has no reasonable expectation of privacy in his movements from one place to another." The Court noted that, in Knotts's case, a police car following a defendant at a distance throughout his journey could have observed him leaving the public highway and arriving at the cabin. "There is no indication that the beeper was used in any way to reveal information that would not have been visible to the naked eye." *Id.* at 285.

Similar to the circumstances in *Knotts,* Skinner was traveling on a public road before he stopped at a public rest stop. While the cell site information aided the police in determining Skinner's location, that same information could have been obtained through visual surveillance.

There is no inherent constitutional difference between trailing a defendant and tracking him via such technology. Law enforcement tactics must be allowed to advance with technological changes, in order to prevent criminals from circumventing the justice system. The Supreme

Court said as much in *Knotts,* noting that, "insofar as respondent's complaint appears to be simply that scientific devices such as the beeper enabled the police to be more effective in detecting crime, it simply has no constitutional foundation. We have never equated police efficiency with unconstitutionality, and we decline to do so now." *Id.* at 284. In drawing this conclusion, the Court discussed *Smith v. Maryland,* 442 U.S. 735, 744–45 (1979), where a defendant was found to have no reasonable expectation of privacy in the numbers he dialed on his phone, even after that information was automated by the phone company. The Court compared this technology to giving the numbers to a telephone operator, where they would not be confidential: "We are not inclined to hold that a different constitutional result is required because the telephone company has decided to automate." *Knotts,* 460 U.S. at 283. Similar reasoning compels the conclusion here that Skinner did not have a reasonable expectation of privacy in the location of his cell phone while traveling on public thoroughfares.

Skinner counters that, unlike *Knotts,* the DEA agents in his case had never established visual surveillance of his movements, did not know his identity, and did not know the make or model of the vehicle he was driving (although they did know it was a motorhome that was accompanied by a pickup truck). Skinner argues that, in this instance, technology was used to supplement, not "augment," the "sensory faculties" of the agents. But even if the agents in *Knotts* momentarily had visual contact of the defendant, and then relied on technology either to reestablish contact or to learn where to initiate visual observation, this was not critical to our analysis. Therefore, no real distinction exists in Skinner's case. . . . As for not knowing his identity, this is irrelevant because the agents knew the identity of Skinner's co-conspirators and could have simply monitored their whereabouts to discover Skinner's identity. Using a more efficient means of discovering this information does not amount to a Fourth Amendment violation. In any event, we determine whether a defendant's reasonable expectation of privacy has been violated by looking at what the defendant is disclosing to the public, and not what information is known to the police.

Although not necessary to find that there was no Fourth Amendment violation in this case, the Government's argument is strengthened by the fact that the authorities sought court orders to obtain information on Skinner's location from the GPS capabilities of his cell phone. The government received authorization from the magistrate judge to receive location information from the cell phone company so that agents could locate and track Skinner's vehicle that was carrying the load of marijuana. When the first cell phone number turned out to be with West in North Carolina, authorities then sought and obtained a second order from the magistrate judge to "ping" the second cell phone number and locate the drugs while they were still en route.

This case is different from the recent Supreme Court decision in *United States v. Jones,* 132 S.Ct. 945 (2012). That case involved the secret placement of a tracking device on the defendant's car, and the Court's opinion explicitly relied on the trespassory nature of the police action. Although Fourth Amendment jurisprudence includes an assessment of the defendant's reasonable expectation of privacy, that "does not erode the principle that, when the Government *does* engage in physical intrusion of a constitutionally protected area in order to obtain information, that intrusion may constitute a violation of the Fourth Amendment." *Id.* at 951. No such physical intrusion occurred in Skinner's case. Skinner himself obtained the cell phone for the purpose of communication, and that phone included the GPS technology used to track the phone's whereabouts. The majority in *Jones* based its decision on the fact that the police had to "physically occupy private property for the purpose of obtaining information." 132 S.Ct. at 949. That did not occur in this case. Indeed, the *Jones* opinion explicitly distinguished *Knotts* on this ground—that trespass was not an issue in *Knotts*—and in no way purported to limit or overrule the Court's earlier holding in *Knotts.* Moreover, *Jones* does not apply to Skinner's case because, as Justice Sotomayor stated in her concurrence, "the majority opinion's trespassory test" provides little guidance on "cases of electronic or other novel modes of surveillance that do not depend upon a physical invasion on property." *Id.* at 955 (Sotomayor, J., concurring).

Skinner's case also does not present the concern raised by Justice Alito's concurrence in *Jones,* 132 S.Ct. at 957–64. There may be situations where police, using otherwise legal methods, so comprehensively track a person's activities that the very comprehensiveness of the tracking is unreasonable for Fourth Amendment purposes. As Justice Alito recognized, prior to certain advances in technology, "practical" considerations often offered "the greatest protections of privacy." *Id.* at 963. For instance, in the situation presented in *Jones,* "constant monitoring of the location of a vehicle for four weeks would have required a large team of agents, multiple vehicles, and perhaps aerial assistance." *Id.* Technology, however, has made it possible to conduct a level of extreme comprehensive tracking, "secretly monitoring and cataloguing every single movement" that the defendant made over four weeks, that previously would have been impossible. *Id.* at 964.

No such extreme comprehensive tracking is present in this case. Justice Alito's concurrence and the majority in *Jones* both recognized that there is little precedent for what constitutes a level of comprehensive tracking that would violate the Fourth Amendment. Skinner's case, however, comes nowhere near that line. While *Jones* involved intensive monitoring over a 28-day period, here the DEA agents only tracked Skinner's cell phone for three days. Such "relatively short-term monitoring of a person's movements on public streets accords with expectations of privacy that our society has recognized as reasonable." *Id.* at 964 (Alito, J., concurring). Here, the monitoring of the location of the contraband-carrying vehicle as it crossed the country is no more of a comprehensively invasive search than if instead the car was identified in Arizona and then tracked visually and the search handed off from one local authority to another as the vehicles progressed. That the officers were able to use less expensive and more efficient means to track the vehicles is only to their credit.

The Supreme Court in *Jones* also distinguished its previous holding in *United States v. Karo,* 468 U.S. 705 (1984), that the installation of a beeper in a container did not constitute a search or seizure, as follows:

> The Government, we said [in *Karo*], came into physical contact with the container only before it belonged to the defendant Karo; and the transfer of the container with the unmonitored beeper inside did not convey any information and thus did not invade Karo's privacy. That conclusion is perfectly consistent with the one we reach here. Karo accepted the container as it came to him, beeper and all, and was therefore not entitled to object to the beeper's presence, even though it was used to monitor the container's location.

Jones, 132 S.Ct. at 952. The same distinction applies even more strongly here: the Government never had physical contact with Skinner's cell phone; he obtained it, GPS technology and all, and could not object to its presence.

Because authorities tracked a known number that was voluntarily used while traveling on public thoroughfares, Skinner did not have a reasonable expectation of privacy in the GPS data and location of his cell phone. Therefore, suppression is not warranted and the district court correctly denied Skinner's motion to suppress.

NOTES AND QUESTIONS

1.   *Fourth Amendment protections for cell-site data.* The *Skinner* case involved GPS data obtained from "pinging" the target's cell phone. Lower courts have divided on the somewhat related question of whether a cell phone user has Fourth Amendment rights in cell-site data concerning the usage of their phone. Whenever a phone is on, it is in contact with local cell towers that are used to route communications to or from the phone. Cell phones usually communicate with the nearest tower, so that a record of which tower was in communication with a particular phone can generate a record of the rough location of the phone's owner over time. Cellular phone companies

automatically generate and store cell-site records whenever a call is placed or a communication is made to or from the phone, allowing the government to obtain cell-site records at those times. Lower courts have divided on whether cell-site records should receive Fourth Amendment protection. *Compare* In re Application of the United States for Historical Cell Site Data, 724 F.3d 600, 613 (5th Cir.2013) (holding that cell site data is not protected) *with* Tracey v. State, 2014 WL 5285929 (Fla. 2014) (holding that cell-site data is protected, at least in the context of real-time access).

2.   In United States v. Stanley, 753 F.3d 114 (3d Cir. 2014), the Third Circuit considered the following question about wireless network surveillance: Does tracing the physical location of a user of an unsecured wireless network constitute a Fourth Amendment search? The court's answer: No, at least when the suspect is using the wireless network without its owner's permission.

In *Stanley*, a Pennsylvania state police officer investigating the distribution of child pornography over peer-to-peer software learned that a computer at a particular IP address was sharing images of child pornography. The investigator, Erdley, obtained a search warrant to search the home associated with the IP address. The search was unsuccessful, however, and Erdley concluded that someone nearby was using the home's unsecured wireless connection without the homeowner's knowledge or permission. With the consent of the homeowner, Kozikowski, Erdley used a software program called "Moocherhunter" to find the physical location of the individual who was accessing Kozikowski's wireless network.

Moocherhunter works by measuring the distance between the wireless router and the computer connecting to it. By moving the antenna of the wireless router, and by knowing the MAC address of the computer connected to the wireless router, Erdley was able to trace the location of the computer connecting to the wireless router to a specific apartment. Erdley then obtained a search warrant and searched the apartment, finding child pornography on the computer of the defendant, Richard Stanley.

The District Court ruled that use of Moocherhunter was not a search under *Smith v. Maryland*, 442 U.S. 735 (1979):

> Based upon *Smith*'s rationale, the court finds Stanley did not have a legitimate expectation of privacy in the wireless signal he caused to emanate from his computer to the Kozikowski wireless router or in the signal being sent from the router back to his computer, and therefore, Erdely's use of Moocherhunter did not constitute a search in violation of the Fourth Amendment. In *Smith*, the pen register was used to record the telephone numbers people voluntarily dialed and thus, conveyed, to the telephone company by monitoring electrical impulses caused when the dial on the telephone was released. Here, Moocherhunter monitored the strength of a signal that Stanley voluntarily caused to send from his computer to Kozikowski's wireless router and to receive a signal back from the

wireless router in order to gain unauthorized access to Kozikowski's internet connection. In both cases, the party seeking suppression of evidence assumed the risk that information disclosed to a third party may be turned over to the police. Notably, Moocherhunter, like the pen register, did not reveal the contents of the communications; it only revealed that communications were taking place.

United States v. Stanley, 2012 WL 5512987 (W.D.Pa. 2012).

On appeal, the Third Circuit agreed with the district court's result but adopted a narrower rationale. According to the Third Circuit, the difficulty with relying on *Smith v. Maryland* was that it might also allow the government to monitor the *contents* of unsecured wireless networks without Fourth Amendment oversight. To avoid this result, the Third Circuit relied instead on the fact that Stanley had accessed the open wireless network without permission:

> While Stanley may have justifiably expected the path of his invisible radio waves to go undetected, society would not consider this expectation "legitimate" given the unauthorized nature of his transmission.

> As noted in Rakas v. Illinois, 439 U.S. 128 (1978), "a burglar plying his trade in a summer cabin during the off season may have a thoroughly justified subjective expectation of privacy, but it is not one which the law recognizes as 'legitimate.'" The defendant's presence in those circumstances is wrongful; his expectation is not one that society is prepared to recognize as reasonable. Similarly, in United States v. Kennedy, 638 F.3d 159, 165 (3d Cir. 2011), we held that an unauthorized driver in a rental car lacks a reasonable expectation of privacy in the vehicle in part because he not only acts in contravention of the owner's property rights, but also deceives the owner of the vehicle.

> Here, the presence of Stanley's unauthorized signal was itself "wrongful." When Stanley deliberately connected to the Neighbor's unsecured wireless network, he essentially hijacked the Neighbor's router, forcing it to relay data to Comcast's modem and back to his computer, all without either the Neighbor's or Comcast's knowledge or consent. Stanley was, in effect, a virtual trespasser. As such, he can claim no "legitimate" expectation of privacy in the signal he used to effectuate this trespass—at least where, as here, the MoocherHunter revealed only the path of this signal and not its contents.

> The presence of Stanley's signal was likely illegal. A large number of states, including Pennsylvania, have criminalized unauthorized access to a computer network. A number of states have also passed statutes penalizing theft of services, which often explicitly include

telephone, cable, or computer services. We need not decide here whether these statutes apply to wireless mooching, but the dubious legality of Stanley's conduct bolsters our conclusion that society would be unwilling to recognize his privacy interests as "reasonable." This is particularly so where the purpose of Stanley's unauthorized connection was to share child pornography.

To recognize Stanley's expectation of privacy as "legitimate" would also reward him for establishing his Internet connection in such an unauthorized manner. As the District Court recognized, had Stanley shared child pornography using his own, legitimate Internet connection, Erdely could have obtained Stanley's address from his Internet service provider—just as he obtained the Neighbor's address from Comcast. Stanley cannot conceal his location by establishing an unauthorized connection and at the same time ask society to validate his expectation of privacy in the signal-strength information that police used to determine that location in a more roundabout manner.

Although the analogy is imperfect, we believe that the MoocherHunter is akin to a drug sniffing dog in that it was only able to detect a signal that was itself unauthorized and likely illegal. The use of a drug sniffing dog, which allows police to detect odors that they could not perceive with their human senses, is not a search under the Fourth Amendment because it "discloses only the presence or absence of narcotics, a contraband item." *United States v. Place,* 462 U.S. 696, 707 (1983). In this way, "the manner in which information is obtained through this investigative technique is much less intrusive than a typical search." Thus, "the legitimate expectation that information about perfectly lawful activity will remain private is categorically distinguishable from a defendant's hopes or expectations concerning the nondetection of contraband." *Illinois v. Caballes,* 543 U.S. 405, 410 (2005).

Here, the MoocherHunter detected only a signal that was itself unauthorized, and as we have characterized it, likely illegal. At the time Erdely used the MoocherHunter, Stanley was connecting to the Neighbor's router without his knowledge or consent. Without that contemporaneous unauthorized connection, the MoocherHunter would have been unable to function. And the MoocherHunter revealed only the path of the signal establishing this connection. It revealed nothing about the content of the data carried by that signal. Accordingly, Stanley's privacy expectations concerning the path of his unauthorized signal are "categorically distinguishable" from expectations he would have had concerning the path of a lawful, legitimate signal.

United States v. Stanley, 753 F.3d 114, 119–22 (3d Cir. 2014). Is the Third Circuit's approach persuasive? Is the district court's reasoning better or worse? Does the answer hinge on whether you agree that using an unsecured wireless access point may be an illegal under unauthorized access or theft-of-services laws?

3.   CONTENT INFORMATION

At the top of page 573, add the following to the end of Note 9:

Does the Fourth Amendment permit warrants to disclose all e-mails in the contents of an e-mail account—or are such warrants overly broad? Courts have recently divided on whether the Fourth Amendment permits the government to obtain "all contents" warrants for e-mail accounts. Some recent decisions have approved such warrants. See, e.g., United States v. Bowen, 689 F.Supp.2d 675, 682 (S.D.N.Y. 2010) (approving such warrants when the account was entirely or largely used for purposes of criminal activity); United States v. McDarrah, 2006 WL 1997638 (S.D.N.Y.2006), aff'd United States v. McDarrah, 351 Fed.Appx. 558 (2d Cir.2009).

On the other hand, consider In re Applications for Search Warrants for Information Associated with Target Email Address, 2012 WL 4383917 (D. Kan. 2012). The government applied for search warrants to obtain the contents of a Yahoo! account and an account with an online service called UnityFax that was linked to a fraud scheme. The application for the Yahoo! warrant asked for an order requiring Yahoo! to disclose:

> the contents of all e-mails associated with the account, including stored or preserved copies of e-mails sent to and from the account, draft e-mails, deleted emails, e-mails preserved pursuant to a request made under 18 U.S.C. § 2703(f), the source and destination addresses associated with each e-mail, the date and time at which each e-mail was sent, and the size and length of each e-mail.

The application for the UnityFax warrant asked for a similarly broad order for fax communications sent and received through UnityFax. The Magistrate Judge who reviewed the applications denied them on the ground that such broad warrants would be unconstitutional:

> The Court finds that the warrants proposed by the government violate the Fourth Amendment. First, the initial section of the warrants authorizing the electronic communications service provider to disclose all email or fax communications (including all content of the communications), all records and other information regarding the account is too broad and too general. The warrants fail to set any limits on the email or fax communications and information that the electronic communications service provider is to disclose to the government, but instead requires the electronic communications service provider to disclose all email or fax communications in their entirety and all information about the account without restriction. Most troubling is that these sections of the warrants fail to limit the universe of electronic communications

and information to be turned over to the government to the specific crimes being investigated.

Second, even if the Court were to allow a warrant with a broad authorization for the content of all email and fax communications without a nexus to the specific crimes being investigated, the warrants would still not pass Constitutional muster. They fail to set out any limits on the government's review of the potentially large amount of electronic communications and information obtained from the electronic communications service providers. The warrants also not identify any sorting or filtering procedures for electronic communications and information that are not relevant and do not fall within the scope of the government's probable cause statement, or that contain attorney-client privileged information.

Although the sections of the search warrants authorizing the government-authorized review of the information provided by the electronic communications service provider are sufficiently particular in that they link the information to be seized to the alleged crimes, the sections requiring the initial disclosure by the electronic communications service provider under 18 U.S.C. § 2703 are not. They fail to create a nexus between the suspected crime and the email or fax communications and related account information to be obtained and searched. The warrants order the electronic communications service provider to disclose the content of *all* communications associated with the account, including deleted communications, as well as all records and information regarding identification of the email or fax account, and other information stored by the account user, including address books, contact lists, calendar data, pictures and files.

Email accounts likely contain large numbers of emails and files unrelated to the alleged crimes being investigated or for which the government has no probable cause to search and seize. The government simply has not shown probable cause to search the contents of all emails ever sent to or from the account or for all the information requested from Yahoo! or to search the contents of all faxes and other electronic communications associated with the account from UnityFax. The government thus has not shown probable cause for the breadth of the warrants sought here.

The warrants also fail to set any limits on the universe of information to be disclosed to and searched by the government, such as limiting the disclosure and search to information relating to a specific crimes being investigated and for which the government has demonstrated probable cause to search. The Court finds the breadth of the information sought by the government's search warrant for the either the fax or email account—including the content of every email or fax sent to or from the accounts—is best analogized to a warrant asking the post office to provide copies of all mail ever sent by or delivered to a certain address so that the government can open and read all the mail to find out whether it constitutes fruits, evidence or instrumentality of a crime. The Fourth Amendment would not allow such a warrant. The Fourth Amendment should therefore not permit a similarly overly broad warrant just because the information sought is electronic communications versus paper ones.

The Court leaves the suggestion of an appropriate procedural safeguard up to the government. While not endorsing or suggesting any particular safeguard, some possible options would be asking the electronic communications service provider to provide specific limited information such as emails or faxes containing certain key words or emails sent to/from certain recipients, appointing a special master with authority to hire an independent vendor to use computerized search techniques to review the information for relevance and privilege, or setting up a filter group or taint-team to review the information for relevance and privilege.

Id. at *8–10.

On page 573, at the end of Chapter 5, add the following case:

UNITED STATES V. AHRNDT
United States District Court for the District of Oregon, 2013.
2013 WL 179326.

KING, DISTRICT JUDGE.

John Henry Ahrndt moves to suppress evidence and statements obtained as a result of a warrantless search made by a police officer's connection to Ahrndt's personal wireless network and opening one of his shared files. Pending before me is Ahrndt's renewed Motion to Suppress. For the following reasons, I grant the motion and suppress evidence agents discovered on Ahrndt's storage media and the subsequent statements he made to them.

BACKGROUND

On February 21, 2007, a woman referred to as JH was using her personal computer at her home in Aloha, Oregon. She was connected to the internet via her own wireless network, but, when her wireless network malfunctioned, her computer automatically picked up another nearby wireless network called "Belkin54G." Belkin54G refers to a wireless router, made by the company Belkin, that broadcasts a wireless signal in a roughly 400 foot radius. Its default setting has no security. At the second evidentiary hearing, defense expert Robert Young testified that JH's laptop would not have automatically connected to Belkin54G the first time she lost her own wireless signal. Instead, her computer would have sent a signal to search for wireless routers within range of her computer and the names of available wireless routers would have appeared in a list on her computer. JH would have clicked on Belkin54G to prompt her computer to connect to that wireless router. If the wireless router was secured, she would have had to enter a password to connect to the wireless router. Because the Belkin54G was not secured, JH connected without entering a password. From that time forward, her computer remembered the available connection and she did not have to select Belkin54G again when her own wireless signal failed. Nevertheless, even after that first time, in order to connect to Belkin54G, JH's computer needed to send a signal into Ahrndt's computer and the router's processor to use the wireless network.

A Belkin54G router comes with an installation CD containing a manual instructing on the "importance of security measures," according to the testimony of Agent Tony Onstad at the first evidentiary hearing. There is no evidence Ahrndt had read or received this manual. The government did not introduce the manual itself.

After JH connected to the internet via the Belkin54G wireless network, JH opened her iTunes software to listen to music. The iTunes software is designed to organize and play audio, video, and image files. The iTunes software also allows users to browse music and video that is stored in the iTunes libraries of other computers on the same network, if those libraries are enabled to "share." In addition, accepting Young's testimony, iTunes software installed on one computer ("computer 2") integrates with LimeWire installed on another computer ("computer 1") so that when the two computers are on the same network iTunes will display media on computer 2 available through LimeWire on computer 1. In this case, when JH opened her iTunes, she noticed another user's library—called "Dad's LimeWire Tunes"—was available for sharing. Young also testified that the name "Dad's LimeWire Tunes" was an automatically generated folder name.

JH opened Dad's Limewire Tunes and observed files with names that prompted her to call the Washington County Sheriff's Office a little before 10:45 p.m. The transcript reflects the following interaction:

> JH: Ok, Um, I just um was looking at my ITunes um and I, you can share music with people that are I guess in your area and I was just um sharing some music with this I guess it's a neighbor of mine, I have no way of knowing where they are or whatever but it's a whole bunch of um underage child pornography. I just wanted somebody to know about that.

She gave her name, address and phone number. When asked, "And how long ago did you get, receive that?" she answered,

JH: Um, Its up there now. I just turned on my computer and turned on my Itunes and just saw that I was sharing music so I just checked it and um I just saw it. I mean I didn't open any of the stuff but the names are all stuff about 11 year old girls and 9 year olds you know, just stuff that I don't it sounds inappropriate.

Washington County Deputy John McCullough arrived a little less than an hour later. Deputy McCullough noted in his police report that JH showed him a "play list of approximately 25 picture and video files. The files had pornographic titles that indicated the images were of underage children." At first, they were not able to open the files or identify an owner. Deputy McCullough called his sergeant. Deputy McCullough testified at the first suppression hearing that he called his sergeant for two reasons: to advise him what he had learned and to "determine if it would be appropriate or not for me to look further into those files and try to determine what was enclosed within them." First Hr'g Tr. 8:8–12. After speaking with his supervisor, Deputy McCullough concluded it would be acceptable to investigate further and he requested that JH attempt to open one of the files. The two saw a sexually explicit image of a boy masturbating. JH's computer then lost the signal and she was unable to open any other files.

JH informed Deputy McCullough that the Belkin54G showed as an available wireless network on her computer when she moved in. At that time, only one resident lived in her new development. She then pointed out an older house nearby, about 150 feet away, which was the only other home she knew was occupied when she moved in. Deputy McCullough subsequently ran the license plates of a car in the driveway of that house and learned that defendant John Henry Ahrndt, a convicted sex offender, lived there. Fredrick Harmon, a friend and tenant of defendant, also lived at the residence.

Two days later, on February 23, 2007, Washington County Sheriff's Office Detective Ray Marcom and Department of Homeland Security, U.S. Immigration and Customs Enforcement, Senior Special Agent James Cole interviewed JH further about the incident. JH repeated to Marcom and Cole much of what she had told Deputy McCullough.

On April 2, 2007, Agent Cole applied to United States Magistrate Judge Dennis Hubel for a search warrant to access the Belkin54G wireless network for the purpose of determining the internet protocol ("IP") address associated with the router. An IP address would allow investigators to find out from an internet service provider who owned the Belkin54G wireless network. Judge Hubel granted the warrant the same day. On April 7, 2007, Agent Cole drove near the house, accessed the Belkin54G network, and determined the network's IP address. Through the American Registry for Internet Numbers, Agent Cole learned that the IP address belonged to Comcast. He served a summons on Comcast and learned that Ahrndt was the Comcast subscriber for the IP address in question.

On April 17, 2007, Agent Cole obtained a second search warrant from Judge Hubel allowing a search of the home for wireless routers, computers, and any files or storage media that could contain images of child pornography. The next morning officers searched defendant's home and seized one tower computer, a Belkin wireless router, various hard drives, numerous disc media and flash media. A subsequent computer forensic examination of the equipment found 20 images, 17 of which depicted children engaged in sexually explicit conduct.

Ahrndt's expert Young testified at the second evidentiary hearing that when LimeWire is installed, the user has the option of directing LimeWire to start automatically when the user logs into his computer allowing the program to start faster. The default then becomes an automatic start for LimeWire when the user logs in to his computer, allowing LimeWire to run the entire time the user is on his computer. Young also explained LimeWire's default setting is to share content "on the Local Area Network and make it accessible for Itunes and other Digital Audio Access Protocol 'DAAP' enabled Players."

There is no evidence Ahrndt was using iTunes or deliberately sharing files. There is evidence Ahrndt had used LimeWire to download child pornography eight months before, but no evidence he had set his program to share files over the internet.

Ahrndt brought a motion to suppress all evidence seized after Deputy McCullough's initial access of Ahrndt's files through JH's computer, on the theory that without Deputy McCullough's actions the first and second warrants would not have issued.

DISCUSSION

I.   *The Private Search*

The Fourth Amendment limits searches conducted by the government, not by a private party, unless the private party acts as an 'instrument or agent' of the government. Here, JH discovered the list of images contained in Ahrndt's LimeWire folder while using her own iTunes program and Ahrndt's unsecured wireless network. Accordingly, JH's report of the filenames she viewed is not subject to suppression.

Although there is a question whether Deputy McCullough could reenact JH's search by asking her to connect to Ahrndt's unsecured wireless network, open her iTunes, and open the folder called "Dad's LimeWire Tunes," as a practical matter Deputy McCullough's duplication of JH's efforts revealed nothing new that would affect my analysis below.

I do note that in my view, under *Jacobsen,* Deputy McCullough could properly view data on JH's computer when JH had previously performed the search. As the Supreme Court explained in *Jacobsen,* "Once frustration of the original expectation of privacy occurs, the Fourth Amendment does not prohibit governmental use of the now-nonprivate information. The Fourth Amendment is implicated only if the authorities use information with respect to which the expectation of privacy has not already been frustrated." 466 U.S. at 117. I am not persuaded by Ahrndt's citation to *United States v. Young,* 573 F.3d 711 (9th Cir.2009), in which the court declined to expand *Jacobsen* to a search of a hotel room, deemed equivalent to a private residence; the invasive action at issue here is a remote search of computer data transmitted on an unsecured wireless network.

I agree with the government, then, that Deputy McCullough saw data on a network that the private party had previously searched. As a result, Deputy McCullough's view of the list of titles in Dad's LimeWire Tunes did not violate Ahrndt's Fourth Amendment rights.

I next consider whether Deputy McCullough's additional step of clicking the image, an action which exceeded the private search, violated Ahrndt's Fourth Amendment rights.

II. *Whether Opening of the Image Violated Ahrndt's Fourth Amendment Rights*

Deputy McCullough directed JH to open an image. She had not previously opened any of the images. The opened image was no longer within the purview of the private search. I liken the unopened image to the unviewed films at issue in *Walter;* in that case, the private party had not viewed the suspect films and, prior to the agents' action of watching the films, "one could only draw inferences about what was on the films. The projection of the films was a significant expansion of the search that had been conducted previously by a private party and therefore must be characterized as a separate search." 447 U.S. at 657. I, furthermore, reject the government's argument that the contents were already exposed.

The next question is whether Deputy McCullough's action of clicking on the image violated Ahrndt's Fourth Amendment rights. In order to assess Ahrndt's Fourth Amendment rights, I must evaluate whether any subjective expectation of privacy was objectively reasonable. The issue is whether it is reasonable to have an expectation of privacy in the contents of a LimeWire file, when there is no evidence of intentional sharing over the wireless network or the internet, on a personal computer connected to an unsecured home wireless network.

As an initial matter, I conclude Ahrndt's reasonable expectation of privacy in the contents of his computer was not eliminated when he attached it to his unsecured wireless network router. Indeed, as the court stated in *Heckenkamp,* "the mere act of accessing a network does not in itself extinguish privacy expectations, nor does the fact that others may have occasional access to the computer." 482 F.3d at 1146–47.

It is true the *Heckenkamp* court went on to comment that privacy expectations may be reduced if the user is advised the information may not remain confidential or communications may be monitored. Here, with respect to Ahrndt's Belkin54G wireless router, the default setting was unsecured. The quick set-up manual did not discuss security measures that could or should be taken. Although defense counsel stipulated the router came with a manual, and the government's expert testified the manual included detailed instructions on setting up wireless security, the only evidence in the record is that the manual warned of the importance of security. I underscore there is no evidence the manual warned Ahrndt that the *content* of files may be accessible to others, as opposed to just internet access, by failing to secure his router. Accordingly, although Ahrndt's failure to secure his network suggests a lesser subjective expectation of privacy, I could not say he lost all expectation of privacy in the contents of files on his personal computer.

The situation is, of course, a bit more complicated; the evidence suggests the content became available to JH by virtue of the fact that the materials were contained in a LimeWire folder. Nevertheless, although the folder appearing in JH's iTunes directory was called "Dad's *LimeWire Tunes,*" there is no evidence Ahrndt was sharing files on the peer-to-peer network, and the government concedes there is no evidence the image in Dad's LimeWire Tunes library that JH and Deputy McCullough opened was accessible over the internet by LimeWire users at the time JH and Deputy McCullough accessed the files, or at any time prior. Accordingly, I could not say Ahrndt had no right to privacy in those files just by virtue of his use of LimeWire to download images.

Instead, accepting Young's testimony, the evidence suggests LimeWire was likely configured to run whenever Ahrndt turned his computer on. The evidence also suggests the program was set to its default mode of sharing content on Ahrndt's "Local Area Network" making that content "accessible for Itunes and other Digital Audio Access Protocol (DAAP) enabled Players." Def's. Ex. 101 (Second Hr'g). As a technical matter, with respect to the content itself, Young could not say whether iTunes was asking, "Anything to share?" or LimeWire was advertising that it had content to share. Regardless, in order to preclude LimeWire from sharing with iTunes on his network, Ahrndt would have had to seek out and uncheck the sharing option, or choose to require a password for those wishing to access the contents of his LimeWire file. Accordingly, there is no evidence Ahrndt intentionally" enabled sharing of his files over his wireless network. Rather, as Young explained, JH's iTunes software could detect files that were shared, by default, by

Ahrndt's LimeWire program. The government offered no evidence to dispute Young's testimony.

The government suggests Ahrndt had no objective expectation of privacy as a result of the automated computer process that shared his folder, but I find the government's supporting case citations inapt. The government first quotes extensively from the *dissent's* opinion in *Lavan v. City of Los Angeles,* 693 F.3d 1022, 1038–39 (9th Cir.2012). The only other Ninth Circuit case referenced by the government is *United States v. Borowy,* 595 F.3d 1045 (9th Cir.2010) (per curiam), but in that case the agent found the images via the internet by browsing the shared content stored in defendant's LimeWire file. Although the defendant had attempted to prevent LimeWire from sharing his files over the internet, his "subjective intention did not create an objectively reasonable expectation of privacy in the face of such *widespread public access.*" 595 F.3d at 1048 (emphasis added); *compare United States v. Sawyer,* 786 F.Supp.2d 1352, 1356 (N.D.Ohio 2011) (somewhat more reasonable expectation of privacy in content shared with "friends" over an open program, but no control over manner in which "friends" used their access, so no objective expectation of privacy). Here, the evidence suggests Ahrndt unknowingly, and by default of the program, shared the content stored in his LimeWire folder over his home wireless network. This was not the widespread public access found to have undermined Borowy's expectation of privacy.

Finally, both *United States v. Procopio,* 88 F.3d 21 (1st Cir. 1996), and *United States v. O'Bryant,* 775 F.2d 1528, 1534 (11th Cir. 1985), involved unintended disclosures of private documents as a result of third party actions, thereby destroying any objective expectation of privacy. Neither case is persuasive. In *Procopio,* a private party stole a safe, leaving it open in a park with papers inside and outside the safe, but the officer did not exceed the scope of the private search as Deputy McCullough did here. In *O'Bryant,* an officer found a stolen briefcase next to a dumpster and the court explained that abandoned valuable property may be inspected to determine the identity of the owner and to inventory the contents. Finally, both of these cases arose outside the Ninth Circuit.

In short, the government does not dispute a person has a reasonable expectation of privacy in the files on his home personal computer. There is no evidence Ahrndt was using iTunes software or any other program to deliberately share files. The evidence is that he had media-enabled files that JH was able to view using her own iTunes program because Ahrndt's files made themselves available, by default, through JH's iTunes. There is no evidence Ahrndt intentionally enabled sharing of his files over his wireless network, and there is no evidence he knew or should have known that others could access his files by connecting to his wireless network. Deputy McCullough's action of clicking on the image in JH's iTunes directory to open the image violated Ahrndt's Fourth Amendment rights.

CHAPTER 6

STATUTORY PRIVACY PROTECTIONS

■ ■ ■

A. THE WIRETAP ACT

1. THE BASIC STRUCTURE

On page 592 at the top, add the following new Note 10:

10. In Joffe v. Google, 746 F.3d 920 (9th Cir. 2013), the Ninth Circuit considered an important and surprisingly difficult statutory question: Does intercepting the contents of unencrypted wireless Internet communications violate the Wiretap Act?

The issue arose in a civil case challenging Google's StreetView program, which allegedly obtained the contents of at least some open wireless communications in the course of its operation. Google responded that the Wiretap Act does not prohibit the interception of unencrypted wireless communications under 18 U.S.C. § 2511(2)(g)(i), which exempts intercepting "an electronic communication made through an electronic communication system" if the system is configured so that it is "readily accessible to the general public." 18 U.S.C. § 2511(2)(g)(i). Under 18 U.S.C. § 2510(16)(A), Google noted, " 'readily accessible to the general public' means, with respect to a radio communication" that the communication is "not . . . scrambled or encrypted." Google argued that open wireless communications are radio communications; because such communications are not encrypted, they are readily accessible to the general public as a matter of law and are categorically exempt from the Wiretap Act.

The Ninth Circuit reached a limited holding in the case that wireless Internet communications are not categorically excluded from the Wiretap Act as a matter of law because they are not "radio communications." Because the Wiretap Act does not define the term "radio communication," the Ninth Circuit applied the plain meaning of the term:

> In common parlance, watching a television show does not entail "radio communication." Nor does sending an email or viewing a bank statement while connected to a Wi-Fi network. There is no indication that the Wiretap Act carries a buried implication that the phrase ought to be given a broader definition than the one that is commonly understood.

> There are two telltale indicia of a "radio communication." A radio communication is commonly understood to be (1) predominantly auditory, and (2) broadcast. Therefore, television—whether

connected via an indoor antenna or a satellite dish—is not radio, by virtue of its visual component. A land line phone does not broadcast, and, for that reason, is not radio. On the other hand, AM/FM, Citizens Band (CB), 'walkie-talkie,' and shortwave transmissions are predominantly auditory, are broadcast, and are, not coincidentally, typically referred to as "radio" in everyday parlance. Thus, we conclude that "radio communication" should carry its ordinary meaning: a predominantly auditory broadcast.

> The payload data transmitted over unencrypted Wi-Fi networks that was captured by Google included emails, usernames, passwords, images, and documents that cannot be classified as predominantly auditory. They therefore fall outside of the definition of a "radio communication" as the phrase is used in 18 U.S.C. § 2510(16).

Joffe, 746 at 928–29. Because wireless Internet communications are not radio communications, the Ninth Circuit held, the meaning of "readily accessible to the general public" that applies to radio communications under 18 U.S.C. § 2510(16)(A) does not apply to Internet communications.

Now consider the important policy question: Should the Wiretap Act prohibit the interception of unencrypted wireless Internet communications? The Ninth Circuit suggested that such communications should be protected from interception by the Wiretap Act:

> Consider an email attachment containing sensitive personal information sent from a secure Wi-Fi network to a doctor, lawyer, accountant, priest, or spouse. A company like Google that intercepts the contents of that email from the encrypted home network has, quite understandably, violated the Wiretap Act. But the sender of the email is in no position to ensure that the recipient—be it a doctor, lawyer, accountant, priest, or spouse—has taken care to encrypt her own Wi-Fi network. Google, or anyone else, could park outside of the recipient's home or office with a packet sniffer while she downloaded the attachment and intercept its contents because the sender's "radio communication" is "readily accessible to the general public" solely by virtue of the fact that the recipient's Wi-Fi network is not encrypted. Surely Congress did not intend to condone such an intrusive and unwarranted invasion of privacy when it enacted the Wiretap Act.

Do you agree?

C. THE STORED COMMUNICATIONS ACT

2. COMPELLED DISCLOSURE UNDER § 2703

On page 660 at the top, add the following new Note 15:

15. *The SCA and civil discovery.* The application of the SCA to civil discovery has become a very important question in civil litigation. If *A* sues *B*, and *A* wants to obtain *B*'s e-mails as part of *A*'s discovery, can *A* subpoena *B*'s e-mail provider for the e-mails? In general, courts have concluded that the SCA applies to block such discovery requests: Because the SCA requires a warrant to compel the contents of communications, a mere civil discovery subpoena cannot be used to compel the provider to disclose contents. See, e.g., Thayer v. Chiczewski, 2009 WL 2957317 (N.D.Ill. 2009) (citing cases); Crispin v. Christian Audigier, Inc., 717 F.Supp.2d 965 (C.D.Cal. 2010). Under these cases, *A* must subpoena *B* directly, and *B* must obtain the contents from the provider by accessing his own account and then handing over the contents to *A*.

3. VOLUNTARY DISCLOSURE UNDER § 2702

On page 671 in the middle, add the following new Note 13:

13. *Court-ordered consent under the Stored Communications Act.* 18 U.S.C. § 2702 generally prohibits an e-mail provider from disclosing the contents of a customer's communications absent a warrant or consent. In some cases, however, courts have ordered a party to consent to disclosure to facilitate access to that party's private communications. Such a procedure raises two questions. First, if a court orders a party to consent to disclosure of the contents of communications under 18 U.S.C. § 2702, and the party consents only because the court order requires it, is that consent valid for purposes of § 2702? And second, if the consent is valid, can the same court then compel the e-mail provider to disclose the contents of the communications without obtaining a warrant?

In Negro v. Superior Court, 179 Cal.Rptr.3d 215 (Cal. App. 2014), the court answered both questions "yes." In civil litigation between Negro and Navalimpianti, Navalimpianti sought copies of e-mails from Negro. Navalimpianti became convinced that Negro was not handing over all of his e-mails, so Navalimpianti served a civil discovery subpoena on Negro's e-mail provider, Google, seeking copies of Negro's e-mails directly from Google. Google declined to comply with the subpoena on the ground that compliance would violate § 2702.

In response, Navalimpianti obtained an order from the trial court ordering Negro to send an e-mail to Google consenting to Google's disclosure of Negro's e-mails to Navalimpianti's counsel. According to Navalimpianti, the trial court's order constituted consent from Negro, taking the disclosure outside the SCA and thus rendering the civil discovery subpoena on Google enforceable. Faced with the threat of discovery sanctions for failure to comply with the trial court's order, Negro sent an e-mail to Google stating that he consented to Google's disclosure of his e-mails.

The California Court of Appeal ruled that Google was required to comply with Navalimpianti's civil discovery subpoena. According to the Court of Appeal, the existence of the trial court order requiring Negro to express his consent did not itself constitute consent. When the order was issued, Negro had not yet consented. On the other hand, when Negro agreed to comply with the order to avoid sanctions, Negro's compliance with the order constituted valid consent under the SCA:

> We emphatically reject Negro's claim that his consent is vitiated by "judicial coercion." Courts in a variety of other settings have compelled parties to consent to a third party's disclosure of material where such consent was a prerequisite to its production.

> If "judicial coercion" were enough to vitiate the resulting instrument, these powers would be illusory. We cannot entertain such a dramatic and disruptive departure from existing law without a far more compelling demonstration than Negro has attempted to make.

> The simple fact is that Negro was not deprived of volition in this matter. He was presented with a choice between facilitating the discovery sought by Navalimpianti, or risking such sanctions as the [trial] court might elect to impose. He seeks to have the best of both worlds by complying with the court's order while denying that his decision to do so should be given legal effect. We reject this contention and hold that the consent expressly given by him pursuant to court order constituted "lawful consent" under the SCA.

Id. at *11–*12.

The Court of Appeal next ruled that the SCA did not prohibit enforcement of Navalimpianti's civil discovery subpoena on Google. Google argued that the consent of a user under § 2702 made disclosure permissive, not mandatory. According to Google, § 2702 gives providers the power to decide whether to disclose by stating that providers "may" disclose when a user consents. *See* 18 U.S.C. § 2702(b), § 2702(b)(3). Assuming Negro's consent was valid, Google had decided not to disclose. Google reasoned that Google's decision should end the matter: A civil discovery subpoena could not trump Google's statutorily-provided discretion and force it to disclose.

The California Court of Appeal disagreed and ordered Google to comply with the subpoena. Specifically, the court rejected Google's argument that the word "may" gave Google the power to decide whether to disclose the e-mails:

> This approach simply does not work in the present context, where the "may" in question is juxtaposed not with a "shall"—real or hypothesized—but with an earlier "shall not"—specifically, the Act's declaration that a service provider "shall not" knowingly disclose protected materials. (18 U.S.C. § 2702(a).) The subdivision where

"may" appears is framed not as a grant of discretionary power *or* as the imposition of a mandatory duty but as a special *exception* to a general *prohibition*.

In such a context all "may" means is that the actor is excused from the duty, liability, or disability otherwise imposed by the prohibition. Stating that the actor "may" engage in the otherwise proscribed conduct is a natural way—indeed the most natural way—to express such an exception. Thus a traffic law might declare that a driver *shall not* proceed against a red light, but *may* proceed, under stated conditions, to make a right turn. This means only that when the stated conditions are present, the driver is relieved of the obligation to wait for a green light. It does not exempt the driver from duties arising under other laws, such as not to obstruct traffic, or to get out of the way of emergency vehicles. The use of "may" in such a context can connote that the actor is not *obliged* in all cases to perform the contemplated action; but it has no tendency, by itself, to excuse the actor from obligations or liabilities arising from other sources.

In sum, we find no sound basis for the proposition that the Act empowers service providers to defy civil subpoenas seeking discovery of materials that are excepted from the Act's prohibitions on disclosure. Insofar as the Act permits a given disclosure, it permits a court to compel that disclosure under state law. It follows that when a user has expressly consented to disclosure, the Act does not prevent enforcement of a subpoena seeking materials in conformity with the consent given.

Id. at *14–*15.

Do you agree? If Congress had intended to require providers to comply with civil discovery subpoenas whenever a user consented, why didn't Congress make such process one of the authorized means of compelled disclosure under § 2703?

CHAPTER 7

JURISDICTION

■ ■ ■

A. FEDERAL POWER

3. PROCEDURAL STATUTORY LIMITS

At the end of page 696, add the following new subsection, "C) Venue":

C) Venue

A third limit on federal power concerns where charges may be brought. In federal criminal law, this concept is known as "venue." Venue has both constitutional and statutory origins. U.S. Const. Art. III, § 2, cl. 3 requires that criminal trials must be held "in the State where the said Crimes shall have been committed." Federal Rule of Criminal Procedure 18 codifies this right by requiring that "the Government must prosecute an offense in a district where the offense was committed."

Importantly, venue in federal criminal law is different from the concept of personal jurisdiction that arises in civil cases. In the context of civil procedure, the Supreme Court has held that notions of due process require "certain minimum contacts with [the forum] such that the maintenance of the suit does not offend traditional notions of fair play and substantial justice." International Shoe Co. v. Washington, 326 U.S. 310, 316 (1945). Venue in criminal cases is different. In criminal law, charges can be brought wherever the crime was committed. Congress has enacted statutes, and courts have created interpretive doctrines, to answer the "place" of where different criminal offenses can be deemed to have occurred.

The venue requirement can raise difficult questions in computer crime cases. Computer crimes routinely cross both district and state lines. When this occurs, where exactly was the computer crime committed?

UNITED STATES V. AUERNHEIMER

United States Court of Appeals for the Third Circuit, 2014.
748 F.3d 525.

CHAGARES, CIRCUIT JUDGE.

This case calls upon us to determine whether venue for Andrew Auernheimer's prosecution for conspiracy to violate the Computer Fraud and Abuse Act ("CFAA"), 18 U.S.C. § 1030, and identity fraud under 18 U.S.C. § 1028(a)(7) was proper in the District of New Jersey. Venue in criminal cases is more than a technicality; it involves matters that touch closely the fair administration of criminal justice and public confidence in it. This is especially true of computer crimes in the era of mass interconnectivity. Because we conclude that venue did not lie in New Jersey, we will reverse the District Court's venue determination and vacate Auernheimer's conviction.

I.

[*Daniel Spitler discovered that the servers that hosted AT&T's website had a security flaw that allowed anyone to collect e-mail addresses of iPad owners who had AT&T wireless accounts. With the assistance of the defendant, Andrew Auernheimer, Spitler created an automated computer program that he called the "account slurper" that visited AT&T's website hundreds of thousands of times and collected 114,000 e-mail addresses and serial numbers known as "ICC-IDs." In an effort to bring attention to their hacking skills, Auernheimer then contacted Ryan Tate, a reporter at the online publication* Gawker, *to advertise how Spitler and Auernheimer created the program. In the course of proving the act to Tate, Auernheimer e-mailed a copy of the e-mail addresses to him.* Gawker *published a story about Spitler and Auernheimer that was picked up by the Drudge Report and became a national news story. Criminal charges followed.*]

Evidence at trial showed that at all times relevant to this case, Spitler was in San Francisco, California and Auernheimer was in Fayetteville, Arkansas. The servers that they accessed were physically located in Dallas, Texas and Atlanta, Georgia. Although no evidence was presented regarding the location of the *Gawker* reporter, it is undisputed that he was not in New Jersey.

Despite the absence of any apparent connection to New Jersey, a grand jury sitting in Newark returned a two-count superseding indictment charging Auernheimer with conspiracy to violate the CFAA, 18 U.S.C. § 1030(a)(2)(C) and(c)(2)(B)(ii), in violation of 18 U.S.C. § 371 (count one), and fraud in connection with personal information in violation of 18 U.S.C. § 1028(a)(7) (count two, commonly referred to as "identity fraud"). To enhance the potential punishment from a misdemeanor to a felony, the Government alleged that Auernheimer's CFAA violation occurred in furtherance of a violation of New Jersey's computer crime statute, N.J. Stat. Ann. § 2C:20–31(a). *See* 18 U.S.C. § 1030(c)(2)(B)(ii).*

Auernheimer moved to dismiss the superseding indictment shortly after it was returned by the grand jury. In addition to asserting several challenges concerning the CFAA violation, he argued that venue was not proper in the District of New Jersey. The District Court acknowledged that neither he nor Spitler was ever in New Jersey while allegedly committing the crime, and that the servers accessed were not in New Jersey, but denied his motion nonetheless. It held that venue was proper for the CFAA conspiracy charge because Auernheimer's disclosure of the email addresses of about 4,500 New Jersey residents affected them in New Jersey and violated New Jersey law. It further held that because venue was proper for the CFAA count, it was also proper for the identity fraud count because proving the CFAA violation was a necessary predicate to proving the identity fraud violation.

Auernheimer's trial lasted five days and resulted in a guilty verdict on both counts. Initially, both parties requested a jury instruction on venue. Venue is a question for the jury and the court must specifically instruct the jury on venue if (1) the defendant objects to venue prior to or at the close of the prosecution's case-in-chief, (2) there is a genuine issue of material fact with regard to proper venue, and (3) the defendant timely requests a jury instruction.

Although Auernheimer objected to venue and requested an instruction, the District Court held that there was no genuine issue of material fact. It concluded that the Government had established that venue was proper in New Jersey as a matter of law and declined to instruct the jury on venue. After denying Auernheimer's post-trial motions, the District Court sentenced him to forty-one months of imprisonment. Auernheimer timely appealed. Our review of the District Court's legal decision regarding venue is plenary.

II.

Although this appeal raises a number of complex and novel issues that are of great public importance in our increasingly interconnected age, we find it necessary to reach only one that has been fundamental since our country's founding: venue. The proper place of colonial trials was so important to the founding generation that it was listed as a grievance in the Declaration of Independence. *See* The Declaration of Independence para. 21 (U.S. 1776) (objecting to "transporting us beyond seas to be tried for pretended offences"). It was of such concern that the Constitution of the United States twice safeguards the defendant's venue right. Article III requires that "the Trial of all Crimes shall be held in the

---

* [Spitler was also charged, but he pled guilty and testified against Auernheimer in exchange for a reduced sentence.]

State where the said Crimes shall have been committed." U.S. Const. art. III, § 2, cl. 3. The Sixth Amendment further provides that "in all criminal prosecutions, the accused shall enjoy the right to a speedy and public trial, by an impartial jury of the State and district wherein the crime shall have been committed." This guarantee is codified in the Federal Rules of Criminal Procedure, which require that "the Government must prosecute an offense in a district where the offense was committed."

Congress may prescribe specific venue requirements for particular crimes. Where it has not, as is the case here, we must determine the crime's *locus delicti*. *See* Black's Law Dictionary 1025 (9th ed. 2009) (defining *locus delicti* as the "place where an offense was committed"). The *locus delicti* must be determined from the nature of the crime alleged and the location of the act or acts constituting it. To perform this inquiry, we must (1) initially identify the conduct constituting the offense and then (2) discern the location of the commission of the criminal acts. Venue should be narrowly construed.

Continuing offenses, such as conspiracy, that are "begun in one district and completed in another, or committed in more than one district, may be inquired of and prosecuted in any district in which such offense was begun, continued, or completed." 18 U.S.C. § 3237(a). In the context of a conspiracy charge, venue can be established wherever a co-conspirator has committed an act in furtherance of the conspiracy. The Government must prove venue by a preponderance of the evidence.

In performing our venue inquiry, we must be careful to separate 'essential conduct elements' from 'circumstance elements.' For example, in *United States v. Cabrales*, 524 U.S. 1, 4 (1998), the Supreme Court considered whether venue for money laundering activities was proper in Missouri. Laundered proceeds were generated by illegal narcotics sales in Missouri, but all acts constituting the money laundering offense took place in Florida. The Court held that venue was improper in Missouri. The Supreme Court, later reflecting on *Cabrales,* observed that the "existence of criminally generated proceeds" was only a "circumstance element" of money laundering. *United States v. Rodriguez-Moreno*, 526 U.S. 275, 280 n.4 (1999). Although it was an element of the crime that the Government had to prove to the jury, it was a 'circumstance element' because it was simply a fact that existed at the time that the defendant performed her laundering acts. Only 'essential conduct elements' can provide the basis for venue; 'circumstance elements' cannot.

A.

Count one charged Auernheimer with conspiracy to violate 18 U.S.C. §1030(a)(2)(C) and (c)(2)(B)(ii). In the indictment and at trial, the Government identified the nature of the conduct constituting the offense as the agreement to commit a violation of the CFAA in furtherance of a violation of New Jersey's computer crime statute, N.J. Stat. Ann.

§ 2C:20–31(a). Venue would be proper in any district where the CFAA violation occurred, or wherever any of the acts in furtherance of the conspiracy took place.

The charged portion of the CFAA provides that "whoever intentionally accesses a computer without authorization or exceeds authorized access, and thereby obtains . . . information from any protected computer shall be punished as provided in subsection (c) of this section." 18 U.S.C. § 1030(a)(2)(C). To be found guilty, the Government must prove that the defendant (1) intentionally (2) accessed without authorization (or exceeded authorized access to) a (3) protected computer and (4) thereby obtained information. The statute's plain language reveals two essential conduct elements: *accessing* without authorization and *obtaining* information.[3]

New Jersey was not the site of either essential conduct element. The evidence at trial demonstrated that the accessed AT&T servers were located in Dallas, Texas, and Atlanta, Georgia. In addition, during the time that the conspiracy began, continued, and ended, Spitler was obtaining information in San Francisco, California, and Auernheimer was assisting him from Fayetteville, Arkansas. No protected computer was accessed and no data was obtained in New Jersey.

This is not the end of our analysis, however, because the Government did not just charge Auernheimer with conspiracy to commit an ordinary violation of the CFAA, but also with conspiring to violate the CFAA in furtherance of a state crime. The Government can increase the statutory maximum punishment for a subsection (a)(2) violation from one year to five years if it proves one of the enhancements contained in § 1030(c)(2)(B). The enhancement relevant here provides for such increased punishment if "the offense was committed in furtherance of any criminal or tortious act in violation of the laws of any State." *Id.* § 1030(c)(2)(B)(ii). Any facts that increase the prescribed range of penalties to which the criminal defendant is exposed' are elements of the crime" that must be proven to the jury beyond a reasonable doubt.[4] This is true even if they are explicitly termed "sentence enhancements" in the statute.

The New Jersey statute allows for criminal liability "if the person purposely or knowingly and without authorization, or in excess of

---

[3]　The Department of Justice's own manual on prosecuting computer crimes provides in its section devoted to venue that "it would seem logical that a crime under section 1030(a)(2)(C) is committed where the offender initiates access *and* where the information is obtained." Computer Crime & Intellectual Prop. Section, Dep't of Justice, Prosecuting Computer Crimes 118, *available at* http://www.justice.gov/criminal/cybercrime/docs/ccmanual.pdf.

[4]　Just because the enhancement is an "element" that the Government needed to prove beyond a reasonable doubt does not mean that it was an "essential conduct element" of a § 1030(a)(2)(C) violation within the meaning of *Rodriguez-Moreno* that could establish venue. For the purposes of this opinion, however, we will assume (without deciding) that the enhancement could contain "essential conduct elements."

authorization, accesses any computer or computer system and knowingly or recklessly discloses, or causes to be disclosed any data or personal identifying information." N.J. Stat. Ann. § 2C:20–31(a). Its essential conduct elements are accessing without authorization (or in excess of authorization) and disclosing data or personal identifying information.

Here, none of the essential conduct elements of a violation of the New Jersey statute occurred in New Jersey. As discussed, neither Auernheimer nor Spitler accessed a computer in New Jersey. The disclosure did not occur there either. The sole disclosure of the data obtained was to the *Gawker* reporter. There was no allegation or evidence that the *Gawker* reporter was in New Jersey. Further, there was no evidence that any email addresses of any New Jersey residents were ever disclosed publicly in the *Gawker* article. The alleged violation of the New Jersey statute thus cannot confer venue for count one.

Just as none of the conduct constituting the CFAA violation or its enhancement occurred in New Jersey, none of the overt acts that the Government alleged in the superseding indictment occurred in New Jersey either. The indictment listed four overt acts: writing the account slurper program, deploying the account slurper program against AT&T's servers, emailing victims to inform them of the breach, and disclosing the emails addresses obtained to *Gawker*. The co-conspirators collaborated on the account slurper program from California and Arkansas and deployed it against servers located in Texas and Georgia. The Government offered no evidence whatsoever that any of the victims that Auernheimer emailed were located in New Jersey, or that the *Gawker* reporter to whom the list of email addresses was disclosed was in the Garden State.

Because neither Auernheimer nor his co-conspirator Spitler performed any "essential conduct element" of the underlying CFAA violation or any overt act in furtherance of the conspiracy in New Jersey, venue was improper on count one.

B.

We now turn to count two of the indictment because venue must be analyzed independently for each count. Count two charged Auernheimer with violating 18 U.S.C. § 1028(a)(7), which punishes anyone who "knowingly transfers, possesses, or uses, without lawful authority, a means of identification of another person with the intent to commit, or to aid or abet, or in connection with, any [federal crime, or state or local felony]." The statute's plain language indicates that the statute punishes someone who (1) knowingly (2) transfers, possesses, or uses without lawful authority (3) a means of identification of another person (4) with the intent to commit, or in connection with, any violation of federal law or any state felony.

The two essential conduct elements under § 1028(a)(7) are transfer, possession, or use, and doing so in connection with a federal crime or state felony. Starting with the latter essential conduct element, the Government charged Auernheimer with committing identity fraud "in connection with" the ordinary violation of CFAA § 1030(a)(2)(C). As should be clear by now, no conduct related to the ordinary CFAA violation occurred in New Jersey.

There was also no evidence that Auernheimer's transfer, possession, or use occurred in New Jersey. The Government advances two theories of how he could have satisfied this essential conduct element. First, it contends that he violated § 1028(a)(7) by knowingly using the ICC-IDs of other people's iPads to access AT&T's servers. Venue fails under this theory because there was no allegation or evidence that he used the ICC-IDs in New Jersey. The alleged conspirators used the ICC-IDs in their account slurper program, which was programmed from California and Arkansas, and did not access any computer or obtain any information in New Jersey.

The Government also argues that Auernheimer violated the statute by transferring the list of email addresses that he obtained to *Gawker* with the intent to violate the New Jersey computer crime statute. But there was no allegation in the indictment or evidence at trial that the *Gawker* reporter to whom he transferred the email addresses was in New Jersey—and no essential conduct element of the alleged violation of New Jersey law occurred in New Jersey either.

Because Auernheimer did not commit any essential conduct of the identity fraud charge in New Jersey, venue was also improper on count two.

III.

Undoubtedly there are some instances where the location in which a crime's effects are felt is relevant to determining whether venue is proper. But those cases are reserved for situations in which an essential conduct element is itself defined in terms of its effects.

Sections of the CFAA other than § 1030(a)(2)(C) do speak in terms of their effects. For example, § 1030(a)(5)(B) criminalizes intentionally accessing a computer without authorization and recklessly causing damage. Because that crime is defined in terms of its effects—the damage caused—venue could be proper wherever that occurred.

Congress, however, did not define a violation of § 1030(a)(2)(C) in terms of its effects. The statute simply criminalizes accessing a computer without authorization and obtaining information. It punishes only the actions that the defendant takes to access and obtain. It does not speak in terms of the effects on those whose information is obtained. The crime is complete even if the offender never looks at the information and immediately destroys it, or the victim has no idea that information was ever taken.

Venue issues are animated in part by the danger of allowing the Government to choose its forum free from any external constraints. The ever-increasing ubiquity of the Internet only amplifies this concern. As we progress technologically, we must remain mindful that cybercrimes do not happen in some metaphysical location that justifies disregarding constitutional limits on venue. People and computers still exist in identifiable places in the physical world. When people commit crimes, we have the ability and obligation to ensure that they do not stand to account for those crimes in forums in which they performed no "essential conduct element" of the crimes charged.

For the forgoing reasons, we will reverse the District Court's venue determination and vacate Auernheimer's conviction.

C. INTERNATIONAL COMPUTER CRIMES

1. UNITED STATES SUBSTANTIVE LAW

On page 734, at the end of Note 6, add the following:

In United States v. Lyons, 740 F.3d 702 (1st Cir. 2014), the First Circuit expressly rejected the defendant's extraterritoriality claim in an Internet gambling prosecution brought under the Wire Act. Lyons and Eremian worked for a sports betting business based in Antigua that did most of its business with customers in the United States. According to the First Circuit, this connection with the United States was sufficient to generate criminal liability under the Wire Act:

> Lyons's and Eremian's convictions were not an improper extraterritorial application of the Wire Act. It is a longstanding principle of American law that legislation of Congress, unless a contrary intent appears, is meant to apply only within the territorial jurisdiction of the United States. The Wire Act expresses such a contrary intent because it explicitly applies to transmissions between the United States and a foreign country. 18 U.S.C. § 1084. The communications giving rise to these convictions had at least one participant inside the United States and therefore fall within the statute's scope.

Id. at 718.

2.   UNITED STATES PROCEDURAL LAW

On page 752, before Section 3 begins, add the following new Note 10:

10. If United States investigators serve a search warrant under the SCA on an e-mail provider for the contents of a target's e-mail account, but the e-mail provider has stored the target's e-mails on a server located outside the United States, do providers still have to comply with the search warrant? *See* In re Warrant to Search a Certain E-Mail Account Controlled and Maintained by Microsoft Corp., 15 F.Supp.3d 466 (S.D.N.Y. 2014) (answering "yes").

3.   MUTUAL LEGAL ASSISTANCE AND INTERNATIONAL TREATIES

On page 760, at the top, add the following new Note 6:

6.   Many U.S.-based Internet service providers serve a predominantly foreign customer base. Imagine a foreign government seeks contents or metadata from a U.S.-based Internet service provider about a foreign suspect in a criminal investigation. How does the Stored Communications Act apply? What rules govern foreign government access to U.S.-stored contents and metadata?

If the foreign government serves a foreign court order for metadata, the SCA allows but does not require the U.S. provider to comply. For statutory purposes, the foreign government is not a recognized government under the statute and voluntary disclosure is permitted. *See* 18 U.S.C. § 2702(c)(6) (allowing voluntary disclosure "to any person other than a governmental entity"); 18 U.S.C. § 2711(4) (defining "governmental entity" as "a department or agency of the United States or any State or political subdivision thereof"). On the other hand, a U.S. provider cannot comply with a foreign court order for contents because § 2702(a)–(b) bans the disclosure absent U.S. legal process under § 2703.

When the SCA bars U.S.-based providers from complying with foreign legal process, foreign government may work with the United States government under an MLAT. In 2009, Congress enacted a new statute, 18 U.S.C. § 3512, to facilitate that cooperation. Section 3512(a)(1) states that "Upon application, duly authorized by an appropriate official of the Department of Justice, of an attorney for the Government, a Federal judge may issue such orders as may be necessary to execute a request from a foreign authority for assistance in the investigation or prosecution of criminal offenses, or in proceedings related to the prosecution of criminal offenses, including proceedings regarding forfeiture, sentencing, and restitution."

Section 3512(a)(2) clarifies that such orders can include SCA warrants, 2703(d) order, and pen/trap orders. The statute also provides specific guidance on the standard for issuing search warrants for foreign governments: "A Federal judge may issue a search warrant under this section only if the foreign offense for which the evidence is sought involves conduct that, if committed in the United States, would be considered an offense punishable by imprisonment for more than one year under Federal or State law." 18 U.S.C. § 3512(e).

Consider additional alternatives for foreign government access to data from U.S. providers. First, foreign governments may be able to persuade U.S. officials to open a U.S. domestic investigation and obtain U.S. court orders. This procedure requires the offense to also be a U.S. crime, and for U.S. investigators to have reason to make the investigation a high priority.

Second, foreign governments could pressure U.S.-based providers to design their networks so that copies of contents of communications are always stored locally, outside the reach of the SCA. Foreign governments can then access the locally-stored copies of communications without needing to comply with U.S. privacy law.

Also consider a third option, albeit one that is more legally dubious. Can foreign governments order U.S. providers to export data from inside the U.S. to a representative or affiliate outside the United States, where the SCA doesn't apply, and then serve legal process on the foreign-stored copy? Or does such a procedure violate the SCA? *See generally* Orin Kerr, *The Next Generation Communications Privacy Act*, 162 U. Pa. L. Rev. 373, 409–10 (2014).